2004

The Cambridge Introduction to
Spanish Poetry

The Cambridge Introduction to Spanish Poetry comprises an extended survey of poetry written in Spanish from the Middle Ages to the present day, including both Iberian and Latin American writing. This volume offers a non-chronological approach to the subject in order to highlight the continuity and persistence of genres and forms (epic, ballad, sonnet) and of themes and motifs (love, religious and moral poetry, satirical and pure poetry). It also supplies a thorough examination of the various interactions between author, text and reader. Containing abundant quotation, it gives a refreshing introduction to an impressive and varied body of poetry from two continents, and is an accessible and wide-ranging reference-work, designed specifically for use on undergraduate and taught graduate courses. The most comprehensive work of its kind available, it will be an invaluable resource for students and teachers alike.

D. GARETH WALTERS is Professor of Hispanic Studies at the University of Exeter. He is the author of *Francisco de Quevedo, Love Poet* (1985), *The Poetry of Francisco de Aldana* (1988) and *Canciones and the Early Poetry of Lorca* (2002).

The Cambridge Introduction to
Spanish Poetry

D. GARETH WALTERS

University of Exeter

CAMBRIDGE
UNIVERSITY PRESS

PUBLISHED BY THE PRESS SYNDICATE OF THE UNIVERSITY OF CAMBRIDGE
The Pitt Building, Trumpington Street, Cambridge, United Kingdom

CAMBRIDGE UNIVERSITY PRESS
The Edinburgh Building, Cambridge CB2 2RU, UK
40 West 20th Street, New York, NY 10011-4211, USA
477 Williamstown Road, Port Melbourne, VIC 3207, Australia
Ruiz de Alarcón 13, 28014 Madrid, Spain
Dock House, The Waterfront, Cape Town 8001, South Africa

http://www.cambridge.org

First published 2002

Printed in the United Kingdom at the University Press, Cambridge

Typefaces Bembo 11/12.5 pt and Univers   *System* LATEX 2$_\varepsilon$ [TB]

A catalogue record for this book is available from the British Library

Library of Congress Cataloguing in Publication data

Walters, D. Gareth.
The Cambridge introduction to Spanish poetry / D. Gareth Walters.
    p.   cm.
Includes bibliographical references and index.
ISBN 0 521 79122 7 (hardback) – ISBN 0 521 79464 1 (paperback)
1. Spanish poetry – History and criticism.   2. Spanish American poetry –
History and criticism.   I. Title
PQ6076 .W35   2002
861.009 – dc21   2002025670

ISBN 0 521 79122 7 hardback
ISBN 0 521 79464 1 paperback

For Christine

Contents

Preface

This is a book about poetry in Spanish, and not about the poetry of Spain. The distinction is crucial for reasons of language and geography. To speak of the poetry of Spain is to imply the presence of poems written in languages other than Spanish. Catalan poetry, particularly in the medieval and modern periods, bears favourable comparison with the major literatures of Europe, while Galician poetry, so important at a formative stage of the Iberian lyric, has also experienced a renewal, although it is not as significant a body of poetry as Catalan. As many histories of Spanish literature still consulted today were written before the death of Franco in 1975, it is opportune to point to this linguistic diversity, encouraged by the policy of regional autonomy.

There is another dimension to 'Spanishness'. As those involved in the promotion of the language as a suitable subject for the school or university curriculum never tire of observing, Spanish is a world language. In this respect it is nearer to English, the language of another early imperial power, than it is to other European languages. It is the language of the greater part of South and Central America and the Caribbean, while it is also spoken by a rapidly growing number of North Americans. The inclusion of Spanish American poetry in this volume, however, is not merely a response to a contemporary politico-linguistic reality. It is because the bonds of a common language and a partially shared literary inheritance are greater than the distinctiveness and independence that Spanish American poets sometimes claim for themselves. Indeed, in the matter of influence and innovation, the movement has by no means been one way: modern Spanish poets, no less than prose writers, have had occasion to learn from their counterparts across the Atlantic.

As this survey does not adopt a chronological approach it may be felt that it is not a history. It clearly does not follow in the long line of histories of Spanish literature that emphasize continuity and period, and that have, as a consequence, a socio-historical priority. Such an approach has both advantages and drawbacks, and I have tried to incorporate the benefits in the Introduction to my study. My emphasis, nonetheless, is upon aesthetic and ideological evolution with the result that the political and the historical are contingent rather than essential issues.

Yet my aim in adopting a synchronic method is perhaps better defined as 'differently historical' rather than purely ahistorical. Poetry involves a sense of community that is less subject to the tyranny and fashion of the present than are other literary genres; tradition in this connection is a far more dynamic concept than it is commonly taken for. In a recent review of *The New Penguin Book of English Verse*, John Carey observes how the arrangement of the poems by the date of publication rather than in poet-by-poet batches frees them from their 'authorial prisons' and thus creates 'one great metrical cataract' where one hears not so much individual voices as the voice of English poetry. Albeit with a different approach, I look to achieve a similar outcome in this study. No survey, of course, will ever equalize the resonance of these voices. Some, inevitably, stand out, such as the seventeenth-century writer Francisco de Quevedo (more a literature than a man according to Borges), and the twentieth-century Chilean poet, Pablo Neruda, who appears to have accomplished everything that one could conceivably define as poetic goals and achievements. Even these poets (to change metaphor) figure as threads in the large tapestry that tells the story of poetry in Spanish. The most valuable kind of history perhaps is one that, in the absence of all other evidence, could fulfil a pseudo-archeological function: to let later generations know what it has meant to be Spanish or Spanish American, and more specifically in the case of my own project, what use these people had for the common language, and what that use entailed in the universal medium of poetry. If I only partly or occasionally achieve such an aim, then I will feel this undertaking to have been worthwhile.

Any survey of this nature will inevitably involve matters of judgement and taste. I may be faulted on both counts, but would invoke the famous adage 'de gustibus' for the latter. As regards the former, I did not feel compelled to follow conventional practice nor engage in tokenism. Some may feel that I have adhered too closely to the canon; others, that I have not been close enough. A more or less equal division of views along these lines would be the only justification I should desire. I have neither confined myself to the major poets nor sought to promote, against the grain, those who would not have contributed somehow to the story. I did not feel under any obligation to respect the implications of a term like 'Golden Age', commonly used as a designation for Spanish literature of the sixteenth and seventeenth centuries, and consequently to include minor poets from that period merely to prove its supposed richness. It seemed to me entirely appropriate to emphasize the achievements of poets like Belli and Rossetti, not merely because they were women poets – though a case could be made for positive discrimination especially when the majority of readers, and certainly of students, are female – but because they shed new light on age-old issues of gender and sexuality that have figured so largely in Spanish poetry. I also make no apology for the predominance of twentieth-century poets. Their claim to inclusion is not on the grounds of quality; indeed to debate whether modern poetry is better or worse than medieval poetry is about as constructive as deciding if an orange is better than an apple. Nor is it because the voices of modern poets are those that we hear most clearly for being the nearest echoes and instigators of our own voices. It is because they deserve to be judged, in some cases for the first time, in the company of familiar predecessors. Finally, for voices to be heard, they need a stage or a platform. For that purpose I have been generous with quotation in accordance with Emerson's precept: 'Next to the originator of a good sentence is the first quoter of it.'

The input to − as opposed to the mere writing of − a study of this nature involves a time-scale that is far longer than with more specialized books. Many of the poems considered here have lived and grown with me over many years. Moreover, one of the pleasures that I have derived from the undertaking has been to turn again to poems that I first read in school and which I have not considered seriously in the interim. The list of acknowledgements for such a project is therefore potentially endless. It should ideally contain all my students as well as my teachers, from whom I have derived, sometimes selfishly, the benefits of dialogue. I confine myself, in the interests of space, to citing, as teachers and mentors, the late Mr Georges Rochat, Professor José María Aguirre, Professor Nicholas Round and Professor Arthur Terry. I am also indebted, more specifically for this book, in a whole variety of ways to Dr Brígida Pastor and Dr Ann MacLaren of the University of Glasgow; Dr Claudio Canaparo of the University of Exeter; Dr Jordi Doce Chambrelán of the University of Oviedo; and Dr María Jesús Pando Canteli of Universidad de Deusto, San Sebastian. I am especially grateful to Dr Linda Bree of Cambridge University Press for her patience, encouragement and valuable advice. My greatest debt is to my wife Christine for her unfailing faith in this enterprise, and for helping to ensure, often in self-sacrificing ways, that this book came to be written.

Introduction

Origins and developments

Any historical survey of Spanish poetry will be confronted with the problem of origins. Only those histories that understand Spanish poetry as the poetry of Spain rather than poetry in the Spanish language have a clear point of departure: Martial and Lucan, poets of Roman Spain. If, however, we think of the distant sources of the traditional popular poetry that was written down from the Middle Ages then we might acknowledge that a kind of song may well have been in existence since the later Paleolithic period (30,000–15,000 BC), and thus contemporary with cave art, some of the finest examples of which are in the north of the Iberian Peninsula. To compound the problem, even the earliest written poetry in Ibero-Romance is by no means a clear-cut issue. The discovery in the mid twentieth century of poetic fragments written in Mozarabic, a Romance dialect employed by those Hispano-Romans who remained in Andalusia after the Moorish invasion of the Peninsula at the start of the eighth century, proved to be one of the most important developments in the literary history of the Middle Ages. According to those scholars responsible for this pioneering investigation, from around the tenth century poets of Al-Andalus (the name given to the Moorish lands of the south of Spain) wrote compositions entitled *muwashashas* in Classical Arabic, and later Hebrew, that contained a final section in Vulgar Arabic or Mozarabic. This tailpiece was called the *kharja* (literally 'going away'). While Arabic scholars have pointed to the coherence of the poem as a whole because of a thematic connection between the *kharja* and the preceding material, the *kharjas*, by dint of their seeming linguistic divergence, have come to be regarded as brief compositions in their own right.¡Such brevity can lend these tiny love poems an intensity of emotion:

> Vaise mio corachón de mib,
> ¡*Ya Rab*!, ¿si se me tornarad?
> ¡Tan mal me dóled *li-l-habib*!
> enfermo yed, ¿cuánd sanarad?[1]

> My heart goes away from me, oh God, will it return to me? So great is the pain for my lover! It is ill, when will it heal?

1

As the *kharjas* were written in Arabic letters, however, consequently no vowels are present, with the result that precise transcription is difficult and in some instances a matter of conjecture. Indeed so problematic is the very matter of deciphering that doubts have been expressed as to whether the passages are in a language that can be proved to be a derivative of the Latin spoken in the Iberian Peninsula.

Despite these reservations, however, a number of commentators have drawn attention to the similarities in theme and subject-matter between the *kharjas* and both the poetry produced in the north-western corner of the Peninsula in the thirteenth and fourteenth centuries and the songs that appeared more widely in the Peninsula but which were only set down in the fifteenth and sixteenth centuries. These connections betray a complexity that goes beyond the diversity of time and place and that again bears on the issue of what is the earliest poetry in Spanish. Of the three traditions that I have identified, only the last to be written down – the *villancicos* – is in Spanish. For the poetry written in the north-west of Spain in the Middle Ages is in Galician-Portuguese, not in Spanish; indeed it is now regarded as the first flowering of the lyric in Portuguese literature. The similarities of subject-matter and presentation, notably the incorporation of a female speaker, have led to speculation about a linear pattern of development in the Iberian Peninsula as a whole with similar origins and derivations. The fuller picture of early European lyric, however, suggests instead a confluence of traditions. If there was a single source it would be difficult to determine which it would be.

The issue of oral and written poetry likewise affects the epic. Only one such poem has survived in Spanish in a near-complete form, the *Poema* [or *Cantar*] *de mío Cid*, which was probably composed at the start of the thirteenth century. Evidence from chronicles and ballad-literature, however, suggests that there would have been a number of epics. Indeed it is likely that one such poem – the *Siete infantes de Lara* – dates from around 1000 and was revised three centuries later. A distinctive feature of the Spanish epic, certainly on the evidence of the *Poema de mío Cid*, was a blend of oral and written, or learned, elements. This text has perhaps provoked more controversy than any other in Spanish literature in recent decades. There has been a debate about the date of the poem, the status of the poet (was he a learned man – a lawyer or a cleric – or a semi-literate minstrel?), and the very identity of poet (does the name at the end of the manuscript refer to the author or merely a copyist?).

If the *Poema de mío Cid* is indeed an anonymous work then the first name in Spanish poetry is Gonzalo de Berceo (*c*.1196–1260?), a monk from the Rioja region, who lived in the first half of the thirteenth century. Even though Berceo was writing not long after the author of the epic poem, however, his poetry reads and looks very differently. The metrical scheme employed in the epic – the *mester de juglaria* – is well suited to oral delivery with the division of each line into manageable units for performance. The verse-form depends on rhythmic pattern, on the number of rhythmic accents per line, or in some cases, perhaps, on the length of time per line required in the recitation of the verse:

> De los sos ojos   tan fuerte mientre lorando
> tornava la cabeça   y estava los catando.[2]

> From his eyes such tears he shed, he turned his head and looked at them.

Contrast this with a stanza from Berceo's best-known work, the *Milagros de Nuestra Señora*:

> Davan olor sovejo   las flores bien olientes,
> refrescavan en omne   las carnes e las mientes;
> manavan cada canto   fuentes claras corrientes,
> en verano bien frías,   en ivierno calientes.[3]

> The sweet-smelling flowers perfumed abundantly, they refreshed the flesh and minds of men; from each corner there issued forth bright flowing fountains, so cool in summer, so warm in winter.

In this latter form – an example of *mester de clerecía* – the two halves of the line are uniformly of equal length unlike the oral or pseudo-oral form. It is not beat or rhythm but syllable count that is the determining factor: lines are made up of carefully counted syllables, each line comprising two hemistichs (half lines) of seven syllables each. There is, too, an unchanging rhyme-scheme (AAAA BBBB CCCC) whereas the epic had relied on assonance, achieved by the repetition of similar vowel sounds, and sometimes known as 'vocalic rhyme'. The stanza I have quoted from Berceo is perhaps a little untypical in that it is unusually euphonious on account of internal rhymes, including the opening words of the first three lines. The *cuaderna vía* (literally 'four-fold way') does not always guarantee such musical effects.

Berceo was not the first poet to employ this form: the anonymous *Libro de Alexandre* on the life of Alexander the Great is a slightly earlier work. The *cuaderna vía* metre was still being used a century later as the dominant form in the *Libro de buen amor* by Juan Ruiz, the Archpriest of Hita (1283? – 1350/1?), where it both performs a narrative function and supplies connective threads between a variety of other verse-forms.

A distinctive feature of poetry produced in the Christian kingdoms of Spain during the Middle Ages was linguistic choice. We tend nowadays to assume that language relates closely to nationality but in Castile until the late fourteenth century genre rather than nationality was a determining factor. For lyric poetry it was Galician-Portuguese not Castilian that was employed. Thus while Berceo's essentially narrative *Milagros de Nuestra Señora* – a versification of a Latin prose text – was written in Castilian, the collection of songs composed at the court of Alfonso X and with the king's active participation, with a narrative element contained within the forms of the song, are accordingly in Galician-Portuguese. If lyric poetry in Spanish, however, was in a sense delayed, it was to flower in the fifteenth century mainly through the emergence of large compilations of songs known as *cancioneros*. The title itself (literally a 'collection of songs') suggests the predominantly lyrical nature of these compositions. Even though there is no Spanish poet of the period of the calibre of François Villon or the Catalan poet Ausiàs March the sheer number of practitioners – over 700 known authors – testifies to the vitality of the new Castilian lyric.

The *cancioneros* continued to be published into the sixteenth century; indeed the finest collection, the *Cancionero general*, compiled by Hernando de Castillo, was republished many times in the decades following its first edition in 1511. Shortly after the appearance of the *Cancionero general* another, however, more radical, development was to affect the evolution of Spanish poetry. The links between Spain and Italy, established mainly through Aragonese and Catalan political involvement during the fourteenth and fifteenth centuries, became stronger as a result initially of the foreign policy of the united crowns of Castile and Aragon and later of the territorial inheritances of Charles V. While Italian poetic forms had been previously introduced into the Peninsula on a modest scale by such poets as Francisco Imperial (mid fourteenth – early fifteenth century) and the Marqués de Santillana (1398–1458) it was only from the 1520s that what would be termed the Italianate manner – principally the adoption of the sonnet form and the hendecasyllabic line – became the norm. The pioneer was Juan Boscán (1487? – 1542), but it was the poetry of his friend Garcilaso de la Vega (1501/3–36) that set the standard by which poets of succeeding generations would be measured.

The Italianate influence on Spanish poetry is part of the larger process of the importation of Renaissance values and ideas. The revaluation of the legacy of Greece and Rome was evident in sixteenth-century poetry in a number of ways. The philosophical background informed not only the content of poetry but in addition the theory, notably Aristotle's theory of imitation. Poets also chose their classical predecessors as models, imitating their words and forms. A notable example was the cultivation of pastoral where the Eclogues of Theocritus and Virgil were avidly digested. Thus at the climax of Garcilaso's *Égloga tercera* there is a close imitation of a passage from Virgil's *Seventh Eclogue*:

Flérida, para mí dulce y sabrosa
más que la fruta del cercado ajeno,
más blanca que la leche y más hermosa
que'l prado por abril de flores lleno[4]

Flérida, for me sweeter and tastier than the fruit in another's field, whiter than milk and more beautiful than the April meadow full of flowers

The use of classical mythology for illustration and metaphor was another common feature, with the result that the briefest of allusions could serve a shorthand or coded purpose, such as Midas for greed and Icarus for rashness. Such devices were a staple feature of the love poetry of the period where the dominant influence was not a classical writer but the fourteenth-century Italian poet Francesco Petrarca, known in English as Petrarch. A collection of his entitled *Canzoniere* was rediscovered and revalued in Italy at the start of the sixteenth century and soon became the most seminal work of the Renaissance and beyond. Both Petrarch and his earliest imitators became influential models that succeeding generations of poets, among them the poets of Golden Age Spain, would seek to imitate and emulate.

In the course of time so hackneyed did the characteristics of the Petrarchan manner become that in a quest for novelty poets were compelled to expand their range of linguistic and stylistic resources. For instance, one of the standard features of Petrarchan descriptions of the woman was that she had blonde hair. Countless poets of the Renaissance happily adhered to the ready-made analogy of hair as gold, but eventually it became a weak, if not a dead, metaphor. The opening lines of a sonnet by Francisco de Quevedo (1580–1645) indicate how the commonplace could be avoided. The description is of the lady with carnations in her hair:

Rizas en ondas ricas del rey Midas,
Lisi, el tacto precioso, cuanto avaro;
arden claveles en su cerco claro,
flagrante sangre, espléndidas heridas.

Minas ardientes, al jardín unidas[5]

You curl in rich waves of King Midas, Lisi, the touch that is as precious as it is greedy; carnations burn in her bright ring, flagrant blood, splendid wounds. Burning mines, joined to the garden

The use of myth in the opening line illustrates its use as a code – Midas is linked to the lady's hair via the notion of gold. The fifth line, however, is more elaborate and unusual: 'mines' refers to the site of the gold and becomes a replacement metaphor though its phonetic similarity to the name 'Midas' encourages us to think of it as a coherent development rather than a mere flight of fancy.

This kind of variation and ornamentation is sometimes described as 'baroque', a term drawn from the visual arts and architecture and applicable when poetry deviates from the standard or symmetrical features of Renaissance structures. A further tendency of later Golden Age poetry was the emulation of the classical writers not only as formal and thematic but, more radically, as linguistic models: the aim was to approximate the Spanish language to Latin by lexical and syntactical means. The leading exponent of this practice known as *cultismo* was Luis de Góngora (1561–1627), perhaps the most controversial of all Spanish poets. He was admired and scorned in roughly equal measure; indeed his detractors coined the term 'culterano' to describe his style by analogy with the word 'luterano' ('Lutheran') which had a clearly negative resonance in Counter Reformation Spain. The Latinate quality of his longer poems is very evident as in these lines from the *Fábula de Polifemo y Galatea* ('Fable of Polyphemus and Galatea'). Striking in this description of the one-eyed Cyclops, Polyphemus, is the dislocation of syntax to the point where a demonstrative pronoun is separated from its noun by a three-line parenthesis:

> Un monte era de miembros eminente
> este (que, de Neptuno hijo fiero,
> de un ojo ilustra el orbe de su frente,
> émulo casi del mayor lucero)
> cíclope[6]

> An eminent mountain of limbs he was, this (the fearsome son of Neptune whose one eye, that almost emulates the greatest light, lights up the orb of his forehead) Cyclops

Much has been made of the rivalry between Góngora and Quevedo. This probably originated in personal antagonism and reciprocal poetic insults and was converted into a literary feud between Góngora's *cultismo* and Quevedo's *conceptismo* – that is, a particularly concentrated form of conceptual wit, such as the lines from the love sonnet quoted above; the term 'wit' describes the quality of mind that could produce conceits, and is applied to the so-called English Metaphysical poets of the seventeenth century such as John Donne. In fact Quevedo is as capable of baroque pomp and the elevated manner as Góngora is of dense word-play and the ingenious metaphor. If there is a difference it is of degree, not of kind.

The *Penguin Book of Spanish Verse*, edited by J. M. Cohen (1960), contains no poetry written between the end of the seventeenth and the middle of the nineteenth centuries. Although extreme and unjust, this omission embodies the low esteem in which Spanish poetry of this long period is generally held. Except for the Mexican nun Sor Juana Inés de la Cruz (1651–95) it is hard to find a poet between 1650 and 1830 of the stature of half-a-dozen and perhaps more of the Golden Age. It would be simplistic to account for this falling-away in either historical or cultural terms. Neither the decline of Spain as a world power nor the growing dependency on French artistic norms with the emphasis on neo-classical adherence to rules and conventions, somehow felt to be alien to the way Spaniards did things, constitute adequate explanations. The decline of Spain is a complex historical issue and in terms of perceptible events is more pronounced at times outside this barren period: that is in the middle of the seventeenth century and at the end of the nineteenth. Again, having regard for the effect of the Italianate influence on sixteenth-century literature it would be rash to cite the foreignness of the French influence as a negative or inhibiting factor. Indeed it could be argued that the restraint and moderation that it offered might have served to animate a literary culture that had burnt itself out through the excesses of Góngora's lesser followers. We do not possess a theory which explains why the arts flourish in certain periods and wither in others; the most that can be asserted is that such mundane reasons as the conditions in which artists and writers have to work, and especially the presence of patronage, are likely to be more significant than speculations based on historical hindsight.

While Spanish poetry of the eighteenth century often bears a superficial similarity to that of the later Golden Age as a result of the imposing legacy first of Góngora, then of Quevedo, there are radical divergences. The neo-classical instinct for balance and clarity contrasts with the intricacy and ingenuity of baroque literature. The characteristics of European art, culture and thought of the eighteenth century are such that they led to designations like 'the Age of Reason' and 'the Enlightenment'. It is as though all shadows, both literal and metaphorical, have been dispelled, hence the predilection for moonlit landscapes, as in the 'Himno a la luna' by Gaspar Melchor de Jovellanos (1744–1811):

> Astro segundo de la ardiente esfera,
> que en el espacio de la noche fría
> suples la ausencia del radiante hermano,
>   fúlgida luna.
> Tú, que la sombra disipando, sacas
> plantas y flores del funesto caos,
> volviendo al suelo, con tu luz dorada,
>   vida y colores[7]

> Second star of the ardent sphere, who in the emptiness of the cold night, replace the absence of your radiant brother, gleaming moon. You, who, as you dispel the shadow, draw out plants and flowers from gloomy chaos, restoring life and colours to the earth with your golden light

During the eighteenth century, too, there were the first manifestations of a shift in sensibility that would lead to a major upheaval in the arts. In some ways these traits, variously described as early Romantic or, in the case of Spain especially, pre-Romantic, represent a reaction against the optimism and radiance of the Enlightenment. The most striking manifestation in European as well as Spanish art is perhaps that embodied in an individual output, that of Goya. The certainty of the Age of Reason yields to doubt and scepticism, and shadows return to darken the landscape, as in a poem by Alberto Lista y Aragón (1775–1848):

> ¡Qué horror! La fiera noche
> ha triplicado el denegrido manto
> de tinieblas sin fin. Huyó del cielo
> el nocturno esplendor: no hay una estrella
> que con su yerta amortiguada lumbre
> hiera la oscuridad del firmamento.[8]

> What horror! The fierce night has tripled the blackened cloak of endless darkness. The nocturnal splendour has fled from the sky: there is not a single star whose fixed, dim light could wound the blackness of the firmament.

The Romantic era was an especially fertile one for poetry in England, Germany and France. This was not so, however, in Spain where the poetry of the first half of the nineteenth century was of a considerably inferior quality; there is no Spanish poet of the period to compare with Shelley, Heine or Hugo. Cultural and historical circumstances – in particular the Peninsular War and the subsequent despotic rule of Ferdinand VII – again do not adequately explain the artistic poetic deficit, as it was in the decades straddling the turn of the nineteenth century that the extraordinary genius of Goya was to flourish. The contrast between the intellectual vitality of English poetry in the first quarter of the nineteenth century and Spanish poetry of the same period is glaring. It is possible, however, to take too negative a view of early Spanish Romantic poetry and disregard important minor poets. The *Romances históricos* of the Duque de Rivas (1791–1865) are significant because they re-establish the traditional Spanish ballad as a worthy vehicle of serious poetry. Rivas also was responsible for establishing the narrative poem as a favoured vehicle for poets who followed him.

Perhaps the greatest poem of the Spanish Romantic era is *El estudiante de Salamanca* by José de Espronceda (1808–42), a re-working of the Don Juan legend. This long narrative poem has many of the hallmarks of European Romanticism, most obviously the eerie setting with its pronounced atmosphere of Gothic horror:

Era más de medianoche,
antiguas historias cuentan,
cuando en sueño y en silencio
lóbrego envuelta la tierra,
los vivos muertos parecen,
los muertos la tumba dejan.
Era la hora en que acaso
temerosas voces suenan
informes, en que se escuchan
tácitas pisadas huecas,
y pavorosas fantasmas
entre las densas tinieblas
vagan y aúllan los perros
amedrentados al verlas.[9]

It was later than midnight, the old tales relate, and with the earth enveloped in sleep and gloomy silence, the living seem as dead, and the dead leave the tomb. It was the time when fearful voices sound disembodied, when silent, hollow footsteps are heard, and terrifying ghosts wander among the deep shadows and dogs howl in horror when they see them.

The change of sensibility that Romanticism implied had a liberating effect on the formal and metrical features of Spanish poetry. This technical revolution can be well illustrated within the work of Espronceda. His earliest poetry is in the neo-classical vein as in this extract from a poem about night:

El arroyuelo a lo lejos
más acallado murmura,
y entre las ramas el aura
eco armonioso susurra.[10]

The stream in the distance murmurs more silently, and between the branches the breeze whispers in harmonious echo.

This final phrase indeed could sum up Espronceda's poetry in this vein: it is smoothly flowing and symmetrical in form and design. In *El estudiante de Salamanca*, however, the range of verse-forms is immense, and determined by the subject and mood of what is being described. Thus the lines that describe the eponymous hero's death convey the last flickers of life in short, breathless lines, culminating in a single-word line that seems to embody physical collapse:

la frente inclina
sobre su pecho,
y a su despecho,
siente sus brazos

lánguidos, débiles
desfallecer.

            (p.177)

He rests his head upon his chest, and despite himself he feels his languid, weak arms give way.

The narrative poem enjoyed such a vogue in the Romantic period that it was not only continued by later poets such as José Zorrilla (1817–93) but also left its mark on other genres. In the late 1850s and 1860s Gustavo Adolfo Bécquer (1836–70), a Sevillian who had settled in Madrid, published a series of *leyendas* ('legends') that often appear like prose equivalents of the Romantic narrative poem. Indeed Bécquer's short stories are arguably, by dint of greater powers of description and evocation, more poetic than the verse equivalents of other poets. Bécquer, however, was the leading Spanish poet of the mid-century period. His verse, influenced by Andalusian folk-song and the lyrics of the German poet Heine, emerges as fresh and imaginative alongside the banal and overblown poetry of contemporaries such as Ramón de Campoamor (1817–1901) and Gaspar Núñez de Arce (1834–1903). Of the former it was said not unreasonably that his was a poetry destined for an illiterate society. Indeed the work of both poets lacks the charm of simplicity for they are frequently verbose, as with the opening of Núñez de Arce's long religious poem 'La visión de Fray Martín':

> Era una noche destemplada y triste
> Del invierno aterido. Lentamente
> La nieve silenciosa, descendiendo
> Del alto cielo en abundantes copos,
> Como sudario fúnebre cubría
> La amortecida tierra. Cierzo helado
> Azotaba los árboles desnudos
> De verde pompa, pero no de escarcha.[11]

It was an unpleasant and sad night of freezing winter. Slowly, the silent snow falling in large drops from the sky on high covered the dead earth like a funeral shroud. The icy wind whipped the trees, devoid of their green pomp but not of frost.

This is a kind of poetry-by-numbers where most concrete nouns attract a predictable adjective. It is a long way removed from the concision and understatement that, as we shall see, are hallmarks of Bécquer's poetry.

After Bécquer's early death in 1870 the finest poetry was produced outside Castile and to a considerable extent not in Spanish: by Rosalía de Castro (1837–85), writing both in her native Galician and in Castilian, and by the poet-priest Jacint Verdaguer (1845–1902) whose entire poetic production was in Catalan.

A much-needed injection of novelty arrived in the shape of South American *modernismo*, a movement whose most influential exponent was the Nicaraguan Rubén Darío (1867–1916). Both Darío and his fellow-poets from the New World took their inspiration, however, from Europe not America, especially from Parnassianism, a literary movement in France in the second half of the nineteenth century that envisaged the poet's role as a sculptor or craftsman who should fashion his poem into something almost tangible, hence the frequent allusions to the plastic arts. As Darío and his followers, however, were less taken with the more intellectually stimulating example of poets such as Baudelaire and Mallarmé, Spanish poetry was enriched purely by an extension of lexicon and by the cultivation of an aesthetic of fantasy and exoticism that looked to other arts, such as painting and music, as in the suggestively titled 'Sinfonía en gris mayor' by Darío:

> La siesta del trópico. El lobo se aduerme.
> Ya todo lo envuelve la gama del gris.
> Parece que un suave y enorme esfumino
> del curvo horizonte borrara el confín.
>
> La siesta del trópico. La vieja cigarra
> ensaya su ronca guitarra senil,
> y el grillo preludia un solo monótono
> en la única cuerda que está en su violín.[12]

> The tropical siesta. The sea-dog falls asleep. Now the gamut of grey covers everything. It seems as if a soft and huge pencil had blurred the line of the horizon's curve. The tropical siesta. The old cicada tries out its hoarse and senile guitar, and the cricket begins a monotonous solo on the single string that is on its violin.

The impact of *modernismo* cannot be overestimated, leaving a deep mark in the longer term on such poets as the young Federico García Lorca (1898–1936). At the same time that *modernismo* was popular, however, Spanish thinkers and writers were preoccupied with a national issue: the state of Spain in the wake of the loss of the overseas possessions of Cuba and the Philippines, in a war with the United States. The Generation of 1898 – the year in which these historical reverses occurred – was mainly a movement comprising essayists and novelists (Unamuno, Baroja, Azorín, Ganivet), but one of the most enduring and popular collections of poetry of the twentieth century, *Campos de Castilla* by Antonio Machado (1875–1939), betrays those same hallmarks of an anguished national and historical awareness that we find in the prose meditations of the period:

> Castilla miserable, ayer dominadora,
> envuelta en sus andrajos, desprecia cuanto ignora.[13]

> Wretched Castile, yesterday so dominant, now wrapped in its rags, it scorns all that it does not know.

The First World War brought about or at least coincided with artistic innovations and upheavals as radical as those associated with the political revolutions in the dawn of the Romantic era more than a century earlier. The arts were transformed by such movements as Dadaism, Futurism and, later, Surrealism, while Spanish poetry was subject not only to such Europe-wide movements but also to innovative tendencies peculiar to Spain and Spanish America, especially in the years of the First World War and immediately after. A derivative of Futurism was *ultraísmo*, founded by Guillermo de Torre (1900–71), one of whose aims was to reflect in poetry the machine age and technological advance. Its poetic language differed sharply from that both of the *modernista* poets and of the poets of the Generation of 1898 towards whom the *ultraístas* adopted a belligerent attitude. A related *avant-garde* movement was that of *creacionismo*, invented by Vicente Huidobro (1893–1948), a young Chilean poet resident in Europe. He had been among the contributors to the magazine *Nord-Sud* founded by Guillaume Apollinaire, a French poet who attempted to introduce Cubist ideas into poetry. In like manner *creacionismo* aimed to achieve Cubist effects by making art not a depiction or reflection of reality but an independent, self-sufficient object: it was meant to complement rather than to represent life – a creation in its own right. The spirit of the movement is summed up in a couple of oft-quoted lines from Huidobro's 'Arte poetica':

> Por qué cantáis la rosa, ¡oh Poetas!
> Hacedla florecer en el poema.[14]

> Why do you sing of the rose, o Poets! Make it bloom in the poem.

Short-lived as these movements were they contributed towards the release of poetic energy in the emergence of several Spanish poets of exceptional talent in the 1920s. Variously known by the collective titles 'Generation of 1927', 'Generation of 1925' and 'The Generation of the Dictatorship', they included Gerardo Diego (1896–1987), whose earliest works betray the influence of *creacionismo*; Pedro Salinas (1891–1951); Jorge Guillén (1893–1986); Rafael Alberti (1902–99); Luis Cernuda (1902–63); and, most famously of all, Federico García Lorca (1898–1936). The last three betray in some of their works features of the Surrealist movement. Unlike their immediate predecessors – the *creacionistas* and *ultraístas* – these poets felt a greater affinity with the poetry of Spain's past, both the traditional-popular poetry of the Middle Ages and Renaissance and the major poets of the Golden Age. *Marinero en tierra*, the first collection of Rafael Alberti, is one of the earliest manifestations of such a new approach, blending the old and the new in a piquant mix, as in a poem entitled 'El aviador' where the machine age meets the Medieval lyric:

> –Madre, ha muerto el caballero
> del aire, que fue mi amor.
>
> Y en el mar dicen que ha muerto
> de teniente aviador.
>
> ¡En el mar!
> ¡Qué joven, madre, sin ser
> todavía capitán![15]

> Mother, the knight of the air, who was my love, has died. And they say he died as a lieutenant pilot in the sea! In the sea! How young, mother, without yet being a captain!

It was to the learned rather than popular poetry of the Renaissance that Alberti's contemporary Luis Cernuda looked for his *Égloga, elegía, oda*. Both the title and lines such as the following evoke the idyllic but stylized world of pastoral poetry:

> Entre las rosas yace
> El agua tan serena,
> Gozando de sí misma en su hermosura;
> Ningún reflejo nace
> Tras de la onda plena,
> Fría, cruel, inmóvil de tersura.[16]

> Among the roses the water lies so serene, enjoying itself in its beauty; no reflection is born beyond the full wave, cold, cruel, immobile in its smoothness.

The revaluation of Góngora by Dámaso Alonso (1898–1990), an influential scholar and minor poet of the Generation of 1927, is a parallel literary-critical activity.

Together with the prodigious talents of the Chilean Pablo Neruda (1904–73), resident in Spain for a period during the 1930s, and the self-taught poet from Orihuela, Miguel Hernández (1910–42), the poets of the Generation of 1927 ensured that Spanish poetry in the 1920s and 1930s enjoyed a second Golden Age. This ended abruptly with the oubreak of the Spanish Civil War in 1936. The majority of writers were sympathetic to the beleaguered Republican cause, supporting it through their artistic activity and sometimes through a commitment to arms. The conflict also spawned poetry for propaganda purposes, much of it of predictably poor quality. A handful of poems by Neruda and Hernández, however, rose above the mediocre, while the rediscovery of the ballad as a tool for oral poetry was an interesting side-effect of the poetry of the Civil War period. The ultimate effect of the conflict, however, was catastrophic for Spanish poetry as indeed it was for Spanish cultural life as a whole. There were individual tragedies among Spanish writers and poets: Lorca was executed by Franco supporters in Granada a month into the Civil War; Antonio Machado died just across the French border shortly after his flight to exile in a vast exodus in early 1939; Hernández died as a political prisoner in 1942. The attempts to resurrect cultural activity in the aftermath of war were crudely linked to the ideology of the dictatorship, with the emphasis on a unitary, Catholic state. The literature of Imperial Spain of the sixteenth century acquired an iconic status, epitomized in the naming of a literary journal *Garcilaso*.

In some respects Spanish poetry of the second half of the twentieth century has mirrored those features that characterize its development over hundreds of years, notably in the way in which developments have occurred mainly by reaction rather than evolving as a continuum. Thus the predominantly social poetry of the 1940s and 1950s, whose leading practitioners were Gabriel Celaya (1911–91) and Blas de Otero (1916–79), yielded to a purer kind of poetry in the following two decades, principally as a result of the work of a group of writers labelled *novísimos*, notably Pere Gimferrer (1945–) and Guillermo Carnero (1947–). Again, as with poetry written in the earlier part of the twentieth century there was evidence of a fascination with the realities and novelties of contemporary life. Thus while the Futurists declared their enthusiasm for machines and the industrialized world so Gloria Fuertes (1918–98) incorporated consumerism, as in her poem 'Galerías preciadas', the title of which plays on the name of a well-known department store – 'Galerías Preciados':

> Todo te viene pequeño
> –o demasiado grande–,
> ni siquiera lo que escoges te va,
> todo te viene pequeño.
> Con el alma desnuda por una cosa u otra
>   imploramos al Tendero.[17]

> Everything is too small for you – or too big –, not even what you choose fits you, everything is too small for you. With our naked souls we beseech the Shopkeeper for one thing or another.

The final line with its capitalization of 'Tendero' strongly suggests that the shopping experience is a metaphor for a profounder existential concern, but the experience is rooted in the most everyday of realities. In 'Chico Wrangler', however, Ana Rossetti (1950–) is content to explore the world of advertising and the exploitation of the body and sexuality for its own sake:

> Dulce corazón mío de súbito asalto.
> Todo por adorar más de lo permisible.

Todo porque un cigarro se asienta en una boca
y en sus jugosas sedas se humedece.
Porque una camiseta incitante señala,
de su pecho, el escudo durísimo,
y un vigoroso brazo de la mínima manga sobresale.[18]

Sweet heart of mine suddenly assaulted. Everything to adore more than what is permitted. Everything because a cigar settles in a mouth and moistens in its juicy silks. Because a provocative tee-shirt indicates the rock-hard shield of his chest, and a vigorous arm protrudes from the flimsy sleeve.

The incorporation of the detail and images of contemporary life by such poets as Fuertes and Rossetti, however, is no more novel or unexpected than the utilization of military metaphors in a Renaissance poem as the verse equivalent, often as a eulogy to a patron, of the court portrait of the sixteenth and seventeenth centuries. At the opening of Garcilaso's *Égloga primera* the poet's depiction of the Duke of Alba engaged in hunting is reminiscent of the equestrian portraits of Velázquez:

resplandeciente, armado,
representando en tierra el fiero Marte;

agora, de cuidados enojosos
y de negocios libre, por ventura
andes a caza, el monte fatigando
en ardiente ginete que apresura
el curso tras los ciervos temerosos[19]

resplendent in your armour, an earthly representative of fearsome Mars, now free of worrying concerns and matters of state, you may have the fortune to ride to hunt, wearying the mountain on an impetuous steed that quickens its stride after the frightened stags

Moreover, when we observe how a poet such as Fernando de Villena (1956–) writes sonnets that seem to have come from the pen of a sixteenth-century writer it serves to remind us that the poetry of Spain in recent years, no less than in the past, displays the dual characteristics of tradition and originality, and thus betrays the same creative tension that has been apparent on various occasions over many centuries.

Versification

Except for the earliest poetry, such as the *Poema de mío Cid*, Spanish verse is classified according to the number of syllables per line. Some of the commoner line lengths, however, also require fixed accents. For example, the hendecasyllabic (eleven-syllable) line will usually have either a single stress on the sixth syllable

> En fin a vuestras m*a*nos he venido

or else two less emphatic stresses on the fourth and eighth syllables

> ¡Oh dulces pr*e*ndas por mi m*a*l halladas

To calculate line length, syllables are counted to the last stressed syllable, and then one syllable-count is added regardless of the number of actual syllables following the final accent. Therefore only when a line ends in a stressed syllable followed by a single unstressed syllable does the total number of syllables counted correspond to the designated length, as with the following octosyllabic line, the standard metre for the *romance* or Spanish ballad:

> Voces de muerte son*a*ron

The following line contains seven syllables, but as it ends in a stressed syllable an extra syllable is 'understood' so that it is also reckoned an octosyllable:

> cerca del Guadalquiv*i*r

Conversely, where the stress falls on the antepenultimate syllable of the line, one syllable is subtracted, as with the following example, which is an octosyllabic line even though it contains nine syllables:

> entre la cruz y la c*ú*pula

If two vowels stand together, either within the single word or at the end of one word and the start of the next, they are usually counted as a single syllable. This is a process known as synaloepha:

> la monja bord*a a*lhelíes

From around the start of the sixteenth century the aspiration of initial *h* disappeared so that surrounding vowels would be affected by synaloepha. Such a process, however, evidently does not occur in a line from a sonnet by Garcilaso dating from the 1520s, where in order to have a hendecasyllabic (eleven-syllable) line, the articulation of the initial *h* in 'hondo' is necessary:

> así yo por l*o h*ondo travesando

Sometimes, again to comply with the needs of the metrical form, contiguous vowels that would normally be reckoned as separate syllables are considered as one — a process known as syneresis:

> qued*ao*s en aquesa playa

The opposite to this – dieresis – involves dividing a normal diphthong into two syllables, whereby 'süave' would be a three-syllable word, and 'jüez' one of two syllables.

Rhyme in Spanish poetry is either consonantal (full rhyme) or assonantal (half rhyme). The former is the norm for the sonnet form; the latter, for the ballad or *romance*. Consonantal rhyme involves the identical repetition of vowels and consonants after the final stressed syllable. It is important to note that this repetition is phonetic not orthographic, thus 'fuente' rhymes with 'mente', and 'muerte' with 'verte'. Assonantal rhyme involves identity between vowels only, so that the consonant that figures in the affected part of the line may vary. Assonantal patterns most commonly occur on even-numbered lines, and will extend over lengthy passages, either a whole poem or a substantial section of a long poem. Assonance is designated by the identification either of two vowels, or, where the line ends in a stressed syllable, of one. This passage from Lorca's *Romancero gitano* involves an assonance on *u-o*:

> Coches cerrados llegaban
> a las orillas de juncos
> donde las ondas alisan
> romano torso desnudo.
> Coches, que el Guadalquivir
> tiende en su cristal maduro,
> entre láminas de flores
> y resonancias de nublos.

Another from the same collection comprises assonance on a single vowel – on *í*:

> Les clavó sobre las botas
> mordiscos de jabalí.
> En la lucha daba saltos
> jabonados de delfín.
> Bañó con sangre enemiga
> su corbata carmesí,
> pero eran cuatro puñales
> y tuvo que sucumbir.

Chapter 1

Poets and readers

Few Spanish poets have been what might be termed professional poets. Lorca, perhaps the best-known of all, is untypical in being as near to a full-time writer as one could envisage. Even the jobbing poet of the Middle Ages – the minstrel – is denied a place of honour in Spanish literature given the dearth of surviving epic poems and the likely learned authorship of the *Poema de mío Cid*. The Middle Ages do, however, provide some of the classic profiles of Spanish poets, notably the figure of the poet-cleric. The contrasting figures of Berceo and the Archpriest of Hita established a trend that was to continue into the Golden Age whereby clerics wrote secular as well as religious poetry. Thus the major figures of the Golden Age include the love poet Fernando de Herrera (1534–97), the holder of a small lay benefice in the church of San Andrés in Seville; Góngora, who entered the Church in order to accept a prebend renounced in his favour by an uncle; the theologian Fray Luis de León (1527–91); and the Carmelite mystic, San Juan de la Cruz (1542–91).

The figure of the poet-courtier, that would be a dominant presence at the start of the seventeenth century in such figures as the Conde de Salinas (1564–1630) and the Conde de Villamediana (1582–1622), is anticipated by such aristocratic poets of the fourteenth and fifteenth centuries as the Marqués de Santillana (1398–1458) and Juan de Mena (1411–56). The Duque de Rivas, an aristocrat and politician, was following in a long line. In his youth Rivas had also been a soldier and was wounded in the Peninsular War. The figure of the soldier-poet can also be traced back into the Medieval period. Because of the Aragonese possessions in Italy the leading Catalan poets of the early fifteenth century, Jordi de Sant Jordi (1400–24) and Ausiàs March (*c.* 1397–1459), had served abroad. This trend was more pronounced a century later when Spain, already unified by the joining of the crowns of Castile and Aragon, acquired further possessions through the accession of Charles V to the throne and his subsequent election as Holy Roman Emperor. The following decades were the heyday of the soldier-poet, the most celebrated of whom, Garcilaso de la Vega, was killed in battle near Nice in 1536. The epitome, however, of the figure of the soldier-poet, representative of Spain's international commitments and ambitions in the sixteenth century, is Francisco de Aldana (1537–78). Of Spanish parentage he grew up at the court of Cosimo de Medici in Florence and served in the Spanish campaigns in the Low Countries in the 1570s. He set foot in Spain for the first time only in 1577 when he was appointed Governor of the fortress of San Sebastian. The following year he died in the service of King Sebastian of Portugal at the battle of Alcazarquivir in North Africa.

The modern era has, for obvious enough reasons, seen the emergence of different types. A characteristic twentieth-century figure is the poet-scholar. The precursor was perhaps Antonio Machado. Although he never attained an elevated academic position – for most of his life he was a provincial schoolteacher – he became increasingly preoccupied with philosophical ideas and metaphysical concerns that had scarcely bothered Spanish Romantics or even the *modernistas*. It was with the Generation of 1927, however, that the poet-scholar came to prominence. The monumental scholarship of Dámaso Alonso has already been mentioned, and to this can be added the influential editorial activity of Gerardo Diego and Emilio Prados (1899–1962), and the academic affiliation, especially after the Civil War, of Pedro Salinas (1891–1951) and Jorge Guillén (1893–1986). The most recent development for Spanish poets perhaps has been a shift from the academic to a greater variety of professions, including law and journalism, although the poet-scholar is still an important figure as in the case of Guillermo Carnero (1947–), who figures in this study both as a poet and as an editor.

The modern image of the process of getting a poem into print – the poet being inspired to write, submitting a manuscript to the publisher, waiting for acceptance, correcting proofs, and seeing his book published and (hopefully) bought for private reading – is precisely that: a modern image. It describes only one – if the most recent – model of the poetic enterprise from conception to fruition and also only one poet–reader relationship. As we have glimpsed already, however, the circumstances of composition and reception of two of the earliest masterpieces of Spanish poetry are far removed from the standard contemporary model. Both these Medieval works appear to have been designed for performance, the *Poema de mío Cid* for entertainment and perhaps propaganda, Berceo's *Milagros de Nuestra Señora* for entertainment and instruction. The former was, as we have seen, likely to have been the work of a learned writer aping the devices of an orally composing poet. The latter was a free translation into rhyming fourteen-syllable lines of a Latin prose text. Berceo did not conceive his role as that of the inspirational poet figure so beloved of the Romantic and modern eras, but as a craftsman, in his words, as a 'leal obrero de Dios' ('loyal workman of God').

In both cases the concept of 'audience' is more specific than a modern understanding might acknowledge. The audience consisted quite simply of those who had turned up. Indeed, until quite recently, audiences and readers have been far more clearly definable, a situation that related to the way in which poetry circulated. Until the seventeenth century – two centuries beyond the invention of printing – Spanish poetry circulated mainly in manuscript form. Such a mode of diffusion was by no means confined to minor or anonymous poets; many works by writers of the stature of Góngora and Quevedo have come down to us in this form, in the process often posing sizeable problems of attribution.

With a restricted public, poets, more consciously than nowadays, wrote mainly with an audience in mind. They knew, as they wrote, who would read their verses, and such a knowledge influenced what they wrote. With an audience of fellow-poets – rivals as well as friends – they might adopt an allusive and playful manner. Emulation and competition were powerful motivators and were consistent with Renaissance precepts about the imitation of good models, contemporary as well as classical. Poetry of this kind was social in implication, again in a way unfamiliar to modern readers. One reason why Spanish poets of the Golden Age were unconcerned about having their works published was that the principal outlets for their poetry were formal literary gatherings. The favoured milieux for the major poets of the seventeenth century were academies in such cities as Madrid, Seville and Valencia. These had their origins in the literary gatherings and performances in Andalusian cities in the time of the Moors and continued sporadically in the Medieval period, especially in the courts of Alfonso X and Juan II of Castile. In more recent times the distinctively Spanish *tertulia* – a semi-formal gathering of friends in a café to discuss literary and other matters – represents an important offshoot of the academy. Lorca's earliest performances of his poems took place at a *tertulia* in the Café Rincón in Granada. Indeed Lorca's own career as a poet epitomizes some of the tensions implicit in an understanding of how poetry and audience can relate. He was a charismatic reciter of his verse, for whom an English-language equivalent might be Dylan Thomas. He was generally diffident, however, about the activities associated with publication. He was remiss in such routine matters as the reading of proofs and showed little urgency about getting completed work published, sometimes leaving near-completed projects tantalizingly unfinished. As a result some works appeared only many years after completion, while others were published posthumously with all the drawbacks that such publications entail. It was as though Lorca acknowledged that once a work was set in print it was no longer his own, not something over which he could enjoy the privileges of sole proprietorship as an author–performer.

The trend in the promotion of poetry over the past five hundred years has been towards a published medium for public sale and private reading, and away from individual ownership for public performance. This has been a trend, however, rather than an unvarying norm. The act of private reading was implicitly recognized as essential during the later Renaissance period for an adequate appreciation of longer poems like the literary epic or coherent groupings of poems such as sonnet sequences. Conversely, on various occasions in the modern era the potency of spoken verse, of poetry recited in public, has been evident. The ballads of the Spanish Civil War and the rich vein of Latin American protest poetry are two such manifestations. Indeed these poems are apt to seem banal and inflated when set down on the page and subjected to the kind of close-reading scrutiny we apply to poetry destined for individual reading. Interestingly the compositional processes of this kind of poetry are reminiscent of the procedure in the *Poema de mío Cid* insofar as we assume a learned, or certainly a literate, poet who creates a work that supposes an illiterate audience, or at least one deprived of the possibility of the written medium.

Modern poetry in particular, however, betrays on occasion a tendency that is the very opposite to this reaching out to a public. The notion of poetry as a private world and a hermetic activity, forbidding in its desire to avoid communication and thus apparently to ignore the reader, has arisen at the same time that poetry has, through lower publication costs and improved technology, become theoretically more accessible. The paradox is more intriguing if we think, say, not of a poet like the introverted Emilio Prados, a member of the Generation of 1927, but of his contemporary Pablo Neruda. The latter's earliest collection, *Veinte poemas de amor y una canción desesperada* was a runaway success. It is not, however, by most definitions, poetry that is readily understood. Its imagery is dense and complex and, through subtle allusion, evokes the baroque poets of Spain, especially Quevedo. We might justifiably posit another model of readership from this case whereby the owning of books is not tantamount to the reading of books, nor to the active appreciation of poetry. It comprises instead what could be described as a form of mass popular bibliophily.

Those non-reading owners of books that one must presume in the case of a poet like Neruda represent an extreme of passive readership. Most formulations of the poet–reader relationship, however, are in fact predicated on an active (poet) – passive (reader) model. In *A Reader's Guide to Contemporary Literary Theory* Raman Selden suggests a scheme for the literary process, based on Roman Jakobson's diagram of linguistic communication, comprising three parts or, conceived in temporal terms, three stages: writer – text – reader.[1] While we conventionally refer to the poetic text as 'the work', a poem *works* only by the involvement of the other two elements: the creator/writer and the receiver/reader. Such a consideration may appear too obvious to be worth stating insofar as it refers to the writer, but it has not always been so in the case of the reader. In an influential survey of the history of modern theory Terry Eagleton argues that the acknowledgement of the reader's role in 'realizing' a poem is a recent phenomenon:

> Indeed one might very roughly periodize the history of modern literary theory in three stages: a preoccupation with the author (Romanticism and the nineteenth century); an exclusive concern with the text (New Criticism); and a marked shift of attention to the reader over recent years. The reader has always been the most underprivileged of this trio – strangely, since without him or her there would be no literary texts at all. Literary texts do not exist on bookshelves: they are processes of signification materialized only in the practice of reading. For literature to happen, the reader is quite as vital as the author.[2]

Such an awareness of the reader's role goes beyond theorizing. It has practical implications for how to read poetry, encouraging us to be more rigorous in defining what happens when we are reading. Apart from this positive contribution (some of whose implications I shall explore in the course of this chapter), affording readers their rightful place in the scheme of things can serve as a corrective to critical fallacies.

A common misconception in approaching poetry is to assume an auto-biographical intent by default: a poem is therefore held to be not only *by* someone but *about* someone. More than that it is assumed to be reflective so that an 'I' in the poem is tantamount to the 'I' that is the poet, and what happens in the poem has also happened in the life. I am not suggesting that poetry does not have an autobiographical aspect. Rather I am urging caution about simplifying and prioritizing it because in the process the reader's hori-zons are artificially narrowed. Let us consider two Spanish poems separated by 400 years. In Garcilaso's *Égloga primera* the shepherd Salicio complains at his abandonment by Galatea, who has chosen another lover; another shep-herd, Nemoroso, mourns the untimely death of his beloved, Elisa. Until quite recently it was commonly accepted that this poem was a close reflec-tion of events in Garcilaso's life: his love for a Portuguese lady-in-waiting by the name of Isabel Freire, who married another man, and her death in childbirth (a detail reproduced in the poem) a few years later. The poem was read effectively as the embodiment of these experiences and through successive generations a romantic myth was created. Not even the discovery that Garcilaso almost certainly did not meet Isabel Freire in the year when it was assumed that he fell in love with her has dented this myth. Yet even to argue over what Garcilaso was supposed to have been doing or feeling when he wrote the poem misses the point. The poem is the same whether Garcilaso was passionately in love for several years or whether he never knew Isabel Freire. One suspects the truth to be somewhere in between but even such a cautious conclusion is unhelpful because it only continues to tell us about the *causes* of the poem. It tells us nothing about effects; and such autobiographical solutions impoverish the reader. To return to Selden's scheme, the emphasis on the author–text relationship is so pronounced that the text–reader relationship is overlooked. In the process it would be easy and tempting to be blind to other considerations. On the one hand we might ignore the fact that in 1527 the Italian poet Luigi Tansillo wrote a poem entitled *I due pellegrini* ('The two pilgrims') that contained the same contrast between betrayal and bereavement as had Garcilaso's poem. Moreover, the biographical reading can curtail text-based activity, for example examining the very structuring of the poem. The equal division of space between the two laments – recalling some of Virgil's *Eclogues* – encourages the reader to think of them as competing rather than just complementary songs, maybe prompting the question 'Which is the greater sorrow?' This competitive aspect and our awareness of a playful dimension is also suggested by the highlighting of imagery for the two shepherds. Salicio's amatory rage is initially conceived in terms of fire – testament to his fierce jealousy:

> ¡Oh más dura que mármol a mis quejas
> y al encendido fuego en que me quemo
> más helada que nieve, Galatea![3]

> O harder than marble to my laments, and more frozen than snow to the blazing fire in which I burn, Galatea!

The image that sets the tone for Nemoroso's lament, however, is the opposite one: water. His, accordingly, is a gentler grief:

> Corrientes aguas puras, cristalinas,
> árboles que os estáis mirando en ellas,
> verde prado de fresca sombra lleno
>
> (p. 128)

> Pure and crystal-clear flowing waters, trees that look at yourselves in them, a green meadow full of fresh shade

Biographical elements figure in a rather different way in Rafael Alberti's *Sobre los ángeles* (*Concerning the Angels*). They appear sporadically as snippets of life – almost as a collage-effect, a characteristic of Surrealist art. Alberti, however, unlike Garcilaso, also supplied what could be described as a confirmative document in the shape of an autobiography – *La arboleda perdida* (*The Lost Grove*). It is therefore possible, as both commentators and editors have done, to set the two texts alongside each other and use the prose autobiography as a critical tool. The danger of this approach is that it is far too limiting and will suppress the deductions and leaps that are part of the reader's task in reading (or even making) the poem. In the case of the poem

'El ángel de las bodegas' ('The angel of the wine-cellars') it is tempting to be content merely with the information that Alberti's family had been involved in the wine trade and that the business was unsuccessful.[4] To explain such lines as the opening – 'Fue cuando la flor del vino se moría en penumbra / y dijeron que el mar la salvaría del sueño' ('It was when the flower of the wine was dying in the shadow / and they said that the sea would save it from sleep') – in terms of what happened to the Alberti family rather than in terms of the negativing of an image with powerful sacramental overtones ('la flor del vino') is to reduce the text.[5] The symbolic potency of such a phrase is thereby all too easily ignored.

If biographical readings have an inhibiting effect the same can be said for context. By this I mean what is sometimes rather vaguely described as the 'background' to a poem, for example the social or historical circumstances in which a poem is written. All too often the background, by a critical leap, becomes the explanation of the poem, its rationale. Again I shall consider two poems separated in time. The first is a sonnet by Francisco de Quevedo that dates from around 1613:

> Miré los muros de la patria mía,
> si un tiempo fuertes, ya desmoronados,
> de la carrera de la edad cansados,
> por quien caduca ya su valentía.
>
> Salíme al campo, vi que el sol bebía
> los arroyos del yelo desatados,
> y del monte quejosos los ganados,
> que con sombras hurtó su luz al día.
>
> Entré en mi casa; vi que, amancillada,
> de anciana habitación era despojos;
> mi báculo, más corvo y menos fuerte;
>
> vencida de la edad sentí mi espada.
> Y no hallé cosa en que poner los ojos
> que no fuese recuerdo de la muerte.[6]

I looked at the walls of my native place, once strong and now dilapidated, weary with the passing of time, as a result of which their strength is now sapped. I went out into the countryside, I saw that the sun drank the streams released from ice, and the cattle complaining that the mountain stole their daylight with its shadows. I went into my house; I saw that it was the rubble of an old, tarnished habitation; my walking-stick, more curved and less strong; I felt my sword overcome by age. And I found nothing on which to set my eyes that was not a reminder of death.

A number of extra-textual factors converge upon this text and distort its impact. Firstly, there is the historical situation. It was written at a time when, according to conventional interpretations assisted by hindsight, the vast Spanish Empire was starting to show signs of crumbling. Secondly, Quevedo was chiefly known as a satirist: a sharply sceptical commentator on the events of his day, someone whom it could be presumed would be alive to the symptoms of a national malaise. If we add to these non-textual issues the word for 'native-land' in the first line of the sonnet and the image of crumbling walls we seem to have all we need to define the piece as a poem that is a memorable summation of a historical process. What we do not yet have, however, is either the remainder of the sonnet or the poems that precede and follow it in the collection in which it appears. Both these make it clear that the subject is of an individual significance, not a national one. We do not need to rely upon even these, however, to challenge the historical interpretation. The word 'patria', commonly taken to mean 'native-land', also had the meaning of 'town', an understanding that in fact relates more readily with 'walls' than does the less concrete and particularized word 'native-land'. Indeed it is feasible that 'muros desmoronados' refers to the walls of Madrid that were being knocked down as the city was being enlarged at the start of the seventeenth century. It is significant that the historical readings of Quevedo's sonnet tend to cite the opening two lines and leave it at that – a glaring omission, for the later part of the sonnet has an obviously personal and individual preoccupation. As we shall see below, however, decoders of poems tend in one way or another to be partial, one mode of partiality being selective quotation. This involves using the text to 'prove' an idea, which in all likelihood will have derived, as here, from non-textual sources.

My second example of the imposition of a historical reading on a poem concerns Antonio Machado's 'El hospicio', the fourth poem in *Campos de Castilla*:

> Es el hospicio, el viejo hospicio provinciano,
> el caserón ruinoso de ennegrecidas tejas
> en donde los vencejos anidan en verano
> y graznan en las noches de invierno las cornejas.
>
> Con su frontón al Norte, entre los dos torreones
> de antigua fortaleza, el sórdido edificio
> de grietados muros y sucios paredones,
> es un rincón de sombra eterna. ¡El viejo hospicio!
>
> Mientras el sol de enero su débil luz envía,
> su triste luz velada sobre los campos yermos,
> a un ventanuco asoman, al declinar el día,
> algunos rostros pálidos, atónitos y enfermos,
>
> a contemplar los montes azules de la sierra;
> o, de los cielos blancos, como sobre una fosa,

caer la blanca nieve sobre la fría tierra,
¡sobre la tierra fría la nieve silenciosa![7]

It is the poorhouse, the old provincial poorhouse, the ruined mansion
with blackened tiles, where the swifts nest in summer, and the crows caw
on winter nights. With its façade to the north, between the two turrets of
an ancient fortress, the squalid building with its cracked and dirty walls is
a corner of eternal shadow. The old poorhouse! While the January sun
casts its weak light, its veiled sad light on the barren fields, pale,
bewildered and sick faces appear at an ugly window as the day ends, to see
the blue hills of the sierra, or from the white skies, as though upon a grave,
white snow falling on the cold world, on the cold earth the silent snow!

This collection is quite reasonably acknowledged as one of the key works
of the Generation of 1898. Machado himself recognized the importance of
the historical theme, although the book itself is varied in content and style,
covering as it does poems written over a period of ten years. Perhaps because
of this authorial self-assessment one critic feels justified in describing the
poem as 'una profunda metáfora para expresar el estado de su España con-
temporánea y de las condiciones de muchos de sus habitantes' ('a profound
metaphor by which to express the state of the Spain of his day and of the
conditions of many of its inhabitants').[8] The problem with this kind of interpretation is not so much that it cannot be shown to be right as that it cannot
be shown to be wrong. The case does not rest on the effects of the poem
but upon the alleged intention. It depends on circumstantial evidence: the
period, the title of the collection, the poet's declared priority. The interpretive method in such instances, however, readily becomes circular. The text
both suggests and eventually confirms (how could it do otherwise?) the initial intuition, which is a combination of biography, history and text. It fails
to address what the text *does* (a process I shall attempt to describe below),
but at least one could not accuse the interpreter of being random. In the
particular case of modern poetry, however, interpretation often depends on
the randomness of word-association.

Let us consider for example the opening of Lorca's 'El rey de Harlem'
('The king of Harlem') from his *Poeta en Nueva York*:

Con una cuchara,
arrancaba los ojos a los cocodrilos
y golpeaba el trasero de los monos.
Con una cuchara.[9]

With a spoon, he tore out the crocodile's eyes and beat the monkeys on
their bottoms. With a spoon.

Derek Harris asserts that this passage presents a 'considerable puzzle'.[10] The
word 'puzzle' is a significant choice. It points to a process that will govern

the approach to the poem: difficulty and solution. For the critic–decoder the more a passage resists explanation by paraphrase the greater the need to illuminate and to define. Undaunted by the challenge Harris sets out to solve the puzzle:

> This is an incantatory, almost magical, statement centred on the African animals of the Zoo. Crocodiles are associated with death in the New York poems, and their blinding may thus be taken to represent a defeat for death. Monkeys are a traditional symbol of trouble, while in Christian symbology they stand for sin, lasciviousness, malice, the base condition of man, and even for the Devil. Their chastisement seems to indicate another defeat for negative forces. The spoon is perhaps an image of the King's sceptre, diminished in status.   (p. 32)

I think it is possible to pinpoint the error of an approach like this in such a way that the objection is not based on either theory or taste. The misconception arises from a questionable critical method, specifically the outcome of an inordinate focus on two images – the crocodiles and the monkeys. Harris attributes to them characteristics ('death', 'trouble', 'sin', etc.) on the basis of (i) imprecise cross-referencing which could be auto-referential, (ii) traditional symbolism and (iii) Christian symbology. Both images are negated (Harris's understanding of 'arrancaba los ojos' and 'golpeaba') hence the 'defeat for negative forces' whatever these may be. Although Harris's statement has the requisite quality of definition, it is, however, on the basis of word-association rather than context. In his fixation on what he decides to be the two key terms he prefers to explore outside the text rather than address what is inscribed within it. He has in the process inverted Wittgenstein's injunction: 'Don't look for the meaning of a word, look for its use.' Consequently he has nothing to say about the incongruities in the text: that a spoon not a knife should be used as the instrument of aggression; that the king of Harlem, of African origin, should be attacking, even if in an inept and comical fashion, creatures with whom he has a kinship. Such a response to the text does not clarify in terms of solving a puzzle but that would be a shortcoming only if we regard poems as little more than riddles. The kind of wondering into which I am led, however, represents an attempt to reflect what happens as a result of the text, what comes out of it. It departs from expectations articulated as questions (e.g., should a king be doing this?) and thus locates contradictions. In short all it defines is the likely knowledge and curiosity of the reader about to embark on the fifth line of the poem. This has been achieved by an awareness of what the poem *has done*, not on the basis of what the poem *has supplied* by way of extractable material. It is a mode of understanding that does not depend upon the inevitable arbitrariness of noun-based deciphering; it has, in short, involved responding to the actions rather than the objects in the narrative of the text.

Let us now look again at Machado's 'El hospicio' and apply a similarly reader-centred approach. The first two stanzas describe the poorhouse from outside; the opening with its deictic intent ('Ah, here's the poorhouse') suggests both a narrator–observer, an implicit first-person presence, and an addressee. The last two stanzas, however, supply an opposite perspective: the eyes are of those within looking out. An awareness of this switch sharpens the reader's perception of the inmates' plight. The move from building to people and from institution to experience yields both a sense of compassion that is emphasized in the pathos of the third stanza and a recognition that compassion is denied in the play on 'tierra fría' and 'fría tierra' – a cold (frozen) earth because it is snowing and a cold (callous) earth because it is uncaring. The contrast of past and present – the crux of Predmore's historical interpretation – does not therefore figure in the development of the poem except as an accompanying irony: the fortress, which was a stronghold, has now become an asylum for the weak and unfortunate. What a historical reading does, rather as Harris does with 'El rey de Harlem', is to extract details and explore them out of context, and thereby sacrifice the fuller awareness of what the poem has made us do. Stanley Fish reminds us that it is easy 'to surrender to the bias of our critical language and begin to talk as if poems, not readers or interpreters, did things'.[11] Let us now consider the effect of such a statement by reference to Lorca's 'Aire de nocturno' from *Libro de poemas*:

> Tengo mucho miedo
> de las hojas muertas,
> miedo de los prados
> llenos de rocío.
> Yo voy a dormirme;
> si no me despiertas,
> dejaré a tu lado mi corazón frío.
>
> '¿Qué es eso que suena
> muy lejos?'
> 'Amor,
> el viento en las vidrieras,
> ¡amor mío!'
>
> Te puse collares
> con gemas de aurora.
> ¿Por qué me abandonas
> en este camino?
> Si te vas muy lejos
> mi pájaro llora

y la verde viña
no dará su vino.

'¿Qué es eso que suena
muy lejos?'
'Amor,
el viento en las vidrieras,
¡amor mío!'

Tú no sabrás nunca,
esfinge de nieve,
lo mucho que yo
te hubiera querido
esas madrugadas
cuando tanto llueve
y en la rama seca
se deshace el nido.

'¿Qué es eso que suena
muy lejos?'
'Amor,
el viento en las vidrieras,
¡amor mío!'[12]

I am very frightened of the dead leaves, frightened of the meadows full of dew. I am going to fall asleep; if you don't wake me I will leave my cold heart at your side. 'What is it that sounds far away?' 'Love, the wind on the glass, my love!' I put necklaces with dawn gems on you. Why do you abandon me on this road? If you go far away my bird weeps and the green vine will not yield its wine. 'What is it that sounds far away?' 'Love, the wind on the glass, my love!' You will never know, sphinx of snow, how much I would have loved you on those dawns when it rains so much and the nest is broken on the dry branch. 'What is it that sounds far away?' 'Love, the wind on the glass, my love!'

There are different presences in this poem, deriving from a first-person controlling voice and an addressee suggesting two identities. The incorporation of direct speech in the guise of a refrain adds to the complexity. The first task is to locate, partly by disentangling, the various voices or presences.

Initially we encounter a child-like attitude: the unfounded fear (why be afraid of the leaves and the meadow?), the worried question in the refrain, the focus on basic activities (sleeping, waking, going away), the sense of insecurity (the subject abandoned on the road). All of this is enunciated in an appropriately direct and simple language. Midway through the poem, however, another voice is perceived: that of the lover. At first this is ill-defined, marked by the abstract terms 'corazón' and 'amor'. In the third and final strophe, however, it emerges clearly, and effectively supplants the child-like voice of the opening. It is a reproach that unexpectedly evokes the terminology of Medieval or Renaissance love poetry: the rebuke and appeal to an indifferent female object – 'esfinge de nieve' ('sphinx of snow').

For these differing subject voices there is but a single response from the addressee: the second part of the refrain – ' "Amor, / el viento en las vidrieras, / ¡amor mío!" ' ('Love, / the wind on the glass, / my love!'). This is clearly (or as clearly as anything could be in this poem) a reassurance to the curious and troubled questioner. To the child-subject these words are those of a mother. The refrain itself, however, is intriguing because it supplies a constant message while the principal strophes embody the changes of addressee and attitude. Moreover, although the origin of the response is maternal, its detail is sufficiently protean to cover the poem's dual emotional configuration. The sound in the distance is both the wind rattling the windows and, in a word, love. Two replies, in effect, but a single voice: tender and consoling, and solely indicative of the motherly presence. It would be inappropriate to attribute to the sphinx of snow the endearment at the end of the refrain.

Having identified, indeed isolated, two likely female presences we could now locate areas where there is ambivalence. The close of the first strophe has within it the abrupt shift from the child's simple utterance – 'Yo voy a dormirme' ('I am going to fall asleep') – to the abstraction of 'corazón' ('heart'). The qualification of 'corazón' as 'frío' ('cold'), however, seems inappropriate for the subject, whether as child or would-be lover, though we will subsequently deem it appropriate for the remote beloved. Additionally, the opening of the second main strophe hints at an idealization – 'Te puse collares' ('I put necklaces on you') – that smacks of a child's disarming endearment as much as of a lover's devotion. We are now starting to wander into the area where we read symbolically, and it is at this stage that a decision about the understanding of the poem might be made.

Interpreting or decoding readers may take their cue from the symbolic implications of the phrase at the start of the second strophe and embark on further 'discoveries'. Before doing this, however, it is very likely that a choice about the poem's meaning or subject will have been made, if only unconsciously. This may well require an unequivocal answer to the question 'with which of the two loves does the poem deal?' – an answer that will compel elimination. This is a process that will not be necessarily recognized as such for habits of interpretation dull the awareness of what we do when we read, whereby what is recognized is outcome – a product rather than a process. The answer to such a question would be without fail erotic love, but what I query is that it should be 'without fail' especially if we keep in mind what the poem *is*, as suggested by my opening comments on the piece, while I have not yet seriously considered what the poem *does*. There are, I hazard, two reasons for such a definitive, unqualified answer. One derives from the fact that it comprises the final impression of the poem read as a sequential unfolding – in other words it is what is at the end, and because of that we deem it to be the poem's end, that is, its objective – and it becomes the abiding impression. The second reason is a matter of custom and practice; I am tempted to say an understanding by default. Most love poems are concerned with erotic love; most of these are about heterosexual love relations; and of these the majority convey an experience that is negative or unfulfilled. The present poem passes all these tests, but an unchallenged expectation has been allowed to become the poem's theme, its foundation.

And on this base a further and familiar process of analysis can now take place. With the erotic scenario in mind the critic is free to 'see the meaning' 'behind the words', 'below the surface' or some such phrase; it is a task that leads towards paraphrase and word–substitution. Let us imagine how it might be with 'Aire de nocturno'. The vine that will not yield wine and the destroyed nest on the dry branch will be read as metaphors of a failed love. There is nothing objectionable about such a reading in itself but it is conducive to a doubly suspect process of understanding. On the one hand it may encourage further and more fanciful decoding whose only validity will be that it is part of the 'general picture', that it fits in with the approach adopted. It will, however, have been forgotten that this 'picture' is the unidimensional one that the critic has extracted from the poem rather than one that recognizes the plural voices and presences within it. In this vein, too, the dead leaves will be categorized with the barren vine and the broken nest as another instance of pathetic fallacy – human emotions reflected in or projected upon inanimate objects – and, consequently, its more immediate, though problematic, point of contact with the image of the dewy meadows will be overlooked. It almost goes without saying that within this interpretive frame the weeping bird can supply the statutory phallic symbol.

What such an interpretation also does, however, is to betray what has been the experience of responding to the poem. For rather than making sense by *completing* the poem we would be imposing meaning by *amending* it. This is ironic, for while decoders may imagine that interpretation offers freedom (hence such observations as 'many interpretations are possible' and 'this is ambiguous') it is an illusory freedom for they are slaves to a way of reading that is restricted by the requisites of the symbolic understanding and, often, of preconception. The outcome of this approach is to sell the poem short because it has rejected what was valid, even troubling, in an intial response. It fails to acknowledge what Stanley Fish has defined as the kinetic quality of literature; it is a kind of criticism that forgets that as we read a book both it and we are moving: the pages turning, the lines receding into the past.

Instead of an interpretation based on 'forgetting', that is elimination, however, one could envisage another, based on incorporation. The cue for this could be the occasional amalgamation of the maternal and the erotic, and its extension so that the alternation of the two loves becomes in this reading a fusion. This supplies the critic with a ready-made solution to the poem in the form of an Oedipal interpretation. One of the problems with this is that it is a *solution*. It treats the *text* (as distinct from the larger concept of the poem) as somehow defective, or incomplete *as text*, and confers a unity upon it. What is registered as plural and incompatible is filtered into a single subject that is an *integration*. So what is the warrant for this leap? Nothing other than the neatness afforded by the structural convenience of joining two disparate elements and the attraction of applying to a poet who was homosexual an interpretation that derives from an understanding (there may not be sufficient ancillary detail to call it a reading) of the psychology of Freud.

The sense I acquire in the poem, however, is not at all about reduction or integration. It is about separateness and incongruity, and the sense that I make of it demands that I acknowledge its uncertainty and its actual *confusion* rather than its presumed *fusion*. This confusion resides not in the attempt to describe the nature of the elements – the two loves, maternal and sexual – but in the attempt to reconcile them. The crucial point is this: the attempt does not need to be successful. This is where I take leave from the orthodoxy of New Critics, who were preoccupied with unity and integrity and not averse to taking short cuts to achieve these desired goals. To admit to failure in an effort at combining the two elements, however, will no less enable us to achieve an understanding of the poem: one that, in my view, better relates to the experience of reading it – the sense of the text.

What is clear too is that this sense is as much a result of our intervention, of our making, as any interpretation, however ingenious it may be. The text supplies fragments of emotional relationships in the form of statements and dialogue. These scraps allow us to perceive the incompatibility of the two loves. One of these is real insofar as it belongs to the present or the past; the other is remote (the 'muy lejos' of the refrain), a thing of the future at most. Put more emphatically, there is a love that has gone or that will shortly go (as the child grows up) and a love which, through its conventional formulation, does not exist and may never be. One can envisage a virtual presence that partakes of these two loves, a poetic subject that experiences both, but in a limited fashion. It is an experience that is ill-formed, unclear, and that lacks the security of definition. A textually analytical description could supply a quantification, essentially a localization, of characteristics.

Only in the unsuccessful struggle for meaning as integration, however, is the experience of disturbance and uncertainty realized. This is not inscribed in the text as substance in the form of images, but is fulfilled in the act of reading whereby we have made sense of the poem.

I offer as an analogy to my observations on the Lorca poem a comparison of two public notices: 'Members only' and 'Guide dogs only'. If we subject these to a textual analysis we see that both involve restriction and are identically formulated: noun plus adverb plus verb understood ('are allowed'). Read purely in these terms, however, what could we conclude? That only members would have access in the case of the former and only guide dogs in the latter. Of course we know that the latter example has a further, unstated qualification: the only kind of dog that is allowed is a guide dog. This knowledge, however, is not in the text as formulated but in our *completion* of the text. We achieve the proper understanding because we are endowed with the capacity for making the leap, for coping with the apparently shorthand version of the message. Such a gift would commonly be called common sense; more specifically the sense that the phrase possesses is made common by the readers of the notice. If it were left to the text alone what we would have would be a nonsense.

The intervention of readers in literary texts is not as seemingly dramatic as this retrieval of sense from non-sense. The alert reader, however, can at the very least enhance a text by the realization of its meaning. Let us consider a passage from Luis de León's 'Vida retirada'. Typically for the sixteenth century it is based on a classical source, the *Odes* of Horace, upon which is grafted the topical theme of the scorn of the city and the praise of the country. The poem is made up of a series of contrasts and antitheses, often in a structurally balanced fashion whereby the exposition of a positive quality will be succeeded by an equal space of text dedicated to the negative one. As a consequence, as we read through the poem we are conditioned to expect a process of alternation. Midway through the poem there is a stanza that describes the poet in his rural idyll:

> Del monte en la ladera,
> por mi mano plantado, tengo un huerto,
> que con la primavera,
> de bella flor cubierto,
> ya muestra en esperanza el fruto cierto.[13]

> On the side of the mountain, planted by my own hand, I have a garden, which shows in the Spring, covered with beautiful flowers, the certain fruit as a sign of hope.

We might well now be awaiting the riposte, and indeed when we read the next two lines our expectations would seem to have been fulfilled:

> y, como codiciosa
> de ver y acrecentar su hermosura.

> and, greedy as it is to see its beauty increase.

A word like 'codiciosa' seems tailor-made for all that is negative about the city or court, suggestive as it is of worldliness and self-seeking, while 'hermosura' will imply in this context a vain, perishable beauty. These two lines, however, have not yet supplied the noun to which the feminine adjective 'codiciosa' refers. The following line – 'desde la cumbre airosa' ('from the proud peak') – continues to deny us the information we seek; indeed the adjective 'airosa' could be read as a hint of the pomp of court life. Finally, and by now surprisingly, we discover that the subject is a fountain – a positive element from the dichotomy:

> desde la cumbre airosa
> una fontana pura
> hasta llegar corriendo se apresura.

> from the proud peak a pure fountain quickens its pace and arrives running.

Such a false trail is not without its purpose. If we extract the conflicting ideas from the poem then they can be represented in terms of a straightforward opposition. To carry out such a structural reduction, however, would be to overlook the character of the voice that speaks through the poem. At the end there appears to be an undisturbed contentment, certainly if we were to extract and list the images that are employed:

> A mí una pobrecilla
> mesa de amable paz bien abastada
> me baste, y la vajilla
> de fino oro labrada
> sea de quien la mar no teme airada.

> Y mientras miserable-
> mente se están los otros abrasando
> con sed insaciable
> del no durable mando,
> tendido yo a la sombra esté cantando.

> A la sombra tendido,
> de hiedra y lauro eterno coronado,
> puesto el atento oído
> al son dulce acordado,
> del plectro sabiamente meneado.

> (p. 74)

> Let a poor little table well stocked with pleasant peace be enough for me, and let the plate worked in fine gold belong to him who does not fear the angry sea. And while others are burning in their misery with an insatiable thirst for the authority that does not last, let me sing as I lie in the shade. Stretched in the shade and crowned with ivy and eternal laurel, with my ear listening closely to the sweet measured sound of the skilfully plucked lute.

Merely to tot up the positive images, however, would not properly represent the poet's state of mind: the scene is not how things are but how the poet would wish them to be – an aspiration rather than a reality. As a result the voice is anxious, not complacent, as these are not the lines of a smug moralist, secure in his superior condition. The effect of the surprise attendant upon the presentation of the fountain image thus operates to a similar end. It instils a matching insecurity in readers, denying them the certainty of the clear-cut distinction and alternation. It raises doubts, and results in a momentary need for readjustment that contributes to an experiencing of the poem that involves a process of emotional response allied to reasoning that is close to that of the poet at the end. It is a salutary reminder that to define the poem as a clash of values would be inadequate; the poem is rather about the *response* to such a clash. Moreover, it is a response to which the reader has contributed.

We are now a long way from the conception of the reader as a passive presence that we take for granted. We have also seen how the reader's contribution to the poem (as distinct from the text) can take different forms. In the case of Lorca's 'Aire de nocturno' the reader's inability to achieve a definition adds to the uncertainty and darkness of the poem; with 'Vida retirada' the tentative way in which we assimilate detail matches the poet's insecurity and uncertainty. The mimetic implications of the reader's involvement in these poems is even more pronounced in the first paragraph of a poem from *En las orillas del Sar* by Rosalía de Castro (1837–85):

> Del antiguo camino a lo largo,
> ya un pinar, ya una fuente aparece,
> que brotando en la peña musgosa
> con estrépito al valle desciende.
> Y brillando del sol a los rayos
> entre un mar de verdura se pierden,
> dividiéndose en limpios arroyos
> que dan vida a las flores silvestres
> y en el Sar se confunden, el río
> que cual niño que plácido duerme,
> reflejando el azul de los cielos,
> lento corre en la fronda a esconderse.[14]

> Along the old path, now a pine grove, now a fountain appears, which bursting forth on the mossy rock descends noisily to the valley. And shining in the rays of sun between a sea of greenery are lost, split in limpid streams that give life to the wild flowers and joining together in the Sar, the river which like a child who sleeps peacefully, reflecting the blue of the skies, flows slowly to be hidden in the foliage.

This is a poem evocative of the poet's native Galician landscape, here perceived at its most enchanting. But 'discovered' might be a better description than 'perceived'. The old path referred to in the first line leads to the traditionally magical location of a fountain and later to a river that divides into various tributaries. If this, however, describes the content of the paragraph I have quoted it does little justice to how we absorb it. Much is made of the secrecy of the location, set deep in the woods. Verbs such as 'se pierden' ('are lost'), 'esconderse' ('to be hidden') and even 'aparece' ('appears'), indicative of something that has been suddenly stumbled upon, hint at the remoteness and inaccessibility of the place. Once again, however, the reader's involvement is not confined to such textual tasks: more than the reception of a message it will entail participating in the poem's unfathomability. This process is centred on what is likely to be a difficulty of comprehension in the long sentence that begins in line 5. We may tentatively admit that the subject of 'se pierden' must be the pine grove and the fountain mentioned in line 2. This is grammatically, at least, a possible solution though on reflection it is not the logical one, because while a fountain can be lost in a sea of green, it is hard to see how a pine grove could, most obviously because it is itself likely to be the sea of green. Moreover, the later part of the first sentence (lines 3–4) clearly refers to the fountain alone because of the use of a verb in the singular – 'desciende' ('descends'). We might then reject the connection of 'se pierden' to the nouns in line 2 and await the appearance of the subject after the verb as commonly happens in Spanish. Indeed the appearance of a gerund – 'dividiéndose' ('dividing itself/themselves') – immediately after the verb suggests that the actions suggested by these two parts of speech are connected not only because of the syntactic link but also a semantic one; as they are divided they become lost. Such an understanding, however, would of course require a plural subject and when a subject appears it is a singular one: 'el río' ('the river'), two lines below. We are as a consequence forced to rethink our syntactical understanding and readjust our mental picture. 'Se pierden' does after all refer to the pine grove and the fountain; the gerund is not linked to the immediately preceding verb but to the one that has the river as its subject, that is 'corre' ('flows'), no fewer than five lines below. The reader thus undergoes a process that mimics the likely venturer into the wood: taking a wrong turning, losing the way and eventually chancing upon the desired location. The confusion to which we are subject is inscribed in as many words in the text, in the verb 'se confunden' ('are confused'), which refers to how the tributaries will be absorbed into the larger river, the Sar.

So, the meaning of the poem – if we can so reduce it – will not be the outcome of the search but the search itself. Or, to put it another way, while the syntactical and grammatical senses of the poem require an effort on our part, but one that ultimately yields a solution, the poem is more than that solution: it is also about the effort. To forget what the discovery has demanded of us would be a perverse deprivation as it would be to deny an essential part of the poetic experience of this particular piece. Nobody would claim that the act of appreciating a poem was comparable to an arithmetical calculation but if we do not acknowledge what has gone into the process of understanding – how it has been for us, what it has meant for us – then that is what we are in danger of doing. Or, as Luis Cernuda, one of the most acute poet-critics of his generation, put it, using the same image as Castro does in the poem we have just examined: 'el poema no debía dar sólo al lector el efecto de mi experiencia, sino [conducirle] por el mismo camino que yo había recorrido, por los mismos estados que había experimentado' ('the poem ought not merely to have supplied the reader with the effect of my experience, but [to have led him] along the same path that I had trod, through the same states that I had experienced').[15] In this connection let us compare two real-life situations. The first envisages someone engaged in a calculation of a trial-and-error nature as one frequently is when buying something. For example: I have a sum of £50 and need to know how many items I could buy at £7.25 each. I initially estimate seven, and then discover, after performing the precise calculation, that it is in fact six. Unless it is something on which I had particularly set my heart, then I am content with the solution, or put another way, *the solution is what matters*. The trial-and-error process is a means, the details of which can be forgotten as soon as completed. Let us consider another event, however. I am travelling on a plane and there is a lot of turbulence. At this point I hear the sounds of the musical chime indicating that a message is about to be relayed. The message goes as follows: 'We are sorry to tell you (*pause*) that it has been necessary for us (*pause*) to cancel the in-flight movie.' Another wrong impression – but we do not as easily dismiss the experience of the erroneous expectation in this case as we would with the miscalculation. The traveller's anxiety was unfounded: it was a momentary panic. It would, however, form a part of the memory of that flight in a way that the incorrect calculation when making the purchase would not remotely approach. Indeed we would conclude that the anxiety was the most real and vivid experience of that flight.

If anyone were to be asked which of these occurrences supplied the better analogy for the impact that poetry has, there would doubtless be unanimous agreement that it would be the traveller's because it possessed an emotional dimension unlike in the case of the buyer. When critics, however, speak of a poem's meaning or, as we have seen, of solving the problems posed by a poem, they are unknowingly engaged in an exercise similar to our purchaser making a calculation. This involves rejecting what does not contribute to what they understand to be the purpose of the poem. Whenever there is a definition of, or sometimes a conclusion about, a poem, it will entail an elimination of that part of the experience – and even that part of the text that provokes the experience – that is unnecessary or complicating for the formulation of such a statement. Over-interpreters invariably forget, through either will or habit, what has brought them to the point of statement. As readers they are, in both senses of the word, partial. Or it may be that they do not consider themselves readers as such; indeed the existence of the term 'ordinary reader' is telling in this regard. What this chapter has sought to explore, however, is the inappropriateness of the distinction between the 'ordinary' reader and the 'extraordinary' interpreter. What the poems examined in this chapter require are readers who participate, readers who make the effort. Only with this intervention can the implications and potential of the text be realized; only with this involvement can the poem be fully *made*.

Chapter 2

The interrelationship of texts

The last chapter was concerned with righting an imbalance in the common perception of the relationships between poets, texts and readers. Any corrective measure, however, always runs the risk of excess so that we exchange a prejudice for a dogma, even one as attractive and provocative as Maurice Blanchot's dictum that a book that hasn't been read is a book that hasn't been written.[1] To compare the poetic text to a sleeping princess that awaits the reader's kiss to bring it to life, however, is to disregard its inherent vitality, even if it is conceded that it depends upon the reader for its completion. Indeed modern criticism focuses as much on the text as on the reader in its reaction to the cult of the author so prevalent in the wake of Romanticism, most famously enunciated in Roland Barthes's article entitled 'The death of the author'.[2] The subject of dispute has not been whether the text was important, but *how* it was important. To summarize the theories and movements engaged in this issue would be quite beyond the scope of this study. In a book dedicated to a survey of the poetry of many centuries, however, it is fruitful to explore at least some of the ways in which texts relate to each other.

Ralph Waldo Emerson, often ahead of his time, observed that every book is a quotation,[3] an idea echoed by Harold Bloom when he asserts that 'the meaning of a poem can only be another poem'.[4] For J. Hillis Miller, a literary text is not a thing in itself, and 'the study of literature is therefore a study of intertextuality'.[5] The term 'intertextuality' was coined by Julia Kristeva in 1966 to signify the interdependence of literary texts. Where this theory was radical was in its repudiation of the concept of influence and the study of sources, common scholarly procedures in the comparison of texts. For Kristeva, intertextuality implies a psychoanalytical understanding involving a transposition of one or several sign systems into others.[6] The operation may therefore involve transference from non-literary and even non-linguistic systems to a literary one. More useful for my purpose, however, is the narrower conception of intertextuality such as is suggested by Gérard Genette's concept of 'transtextuality' – that is, everything, be it explicit or latent, that links one text to others. A survey of Spanish poetry will inevitably yield evidence of varieties and nuances in these connections.

The multiple nature of such linkages has been well summed up by Mikhail Bahktin, a scholar from whom Kristeva derived her theory of intertextuality. Although he is specifically describing the relationship of 'the other's word' in the Middle Ages the description is appropriate for a general understanding of intertextuality:

> The role of the other's word was enormous at that time: there were quotations that were openly and reverently emphasized as such, or that were half-hidden, completely hidden, half-conscious, unconscious, correct, intentionally distorted, unintentionally distorted, deliberately reinterpreted and so forth. The boundary lines between someone else's speech and one's own were flexible, ambiguous, often deliberately distorted and confused. Certain types of texts were constructed like mosaics out of the texts of others.[7]

Terms commonly used to indicate the relationship of one text to another are 'imitation' and 'influence'. In broad terms 'imitation' implies a conscious borrowing whereas 'influence' encompasses unconscious as well as conscious indebtedness, and has in recent times become an issue concerned with the very nature of poetry itself, not merely the linkages between individual poems. Such has been the focus of much of the critical writing of Harold Bloom to which I shall return below.

Imitation in Aristotle's understanding implied representation, a precept that during the Renaissance envisaged art as the depiction of nature. Classical writers, however, also advocated the adoption of the style of a previous writer, thus giving rise to a mode of creativity that entailed the imitation of good models. This procedure was both popular and prestigious until the Romantic era when it came into conflict with the cult of individuality and personality. Before examining instances of imitation in its respectable and re-creative guise let us consider its unacceptable face – the most disreputable of all relationships between texts: plagiarism. If imitation constitutes borrowing then plagiarism may be justifiably labelled as theft. Not so much because it is taking without permission – for the imitation that is borrowing does not ask permission either – but rather because the plagiarist, for all that his offence may be blatant, is essentially a clandestine operator, unlike the imitator who is only too happy to proclaim his indebtedness.

A good example of the plagiarist's stealthy activity is offered by José Iglesias de la Casa (1748–91), a little-known eighteenth-century poet from Salamanca. The few commentators who mention Iglesias regard him as one of the leading poets of his day, but they are evidently unaware of his shameless plagiarism. The object of his plunder was Quevedo, and in particular his sonnets to Lisi. Iglesias attempts to cover his tracks in simple but effective ways. Firstly, while he has relied exclusively on Quevedo's sonnets none of his own poems are in this form. Had they also been sonnets, of course, recognition as a result of similar structural and associated syntactical patterns would have been much easier. Iglesias's poems are longer lyrical forms entitled *Idilios*, nearly all of which make use of a five-line stanza, a sub-unit that is unlike those that make up the sonnet. Moreover, in slightly over half the set the speaker is clearly female, a feature that distinguishes Iglesias not only from Quevedo but from virtually every sonnet writer in Golden Age Spanish literature. Iglesias also escaped detection by a number of textual strategies. His borrowings occur more frequently nearer the end rather than the start of the poem, and are thus less obvious if only for the reason that poems – even those with titles – are sometimes identified by their first lines. It is also a well-attested fact that people easily remember the opening lines of poems and songs but have more difficulty as they proceed. Indeed in his sixth *idilio*, that draws on two sonnets by Quevedo, Iglesias clearly sets a false trail by opening with a brief recall of a sonnet by Herrera. Thus the earlier poet's opening –'Osé i temí: mas no pudo la osadía' – becomes in Iglesias:

> Osé y temí, y en este desvarío,
> Por la alta frente de un alto escollo pardo . . .[8]

> I dared and was afraid, and in this delirium, along the lofty ledge of a dark high ridge . .

This opening-line imitation comprises a common and 'legitimate' imitative practice of a kind we shall see again below. It also serves, however, as a smokescreen, for the immediately following phrase is a near-copy of the opening line of a Quevedo sonnet: 'Por yerta frente de alto escollo, osado . . .'.[9] Much of the *idilio* derives, however, from Quevedo's sonnet 'Amor me ocupa el seso y los sentidos', to such an extent that, apart from the first quatrain, every line, if not every phrase, of the sonnet is plundered by the later poet. I print the sonnet alongside the pertinent section of the *idilio* to highlight what Iglesias has attempted to disguise:

Por el hondo distrito y dilatado	Amor me ocupa el seso y los sentidos;
Del corazón, en fuego enardecido,	absorto estoy en éxtasi amoroso;
Se explayó el gran raudal de mi gemido	no me concede tregua ni reposo
Y la dulce memoria de mi amado	esta guerra civil de los nacidos.
Hundió en eterno olvido.	Explayóse el raudal de mis gemidos
	por el grande distrito y doloroso
Soy ruinas toda, y toda soy destrozos	

Escándalo funesto y escarmiento
A los tristes amantes, que sin
    tiento
Levantaron de lágrimas sus gozos,

Gozos de inútil viento.
Los que en la primavera de sus
    días
Temieron el desdén de sus
    amores,
Envidien el tesón de mis dolores,
Y luego aprendan de las ansias
    mías,
Los finos amadores.

del corazón, en su penar dichoso,
y mis memorias anegó en olvidos.

Todo soy ruinas, todo soy
    destrozos,
escándalo funesto a los amantes,
que fabrican de lástimas sus
    gozos.
Los que han de ser, y los que
    fueron antes,

estudien su salud en mis sollozos,

y envidien mi dolor, si son
    constantes.

Along the deep and
distended district of the
heart, inflamed in my fire,
the great torrent of my
lament overflowed and the
sweet memory of my lover
was sunk in eternal oblivion.
I am all ruins, and all
fragments, a disastrous
example and a warning to
the sad lovers, who carelessly
raised their joys from tears,
joys of useless wind. May
those who in the springtime
of their days feared the
scorning of their love envy
the tenacity of my grief, and
may the refined lovers learn
from my sorrows.

Love occupies my mind and
my senses; I am absorbed in
amorous ecstasy; this civil war
of my innate faculties yields me
neither truce nor rest. The
torrent of my lament
overflowed through the great
and grievous district of my
heart, joyful in its sorrow, and
it drowned my memories in
oblivion. I am all ruins, and
fragments, a disastrous
example to the lovers who
manufacture their joys from
pity. Let those who are yet to
come and those who were
before study their health in my
sobbing, and envy my sorrow,
if they are constant.

Iglesias tinkers rather than recreates. There is an inversion of the syntax of lines 5–7 of the sonnet, caused by the postponement of the subject of the sentence ('el gran raudal de mi gemido'). He makes much use of synonyms and paraphrase: 'gemidos' becomes 'gemido', 'grande distrito' becomes 'hondo distrito', 'doloroso' becomes 'dilatado'. Paraphrase is allied to amplification: 'memorias' becomes 'dulce memoria', 'anegó en olvidos' is changed to 'hundió en eterno olvido', and 'envidien mi dolor' to 'el tesón de mis dolores'. The exchange of singular for plural and *vice versa* – hardly the most imaginative re-writing – is evidently very common. In conclusion such fastidious but undemanding tampering bears the hallmarks of an out-and-out plagiarist. All one can say in his defence is that Iglesias had good taste and that he was ahead of his time in recognizing something worth copying in Quevedo's love poetry.

The true nature of Iglesias's lack of scruples becomes clearer when we examine 'true' or legitimate imitators. Unlike the plagiarist the imitator openly displays his debts. As a consequence, first-line imitations are the norm rather than the exception in order that they might leave a surer impact on the reader. In the Renaissance, when imitation of this sparingly allusive kind was especially cultivated, the later poet viewed the imitative act not as a covert activity but as a stimulus and a challenge. Imitation invited emulation, whether of the poets of antiquity or of the poet's immediate predecessors. Imitative processes were often complex, sometimes involving imitations of imitations.

As we have already seen, one of the most influential and imitated poets of the Renaissance was Petrarch. He was best known in his own day for his Latin works, but from the early sixteenth century onwards Petrarchism was synonymous with the *Canzoniere*. The work departs from a biographical detail – Petrarch's love for a Florentine noblewoman, Laura – to become the prototype for the sonnet sequence. The second part of Petrarch's cycle comprises poems written after the death of Laura in which sorrow for her death combines with a penitential mood. One of the most anguished of these poems is one that recalls the occasion of the first sight of Laura, a date that is also the date of her death. The opening line, in translated form, became one of the most quoted in Golden Age Spanish poetry: 'Quand'io mi volgo in dietro a mirar gli anni' ('When I turn around to look at the years').[10] It is not in itself an especially memorable line as it is little more than a scene-setter, indicative of the poem's retrospective note. When a poet cited such a line, however, Petrarch's poems were so well known that it would evoke the remainder of the sonnet – its mood and its ethos. Imitation here is creatively allusive in that the later poet will not seek to duplicate but rather to complement, perhaps even to supplant, the earlier text – what Gérard Genette labels the hypotext. The later text, or 'hypertext', responds to the other in ways that range from slight variation to significant amendment, a procedure enhanced by the informed reader's instinctive comparison of the two texts.

One of the earliest imitations of Petrarch's sonnet is a poem that, with good reason, was placed first among the group of sonnets by Garcilaso published posthumously in 1543:

> Cuando me paro a contemplar mi 'stado
> y a ver los pasos por dó me han traído,
> hallo, según por do anduve perdido,
> que a mayor mal pudiera haber llegado;
> mas cuando del camino 'stó olvidado,

a tanto mal no sé por dó he venido;
sé que me acabo, y más he yo sentido
ver acabar comigo mi cuidado.
Yo acabaré, que me entregué sin arte
a quien sabrá perderme y acabarme
si quisiere, y aún sabrá querello;
que pues mi voluntad puede matarme,
la suya, que no es tanto de mi parte,
pudiendo, ¿qué hará sino hacello?[11]

When I stop to contemplate my condition and to look at the steps that
have brought me to where I am, I discover, with thought of how I strayed,
that I could have arrived at a greater evil; but when I am forgotten by the
path, I do not know how I have come to such an ill; I know that I am
ending, and it has grieved me more to see my passion end with me. I shall
reach my end, for I surrendered myself guilelessly to one who will know
how to be my perdition and my end if she should wish, and will even
know how to wish it; so, as my will can kill me, what will hers, which is
not partial to me, achieve except the same thing?

There is a different emphasis here, While Petrarch emphasizes his spiritual
dejection – the 'basso stato' ('low state') of his last line – Garcilaso's sonnet is
ultimately an amatory lament that through the irony of the concluding tercet
is also a complaint. Such a note would, of course, have been inappropriate
for Petrarch as the object of his love was dead. The concept of death in the
Garcilaso sonnet is metaphorical: the death-in-life of the hapless lover.

The retrospective theme is also present in the first of the *Rimas sacras* by
Lope de Vega (1561–1635):

Cuando me paro a contemplar mi estado
y a ver los pasos por donde he venido,
me espanto de que un hombre tan perdido
a conocer su error haya llegado.
Cuando miro los años que he pasado
la divina razón puesta en olvido,
conozco que piedad del cielo ha sido
no haberme en tanto mal precipitado.
Entré por laberinto tan extraño
fiando al debil hilo de la vida
el tarde conocido desengaño,
mas de tu luz mi escuridad vencida,
el monstruo muerto de mi ciego engaño
vuelve a la patria, la razón perdida.[12]

When I stop to contemplate my condition and to look at the steps along
which I have come, it frightens me that a man who was so lost should
have managed to get to know the error of his ways. When I look at the

years that I spent with my god-given reason cast into oblivion, I recognize
that it is because of heaven's mercy that I have not been plunged into so
much evil. I entered a strange labyrinth, entrusting life's frail thread to a
belatedly acknowledged disillusion, but with my darkness defeated by
your light, the dead monster of my blind deceit returns to its native-place,
with its reason lost.

Imitation here partakes of that complexity to which I referred previously.
As befits the title of the collection to which it belongs, Lope's sonnet
follows the penitential aspect of Petrarch's far more than does Garcilaso's.
Nonetheless the latter's poem was evidently in Lope's mind when he
wrote his own for he has not only followed Garcilaso's first line to the
letter rather than translate the Italian closely but also adhered closely to
his Spanish predecessor for his second line as well. There are indications
in the Lope sonnet that his 'error' is amatory in nature by his use of the
image of the labyrinth and the invocation of blind illusion and subsequent
disillusionment. Evidently one of the attractions of the Petrarch sonnet for
the inventive imitator was its protean character, unspecific and potentially
complex.

Similar in mood to the Lope sonnet is a poem from a collection of poems
about sin and repentance written at virtually the same time by Quevedo.
The ninth poem of his *Heráclito cristiano* ('Christian Heraclitus') is above all
a meditation on the passing of time. I cite the opening:

> Cuando me vuelvo atrás a ver los años
> que han nevado la edad florida mía;
> cuando miro las redes, los engaños
> donde me vi algún día,
> más me alegro de verme fuera dellos,
> que un tiempo me pesó de padecellos.[13]

> When I turn around to look at the years that have dropped snow on the
> flowers of my youth; when I look at the nets, the deceits where I once
> found myself, my joy at seeing myself free of them is greater than the
> suffering they formerly caused me.

What is immediately noticeable about this imitation is that, unlike Garcilaso
and Lope, Quevedo has not used the sonnet form. It is not the same,
however, as when he himself is plagiarized by Iglesias; the well-known line
comes in its due place at the start. Quevedo's principal source is clearly
Petrarch, not Garcilaso, unlike in the case of Lope. His, initially, is an
imitation by translation: Petrarch's 'years' are maintained, and the verbal pe-
riphrasis 'mi volgo in dietro' is faithfully rendered as 'me vuelvo atrás'. The
complexity of this imitation is thus achieved in a different way from Lope's.
Quevedo invokes the original pre-text, to which the Garcilaso resemblances

will inevitably attach themselves. For Quevedo's text is also imbued with erotic overtones, as in the reference to the nets and illusions of line 3.

All of these instances of imitation could, in their differing ways, be termed 'citation for enrichment'. Imitation in its fullest sense, however, meant more than this for Renaissance poets, as I have already indicated: it involved a whole approach to their art. Modern poets, however, do not largely adopt the same aesthetic of imitation, but have in its place re-discovered and refined the concept of citation and allusion so that the potential for such enrichment has been increased.

At the most obvious level the custom of creating a title by quotation from another work is a fairly common practice among twentieth-century novelists. It is less common in poetry and as with novelistic citation rarely amounts to more than a sound-bite, a fleeting echo that lacks the resonance of Renaissance imitators. Nonetheless titles are occasionally very significant. One of the major Spanish love poems of the first half of the twentieth century was *La voz a ti debida* ('The voice indebted to you') by Pedro Salinas. The source of the quotation for this title is a line near the beginning of Garcilaso's *Égloga tercera*:

> mas con la lengua muerta y fría en la boca
> pienso mover la voz a ti debida[14]

> but with my tongue dead and cold in my mouth I intend to move the
> voice that is indebted to you

This is not a declaration of love as it is in the twentieth-century work. It occurs as part of the dedication of the poem and is directed to the wife of Don Pedro de Toledo, Viceroy of Naples and Garcilaso's patron. The poet hopes that his poem will endure so that his praise of the dedicatee will be immortalized. Despite the surface differences, however, Salinas's work articulates an aspiration that in its desire to go beyond the here and now approximates to Garcilaso. The yearning to transcend the limitations of time and the individual life that the sixteenth-century poet envisages is modified in Salinas into a metaphysical or pseudo-mystical vision.[15]

The most celebrated poem on the subject of how love can transcend the limitations of mortality is Quevedo's sonnet 'Amor constante más allá de la muerte':

> Cerrar podrá mis ojos la postrera
> sombra que me llevare el blanco día,
> y podrá desatar esta alma mía
> hora a su afán ansioso lisonjera;

> mas no, de esotra parte, en la ribera,
> dejará la memoria, en donde ardía:

nadar sabe mi alma la agua fría,
y perder el respeto a ley severa.

Alma a quien todo un dios prisión ha sido,
venas que humor a tanto fuego han dado,
medulas que han gloriosamente ardido,

su cuerpo dejará, no su cuidado;
serán ceniza, mas tendrá sentido;
polvo serán, mas polvo enamorado.[16]

The last shadow that takes white day from me will be able to close my eyes, and there will arrive an hour that, indulgent to the anxious yearning of this soul of mine, will release it; but it will not leave the memory of where it burnt on the other shore: my flame can swim across the cold water, and lose its respect for the harsh law. A soul which has been a prison to a whole god, veins that have given humour to so much fire, marrows that have gloriously burnt: it will abandon its body, but not its love; they will be ashes, but it will still have its feeling; they will be dust, but dust in love.

It is in some ways a desperate and unavailing poem whose sonorous rhetoric is akin to the shake of a fist at the fact of mortality. It is a futile gesture and a hollow triumph for, as Arthur Terry has pointed out, its reasoning is fallacious: 'flames can't swim through water, any more than the soul can behave as if it were the body'.[17]

In the opening poem of his collection *A modo de esperanza*, José Angel Valente (1929–2000) alludes directly to Quevedo's sonnet, both in the title ('Serán ceniza') and in the conclusion:

Cruzo un desierto y su secreta
desolación sin nombre.
El corazón
tiene la sequedad de la piedra
y los estallidos nocturnos
de su materia o de su nada.

Hay una luz remota, sin embargo,
y sé que no estoy solo;
aunque después de tanto y tanto no haya
ni un solo pensamiento
capaz contra la muerte,
no estoy solo.

Toco esta mano al fin que comparte mi vida
y en ella me confirmo
y tiento cuanto amo,
lo levanto hacia el cielo

> y aunque sea ceniza lo proclamo: ceniza.
> Aunque sea ceniza cuanto tengo hasta ahora,
> cuanto se me ha tendido a modo de esperanza.[18]

> I cross a desert and its secret, nameless desolation. My heart has the
> dryness of stone and the nocturnal explosions of its material or its
> nothingness. There is, however, a light in the distance, and I know I am
> not alone; although after so much there isn't even a single thought that
> can confront death, I am not alone. I touch this hand at last that shares
> my life and in it I am confirmed and I feel all that I love and raise it
> towards the sky and even if it be ash I proclaim: ash. Even if all I have till
> now, all that has been yielded to me by way of hope, is ash.

Life is seen as a difficult journey through a wilderness. This is a common
symbol that Valente relates – appropriately in view of the connection with a
Golden Age love poem – to the Petrarchan topic of a dejected persona en-
countering an affinity with a barren landscape. The notion of a distant light
that may offer an alleviation of the speaker's plight is likewise a common idea
in Renaissance poetry, suggesting the possibility that the lady may relent.
The ray of hope hinting that the poet is not alone leads to an ambiguous idea:
is the hand he touches that of another or merely his own?[19] Where Valente
treads the same ground as Quevedo is in his defiant assertion of the validity of
his experience. '[T]iento cuanto amo' ('I feel all that I love') suggests all that
has been dear to him rather than someone he has loved, but what is common
to both poets is the unwillingness to yield in the face of death. Valente is admittedly more restrained in his conclusion than Quevedo, but his title cannot
fail to evoke, even if the poem does not exactly mimic, the impossible claim.

   Quevedo's oracular phrasing and sheer flamboyance have not convinced
many poets, as Douglas Sheppard has pointed out.[20] He cites an amusingly
wry reflection on Quevedo's pyrotechnics by Luis Jiménez Martos (1926–):

> Don Quevedo, Francisco: yo me ahorro
> de acercarme a la lírica ensalada . . .
> Me prohibo bajar a los infiernos
> retórico-mortales. No resisto
> el ayayay marcial que a tango suena.

> Don Quevedo, Francisco: I'll spare myself the trouble of approaching
> your lyrical concoction . . . I forbid myself from going down to the
> rhetorico-mortal realms of hell. I can't stand the martial exclamation that
> smacks of the tango.

A similar scepticism is displayed by the Mexican poet Octavio Paz (1914–
98), but in his case by direct citation rather than merely negative appraisal.
While Valente quotes from Quevedo's sonnet by way of enhancement rather
in the manner of imitating Renaissance poets, Paz attacks the very words
of the sonnet in a poem that fragments rather than integrates the source

phrases. The title, 'Homenaje y profanación' ('Homage and profanation'), however, suggests attachment as well as rejection, respect as well as destruction. It is as though Paz is compelled to acknowledge, despite himself, the daunting monumentality of Quevedo's sonnet. First comes the Quevedo sonnet printed, in its entirety, followed by sections entitled 'Aspiración' ('Aspiration'), 'Espiración' ('Expiration') and 'Lauda' ('Lauds'). Paz's procedure as successor poet is to isolate words and phrases from the sonnet and then repeat them obsessively in his own poem. Thus 'blanco día' ('white day') from Quevedo's second line spawns the opening of 'Aspiración':

> Sombras del día blanco
> Contra mis ojos. Yo no veo
> Nada sino lo blanco.
> La hora en blanco. El alma
> Desatada del ansia y de la hora.
>
> Blancura de aguas muertas,
> Hora blanca, ceguera de los ojos abiertos.[21]

> Shadows of the white day against my eyes. I see nothing but the
> whiteness. The blank hour. The soul released from anxiety and the hour.
> Whiteness of dead waters. White hour, blindness of open eyes.

The poem betrays its mocking yet playful character in various ways. At the profoundest level there is deliberate misquotation so that Quevedo's line about how the soul has been a prison to the god of love is rendered through conflation with the subsequent reference to the body as the location of the soul as 'Cuerpo de un Dios que fue cuerpo abrasado, / Dios que fue cuerpo y fue cuerpo endiosado' ('Body of a God that was a burnt body, / God that was body and was a body made god'). Paz also seizes on the paradox of the flame that can survive water in the seventh line of the sonnet to create his own antitheses, as in the unpunctuated third part of 'Aspiración'

> Ardor del agua
> Lengua de fuego fosforece el agua
> Pentecostés palabra sin palabras
> (p. 135)

> Ardour of the water tongue of flame phosphoresces the water Pentecost
> word without words

and in the allusion to the Mexican Day of the Dead in the second section of 'Espiración':

> Vana conversación del esqueleto
> Con el fuego insensato y con el agua
> Que no tiene memoria y con el viento
> (p. 136)

> Futile conversation of the skeleton with the senseless fire and with the
> water that has no memory and with the wind

Later he explicitly links Quevedo's marmoreal erotic vision to the extrava-
ganza of the Mexican funeral: 'El entierro es barroco todavía / En Mexico'
('The funeral is still baroque / in Mexico') (p. 137). He also creates effects
of bathos by undermining the transcendental and apocalyptic implications
of the Quevedo sonnet, as at the opening of 'Espiración':

> Cielos de fin de mundo. Son las cinco.
> Sombras blancas: ¿son voces o son pájaros?

> Skies of the end of world. It is five o'clock. Are the white shadows voices
> or birds?

In its word-play, moreover, Paz's poem is flippant, as when he elaborates
upon the verb 'nadar' from the seventh line of the sonnet, one of whose
forms is a homonym for the word 'nothing' ('nada'):

> Mas la memoria desmembrada nada
> Desde los nacedores de su nada
> Los manantiales de su nacimiento
> Nada contra corriente y mandamiento
> nada contra la nada   (p. 135)

> But the dismembered memory swims from the birthings of its
> nothingness the springs of its birth swims against the current and the
> commandment swims against the nothing

In like vein is the coining of the word 'salombra' by a combination of the
opposing words 'sol' ('sun') and 'sombra' ('shadow'), as in 'Sombra del
sol salombra segadora' (p. 135) and 'Sol de sombra Solombra cegadora'
which contain an additional pun in the homophones 'segadora' ('woman
reaper') and 'cegadora' ('blinding') arising from the Mexican pronunciation
of Spanish [z] as [s].

In the final section 'Lauda', the process of destruction – or profanation,
to employ the poem's designation – is taken to an extreme by disembodiment whereby words lifted from the sonnet are presented in a nonsensical
sequence:

> ojos medulas sombras blanco día
> ansias afán lisonjas horas cuerpos
> memoria todo Dios ardieron todos
> (p. 137)

> eyes marrows shadows white day anxieties eagerness flattery hours body
> memory all God they burnt everything

The concluding lines constitute the ultimate iconoclastic act: the poem's sense is literally subsumed in the senses, and the last line is the epitome of meaninglessness – a string of words, each of which contradicts the previous one:

> Olfato gusto vista oído tacto
> El sentido anegado en lo sentido
> Los cuerpos abolidos en el cuerpo
> Memorias desmemorias de haber sido
> Antes después ahora nunca siempre
>
> (p. 139)

> Smell taste sight hearing touch the sense overwhelmed in the senses the bodies abolished in the body memories unmemories of having been before after now never always

Paz's rough treatment of Quevedo's text is an extreme instance of citation for enrichment, or how one poem can be the subject for another. At first sight at least, the following poem by Antonio Machado represents a more acquiescent attitude to a precursor text, the *Coplas por la muerte de su padre* ('Verses upon the death of his father') by Jorge Manrique (1440–79), lines from which appear at the start of Machado's poem:

> *Nuestras vidas son los ríos*
> *que van a dar a la mar,*
> *que es el morir.* ¡Gran cantar!
>
> Entre los poetas míos
> tiene Manrique un altar.
>
> Dulce gozo de vivir:
> mala ciencia del pasar,
> ciego huir a la mar.
>
> Tras el pavor del morir
> está el placer de llegar.
>
> ¡Gran placer!
> Mas ¿y el horror de volver?
> ¡Gran pesar![22]

> *Our lives are rivers which will run into the sea which is death.* A great utterance! Among my poets Manrique has an altar. Sweet joy of living, bad science of passing, blind flight to the sea. Beyond the fear of death is the pleasure of arriving. Great pleasure! But, what about the horror of returning? Great sorrow!

While Paz's homage was at best an acknowledgement that Quevedo's text existed and that it was a disturbing one, Machado appears to endorse the solemn commonplace about life that is symbolically enunciated in the earlier text. Where Manrique, however, articulates a serene Christian truth his successor's vision is anything but. Machado conceives the movement from life to death – Manrique's stately river – as a headlong rush, and admits that death induces panic. The conclusion is especially anguished. The 'great pleasure' that dying represents (that is, arriving at the sea) is certainly ironic but no sooner has this experience been registered than the hypothetical alternative that he contemplates – returning to live one's life again – is seen to be equally loathsome. So in place of the security of Manrique's faith we perceive an emotional dilemma.

In their different ways both Paz and Machado betray an unease with the original text. They are intimidated by the earlier poem which stands at the head of their own poems rather like a flung gauntlet. Neither the playful vandalism of Paz nor the measured scepticism of Machado can remove the dazzling glare of the precursors despite the fact that their own poems develop into counter-statements that seek to make us concede the inappropriateness of the earlier poems. Much of Harold Bloom's criticism has addressed the matter of how later (or in his terms 'belated') poets fear that their poetic predecessors will have already used up all the available poetic inspiration. Major or 'strong' poets are compelled to define the originality of their work against the achievement of their predecessors or fathers – Bloom's choice of the masculine form is in order to evoke the Freudian Oedipus Complex. According to his highly idiosyncratic but precisely reasoned theory, later poets have evolved various strategies for the inevitable confrontation with the precursor: for resolving, or at least appeasing, the 'anxiety of influence' that they experience. Such strategies entail a creative misreading, or 'misprision', achieved by different responses and approaches to the precursor text. It is not necessary for our purposes to detail all six of these, but one of the key ideas involves what Bloom terms a 'swerve', where the latecomer turns away from the earlier poet.[23]

It might seem an understatement to consider the iconoclasm of Paz and the inversion of Machado by such a mild term as 'swerve' even if their relationship to their respective predecessors smacks of the anxiety of influence. Bloom's conception of influence, however, is not essentially a similarity of text; like Kristeva he downplays the idea of sources. For him: 'Poetic influence, in the sense I give to it, has almost nothing to do with the verbal resemblances between one poet and another... Poets need not *look* like their fathers, and the anxiety of influence more frequently than not is quite distinct from the anxiety of style.'[24]

The value of Bloom's concept of influence, even if one may not entirely yield to some of its more mystical implications – such as a poet being chosen by rather than choosing his precursor – is that it conveniently enables us to skirt around the often insoluble problem of intention.[25] We do not need to ascertain if the influence is a conscious act of borrowing or an unconscious echo, and many 'in-flows' may occur within a process that may be neither purely one nor the other.

It is clear, though, that misreading comes as naturally to modern poets as imitation did to their medieval and Renaissance counterparts. As with the earlier poets it can involve both immediate precursors and more distant antecedents. In the former instance it often functions as a reaction. Let us take as an example the poetry of Lorca. In November 1921 he wrote the bulk of the poems that would be published ten years later as *Poema del cante jondo*. His interest in Andalusian primitive song was at that time stimulated by his friendship with Manuel de Falla with whom he organized a *cante jondo* festival in Granada in 1922. The motive for this event – effectively a series of competitions – was a determination to restore the forms of *cante jondo* to their former purity as they had been commercialized as a shallow form of café entertainment. Lorca's poems of 1921 likewise emerge as an attempt to recapture the essence of *cante jondo*: to evoke rather than to overstate, and to seek mystery rather than trade in clichés. His work could be seen as a misreading of a number of poems written a decade earlier by Manuel Machado (1874–1947), the brother of Antonio. A poem of Manuel's entitled 'Cantares' opens with a blend of definition and depiction:

> Vino, sentimiento, guitarra y poesía,
> hacen los cantares de la patria mía...
> Cantares...
> Quien dice cantares, dice Andalucía.
>
> A la sombra fresca de la vieja parra,
> un mozo moreno rasguea la guitarra...
> Cantares...
> algo que acaricia y algo que desgarra.[26]

> Wine, sentiment, guitar and poetry make the songs of my region... Songs... Whoever says songs says Andalusia. In the fresh shade of the old vine a dark youth strums the guitar... Songs... Something that caresses and something that tears.

When the teenage Lorca was starting to write poetry a few years later he could hardly improve on this mediocre listing of commonplaces:

> ¡Ah Jueves Santo de Andalucía!
> Vino, guitarra, llanto y saetas.
> Cópulas hondas entre miradas.
> Quedan las almas enmarañadas
> En las mantillas vagas e inquietas.[27]

> Oh, Holy Thursday of Andalusia! Wine, guitar, lament and *saetas* [improvised religious songs]. Deep copulas between glances. The souls remain tangled in the vague and troubled mantillas.

When he wrote a poem like 'La guitarra' for the *cante jondo* collection, however, he eschewed crude visualization and instead supplied an evocation. This entailed a distinctively novel envisaging that comprised a re-writing of *cante jondo* images and ideas:

> Empieza el llanto
> de la guitarra.
> Es inútil
> callarla.
> Es imposible
> callarla.
> Llora monótona
> como llora el agua,
> como llora el viento
> sobre la nevada.[28]

> The lament of the guitar begins. It is futile to silence it. It is impossible to silence it. It weeps monotonously like the water weeps, like the snow weeps on the snowfield.

He is by now unconcerned about precise or picturesque detail, and instead concentrates on expanding the horizons of imagination and understanding. The similes are elemental rather than pictorial and as a consequence the *cante jondo* experience is invested with a mysterious dignity, not reduced to a one-dimensional impression.

In the same year that he wrote *Poema del cante jondo* Lorca published his first book of poetry, *Libro de poemas*. In many ways this is a transitional book, one that leads from the juvenilia into the mature work. As such it is an uneven collection that has been little studied. It is essentially an anthology compiled by the poet himself, lacking an obvious structure, and commentators have found it a difficult work to get into focus. It contains poems of an acute artistic sensitivity, however, that offer evidence of a struggle between a burgeoning talent and the heavy baggage of antecedents. Lorca's youthful compositions were coloured by the language of *modernismo*, in particular of Rubén Darío. In *Libro de poemas*, however, we sense an act of disassociation very much in terms of a misreading, of Bloom's misprision. Certainly when we compare parts of the following two poems it is appropriate to consider the relationship as antagonistic. The precursor poem is Darío's sonnet 'Pegaso':

Cuando iba yo a montar ese caballo rudo
y tembloroso, dije: 'La vida es pura y bella'.
Entre sus cejas vivas vi brillar una estrella.
El cielo estaba azul, y yo estaba desnudo.

Sobre mi frente Apolo hizo brillar su escudo
y de Belerofonte logré seguir la huella.
Toda cima es ilustre si Pegaso la sella,
y yo, fuerte, he subido donde Pegaso pudo.

¡Yo soy el caballero de la humana energía,
yo soy el que presenta su cabeza triunfante
coronada con el laurel del rey del día;

domador del corcel de cascos de diamante,
voy en un gran volar, con la aurora por guía,
adelante en el vasto azur, siempre adelante![29]

When I was about to mount the rough and trembling horse, I said: 'Life is pure and beautiful'. Between his lively eyebrows I saw a star shine. The sky was blue and I was naked. On my forehead Apollo shone his shield and I managed to follow the tracks of Belerophon. Every peak is illustrious if Pegasus seals it, and I have been strong enough to climb to where Pegasus has been. I am the horseman of human energy, I am he who presents his triumphant head crowned with the laurel of the king of daylight; the tamer of the steed with diamond helmets, I am on a great flight, with dawn as my guide, striving onwards in the vast azure, ever onwards.

Lorca's 'Sueño', dated May 1919, offers an instance of what in Bloom's theory of influence might be termed *clinamen* – 'A poet swerves away from his precursor, by so reading his precursor's poem as to execute a *clinamen* in relation to it. This appears as a corrective movement in his own poem, which implies that the precursor poem went accurately up to a certain point, but then should have swerved, precisely in the direction that the new poem moves'.[30]

Iba yo montado sobre
un macho cabrío.
El abuelo me habló
y me dijo:
'Ese es tu camino.'
'¡Es ése!', gritó mi sombra,
disfrazada de mendigo.
'¡Es aquel de oro!', dijeron
mis vestidos.
Un gran cisne me guiñó,

diciendo: 'Vente conmigo!'
Y una serpiente mordía
mi sayal de peregrino.

Mirando al cielo, pensaba:
'Yo no tengo camino.
Las rosas del fin serán
como las del principio.
En niebla se convierte
la carne y el rocío.'

Mi caballo fantástico me lleva
por un campo rojizo.
'¡Déjame!', clamó, llorando,
mi corazón pensativo.
Yo lo abandoné en la tierra,
lleno de tristeza.
                    Vino
la noche, llena de arrugas
y de sombras.
                    Alumbran el camino,
los ojos luminosos y azulados
de mi macho cabrío.[31]

I was riding along on a billy goat. My grandfather spoke to me and told me: 'This is your path.' 'It is this one', shouted my shadow, disguised as a beggar. 'It's that golden one!', said my clothes. A great swan winked at me saying: 'Come with me!' And a snake was biting my pilgrim's smock. Looking at the sky I thought: 'I have no path. The roses of the end will be like those at the start. Flesh and dew will be converted to mist.' My fantastic horse takes me through a reddish field. 'Leave me', my pensive heart shouted tearfully. I left it on the ground, full of sadness. Night came, full of wrinkles and shadows. The luminous and bluish eyes of my billy goat light up the path.

Lorca's misreading is achieved by an undermining, often through irony, of the precursor text. The winged horse of the gods becomes the billy goat, earthbound in its roaming. The pure light of the star perceived in the eyes of Darío's Pegasus is converted into the menacing illumination of the goat's glance. The radiant heralding of day in the earlier text is countered by the gloomy (literally wrinkled) shadows of night in Lorca, and the onward drive of the former is belied by the purposelessness of the latter. Most conspicously, the single-minded certainties of Darío's imagining are replaced by the conflicting instructions and summonses of 'Sueño', which lead to an unequivocal negation: 'Yo no tengo camino' ('I have no path'). Among the presences that the speaker denies are the grandfather – the voice of tradition and authority – and the swan – the emblem of *modernismo*.

The unbridled nature of the journey in Lorca's poem – the pensive heart is left behind – has a dark, Dionysian quality that is the opposite of the Apollonian realization in 'Pegaso'. Not for the speaker in the later text the laurel crown of achievement, only the unpredictability of the journey. Lorca's poem is surely the very embodiment of Bloom's dictum that 'a poem is not an overcoming of anxiety, but is that anxiety'.[32]

Both cases of Lorca as misreader involve immediate precursors. For evidence of long-distance influence I turn to the poetry of Rosalía de Castro and specifically the area of religious experience. In her poem 'Santa Escolástica' the speaker wanders through the streets of Santiago in a state of spiritual anguish. At the end she achieves a momentary and perhaps hollow consolation when she enters a church and casts her eyes on the sculptures within. The final line – ' "¡Hay arte! ¡Hay poesía...! Debe haber cielo. ¡Hay Dios!" ' (' "There is art! There is poetry...! There must be heaven! There is God!" ')[33] – emerges as a sign of relief rather than conviction. Indeed the poem as a whole could be interpreted as a misreading of its location: Santiago de Compostela, the place of pilgrimage, the inspiration for a religious experience, is for the speaker a place that entails a fruitless and soul-sapping quest.

The poem of Castro that offers the clearest misreading of earlier poetry is, I believe, the one that begins 'Una luciérnaga entre el musgo brilla' ('A glow-worm shines among the moss'). It is a deeply despairing poem that concludes with the acknowledgement that the soul's cry cannot reach as far as God. We do not have to read that far, however, to ascertain how truly negative it is. The opening lines are arguably the bleakest in Spanish poetry:

> Una luciérnaga entre el musgo brilla
> y un astro en las alturas centellea;
> abismo arriba, y en el fondo abismo;
> ¿qué es al fin lo que acaba y lo que queda?
>
> (p. 74)

> A glow-worm shines among the moss and a star twinkles in the heights; abyss above, and in the depths, an abyss; what finally ends and what remains?

What makes this so profoundly abject is not only the surprising paradox afforded by the equation of images of light with the abyss. The description implies movement: the poet gazing up at the night sky after noticing the brilliance of the glow-worm in the moss. A similar visual focus informs one of the most famous philosophico-religious poems of the sixteenth century, Luis de León's 'Noche serena':

> Cuando contemplo el cielo
> de innumerables luces adornado,

> y miro hacia el suelo
> de noche rodeado,
> en sueño y en olvido sepultado...[34]

> When I contemplate the sky adorned with innumerable lights, and I look
> towards the earth surrounded by night, buried in sleep and oblivion...

While Luis de León, however, in accordance with the Christian Neoplatonic
world-view, securely contrasts the poverty of 'down here' with the riches
of 'up there', Castro sees the star in the heavens as no less abysmal than the
lowly glow-worm. Her poem evokes the appalling void, and what is more
sets its face against transcendence as the closing lines remorselessly indicate:

> 'Pobre alma, espera y llora
> a los pies del Altísimo;
>   mas no olvides que al cielo
> nunca ha llegado el insolente grito
> de un corazón que de la vil materia
> y del barro de Adán formó sus ídolos.'
>   (p. 75)

> 'Poor soul, wait and weep at the feet of the Almighty; but do not forget
> that the insolent cry of a heart which formed its idols from vile matter and
> the mud of Adam has never reached heaven.'

The agony of the earth-bound soul is acutely registered as a loss because of
what the poem has failed to articulate, a failure that is pinpointed by the
allusion to and the denial of the sixteenth-century precursor.

Another misreading is suggested by these lines:

> Desierto el mundo, despoblado el cielo,
> enferma el alma y en el polvo hundido
>   el sacro altar en donde
> se exhalaron fervientes mis suspiros,
>   en mil pedazos roto
>   mi Dios, cayó al abismo,
> y al buscarle anhelante, sólo encuentro
> la soledad inmensa del vacío.   (p. 75)

> The earth deserted, the sky unpopulated, the soul sick and the sacred altar
> where my sighs were fervently exhaled now collapsed into the dust, my
> God broken into a thousand pieces, he fell into the abyss, and on seeking
> him with anxious longing all I find is the immense loneliness of the void.

The first line echoes the doubly negative image at the opening. What is
evoked here is terror of the void – of empty spaces never to be filled. How
different this is from the space that awaits the illumination of God's love in
a poem by Luis de León's contemporary, San Juan de la Cruz:

¡Óh lámparas de fuego,
en cuyos resplandores
las profundas cavernas del sentido,
que estaua oscuro y ciego,
calor y luz dan junto a su querido.[35]

O lamps of fire, in whose splendours the profound caverns of the sense,
that was dark and blind, together lend heat and light to their beloved.

But for the mystic the darkness and the silences are a necessary prelude to an
evacuation of the senses – a route to spiritual fulfilment. For the successor
poet the spaces are merely emptiness: there is nothing that can occupy them.

The clearest stylistic imprint on the poetry of Castro – what we would
conventionally term a 'source' – is that of Gustavo Adolfo Bécquer.
Although only a year Castro's senior, Bécquer was an established, if un-
derrated, poet when she was launching her own career. Indeed by the time
she was writing *En las orillas del Sar* Bécquer had died and his posthumous
Rimas had been in print for several years. A textual indebtedness to Bécquer
is discernible in several of Castro's poems, but their relationship is more
than a matter of echoes, of remembered phrases or images. It involves an
intertextuality that is as conflictive as the one that arises from the connection with the religious poets of the Golden Age. Among several possible
examples I single out Bécquer's tenth *rima*:

Los invisibles átomos del aire
en derredor palpitan y se inflaman,
el cielo se deshace en rayos de oro,
la tierra se estremece alborozada.
Oigo flotando en olas de armonías
rumor de besos y batir de alas;
mis párpados se cierran... ¿Qué sucede?
¿dime?... ¡Silencio! ¡Es el amor que pasa![36]

The invisible atoms of the air throb all around and catch fire, the sky is
undone in golden rays, the earth shudders in joy. I hear floating in waves
of harmony the sound of kisses and the beating of wings; my eyelids close
... What is happening? Tell me?... Silence! It is love that passes by!

This poem conveys the imminence of love in cosmic terms; just to say that
it refers to the natural world would be to downplay its elemental character.
It communicates a seething energy; it is a dynamic evocation of love as
creation. In the context of the *Rimas* as a whole it presages the dawning of
human love though that is no more than a fleeting anticipation here.

A similar excitement is present at the opening of a poem from Castro's
En las orillas del Sar:

Adivínase el dulce y perfumado
    calor primaveral;
los gérmenes se agitan en la tierra
con inquietud en su amoroso afán,
y cruzan por los aires, silenciosos,
átomos que se besan al pasar.[37]

The sweet and perfumed heat of Spring is now perceived; the seeds are
stirring restlessly in the earth in amorous yearning, and through the air
atoms silently cross, kissing as they meet.

We discover identical images – the atoms, the kiss – while the reference to
Spring enhances the amatory mood. The positive note is consolidated in
the second stanza with its mention of the joyous restlessness of youth and
the prospect of apparently boundless life:

Hierve la sangre juvenil, se exalta
lleno de aliento el corazón, y audaz
el loco pensamiento sueña y cree
que el hombre es, cual los dioses, inmortal.

Youthful blood seethes, the heart exalts, full of aspiration, and in its daring
the mad thought dreams and believes that man, like the gods, is immortal.

But in the final stanza there is what Bloom would describe as a 'swerve',
as the successor poet veers away from the radiance in the precursor text to
supply a contrasting perception: Spring yielding to the destructive heat of
Summer:

¡Pero qué aprisa en este mundo triste
    todas las cosas van!
¡Que las domina el vértigo creyérase!
La que ayer fue capullo, es rosa ya,
y pronto agostará rosas y plantas
    el calor estival.

But how speedily in this sad world all things go away. One would have
thought that they were controlled by vertigo! What yesterday was a bud is
now a rose and soon the Summer heat will wither roses and plants.

It is as though the final verb of the Bécquer poem – 'pasa' ('passes by') –
has been misread as a sign of transience: the rapid passing, that is to say
disappearance, of the things of this world.

Bécquer's influence, however defined, on subsequent generations was
considerable, not least in Spanish America. This is not altogether surprising
if we bear in mind that the image of the poet that most endured during the
twentieth century was a Romantic one, and the work of Bécquer fits the bill
perfectly even if in strict literary-historical terms he might be considered to
belong to a later era than that of mainstream Spanish Romanticism. Among

many Spanish American poets who bear his imprint is the contemporary
Nicaraguan poet Gioconda Belli (1948–).[38] Her poem 'Signos' contains an
epigraph by Borges: 'Es el amor, tendré que ocultarme o huir' ('It is love,
I shall have to hide myself or flee'). Her poem itself, however, appears to
acknowledge a Becquerian use of the opening phrase of the epigraph as with
the concluding line of the poem quoted above. Moreover the enumerative
technique allied to the evocation of nature at its most elemental clearly
echoes the manner of several of Bécquer's poems:

> Es el amor con su viento cálido,
> lamiendo insistente la playa sola de mi noche.
> Es el amor con su largo ropaje de algas,
> enredándome el nombre, el juicio, los imposibles.
> Es el amor salitre, húmedo,
> descargándose contra la roca de mi ayer impávida dureza.[39]

> It is love with its warm wind, lapping insistently at the sole beach of my
> night. It is love with its long apparel of seaweed, tangling up my name, my
> judgement, the impossible things. Love is saltpetre, moist, unloading itself
> on the rock of my former impassive hardness.

The same enumerative traits are present in the poem entitled 'Yo, la que te
quiere' ('I, the one who loves you'), which is a misreading of several Bécquer
poems which involve the use of the first-person form not as the vehicle for
the *persona* but for such things as the spirit of poetry and for realizations of
ideal woman. In *rima* XI the poet envisages encounters with three women:

> –Yo soy ardiente, yo soy morena,
> yo soy el símbolo de la pasión,
> de ansia de goces mi alma está llena.
> ¿A mí me buscas?
> –No es a ti: no.

> –Mi frente es pálida, mis trenzas de oro,
> puedo brindarte dichas sin fin.
> Yo de ternura guardo un tesoro.
> ¿A mí me llamas?
> –No: no es a ti.

> –Yo soy un sueño, un imposible,
> vano fantasma de niebla y luz;
> soy incorpórea, soy intangible:
> no puedo amarte.
> –Oh, ven; ven tú.[40]

> 'I am ardent, I am dark, I am the symbol of passion, my soul is full of the
> desire for pleasures. Is it me whom you seek?' 'It is not you. No.' 'My
> forehead is pale, my tresses are golden, I can offer you endless happiness.

I possess a treasure-house of tenderness. Is it me whom you call?' 'No, it is not you.' 'I am a dream, an impossible being, a vain phantasm of mist and light; I am incorporeal, I am intangible: I cannot love you.' 'O, come; do come.'

He rejects the first two in favour of the one who is inaccessible. Belli's poem opens very much in the spirit as well as in the style of Bécquer:

> Yo soy tu indómita gacela,
> el trueno que rompe la luz sobre tu pecho.
> Yo soy el viento desatado en la montaña
> y el fulgor concentrado del fuego del ocote.[41]

> I am your indomitable gazelle, the thunder that breaks the light on your breast. I am the wind that is unleashed on the mountain and the concentrated flash of the fire of the ocote pine.

As the poem proceeds, however, we come to realize that the images that in Bécquer are evocative of distance, mystery and non-attainment have an opposite function in his Nicaraguan successor. They lead instead to the enunciation of a love that is the union, not the separation, of poet and loved one:

> Yo soy un nombre que canta y te enamora
> desde el otro lado de la luna,
> soy la prolongación de tu sonrisa y tu cuerpo.

> I am a name that sings and makes you fall in love from the other side of the moon, I am the prolongation of your smile and your body.

Perhaps not coincidentally both Castro and Belli are women poets misreading a male poet whose inherited focus involves an idealization of Woman and Love. In such cases misreading appears to be prompted by a desire to challenge an understanding of experience which doesn't ring true for them. This is an issue I shall return to in Chapter 6 with reference to the poetry of Ana Rossetti.

Chapter 3

The epic and the poetry of place

The term 'epic' has suffered a curious fate. In modern times it is used quite indiscriminately to refer to something that is grand, large-scale or momentous, ranging from buildings to films and to sporting encounters. Yet it is seldom if ever employed for its original purpose: to refer to a specific poetic genre. Indeed one may wonder if its disappearance as a definition for long and ambitious modern poems is a fastidious reaction to its devaluation as a distinctive designation or a simple recognition that no such poems are composed nowadays because we live in unheroic times. What I believe to be beyond dispute, however, is that the idea, if not the form, of epic has been very much alive in the poetry of Spain and, more particularly, Spanish America in the last century, although the relationship of such derivatives or resonances of epic to epic proper betrays that creative unease associated with intertextuality.

Epic poetry is found in many civilizations and cultures. Although not as universal as folk-song or primitive song it nevertheless occurs over a wide time-scale: the earliest extant poem, the Sumerian epic *Gilgamesh* dates from around 3000 BC. This together with the Homeric epics, *Iliad* and *Odyssey*, of some two thousand years later are examples of oral, or what is also known as primary, epic. In this context *Beowulf*, a work composed between the eighth and tenth centuries, is a comparatively recent poem. Secondary epic, by contrast, involves a written medium, and although it includes poems such as Virgil's *Aeneid* that pre-date a number of oral epics, it is by and large the form of epic that has flourished in more recent times, particularly during the Renaissance. Such broad definitions, however, are not always adequate. For example, the Serbian cycles had been collected and recorded in the nineteenth century but were still being composed and recited according to ancient oral tradition in the 1960s. Moreover, as we saw in Chapter 1, an epic like the *Poema de mío Cid* indicates a degree of overlap between the oral tradition and the written medium.

Although the secondary epic is more sophisticated in its treatment of subject-matter it nonetheless shares many of the thematic keynotes of primitive epic: a protagonist of heroic, if not supernatural, stature; the presence of challenges or quests, frequently involving perilous journeys; and a supernatural dimension. C. M. Bowra's definition of epic as 'the pursuit of honour through risk' is neatly precise.[1] What is evident too is that epic in one way or another is very concerned with a sense of place. This not only involves place in terms of the hero's travels and discovery, as is common in primitive epic, but place as a mode of establishing an identity, whether individual or collective.

Both these notions are to the fore in the *Poema de mío Cid*. Unjustly banished by the king, Alfonso VI, the Cid is compelled to survive by fighting a series of battles against the Moors of Spain. The first part of the poem is mainly a narrative of the hero's military successes, which bring with them the acquisition of towns and new territory, deeds that anticipate the more overtly crusade-like nature of the later victories. The transition between these two kinds of exploit – or between what might be tendentiously termed the mercenary and the pious Cid – comes with the conquest of Valencia. With this triumph the Cid finally regains the king's favour. As a reward he obtains permission for his wife and daughters to visit him in the newly captured city. This reunion comprises one of the most elaborate episodes in the whole work, rivalling the court-scene in the final section, where the Cid obtains redress from his enemies. Rather than a single scene, however, the reunion is, in fact, several scenes that form an elaborate ceremonial involving journeys of greeting and leave-taking. These occupy over 300 lines (nearly 10 per cent of the entire poem) and the modern reader might be tempted to skim over them especially when there are so many more obviously dramatic parts. The reunion episode, however, is crucial for understanding the momentous nature of the Cid's achievement for it marks simultaneously the discovery of place and the recovery of identity through a regained status. A summary of the events is necessary to appreciate the climactic character of the reunion. It begins when Minaya, the Cid's lieutenant and adviser, asks the king to allow the Cid's wife Jimena to join him at Valencia. Having obtained the necessary permission Minaya sets out to accompany Jimena and also sends out an advance body to inform the Cid, who, in turn, instructs an escorting group to meet his wife and Minaya's retinue. They join up and spend the night at Medinaceli. As they approach Valencia the following day they are greeted by a welcoming party sent out by the Cid, and finally the hero himself receives them with much pomp and emotion. The culmination of this apparently endless succession of formal journeys and encounters comprises a passage where the Cid takes his family to the top of the *alcázar* at Valencia so that they may survey the scene:

> Adeliñó mio Çid   con ellas al alcaçar
> ala las subie   en el mas alto logar.
> Ojos velidos   catan a todas partes,
> miran Valencia   commo yaze la çibdad

e del otra parte	a ojo han el mar;
miran la huerta	espessa es e grand;
alçan las manos	por a Dios rogar
destaganançia	commo es buena e grand.
Mio Çid e sus compañas	tan a grand sabor estan.
El ivierno es exido	que el março quiere entrar.[2]

The Cid led them up to the fortress and conducted them to the highest point. Their fair eyes looked everywhere, and saw how the city of Valencia lay before them on one side with the sea on the other, and they saw the wide, rich expanse of the plains; they raised hands to thank God for the great and good reward. The Cid and his companions were well pleased. Winter had gone, and now March was coming in.

This passage communicates with remarkable vividness the wonder experienced by the women as they cast their eyes on an abundance of new sights: the southern city, the sea, the fertile, irrigated plain. That they should be coming from a Castilian Winter to a Valencian Spring makes the novelty all the greater.

The scene consequently suggests a sense of geographical expansion – Spain, not merely Castile – and with it a sense of enhanced identity. It is significant that the lines that immediately succeed the above quotation should imply a further extension in space and with it a sense of historical destiny:

Dezir vos quiero nuevas	de alent partes del mar,
de aquel rey Yuçef	que en Marruecos esta.

I wish to give you news from beyond the sea, of King Yusuf who is in Morocco.

According to Mircea Eliade heroic myths were cosmogonic, reliving the myth of the origin of the world when 'what was' had to be destroyed so that the world could be created.[3] Peter Dunn suggests a variant of this idea for the less primitive *Poema de mío Cid* which is epitomized in the above scene. The work presents a model which represents 'a new and important phase of cultural identity. It celebrates the unity of Castile and León, a growing ascendancy over Islam, the emergence of new order'.[4]

It can hardly be defined as the epic of the Reconquest, however, even if the idea of territorial expansion is prominent. What is termed the Reconquest was not so much a single event as a lengthy and protracted process. That the historical Cid should have formed an alliance with a Hispanic Moor against his fellow-Christians is symptomatic. In the same year, 1492, that the Reconquest was completed by the capture of Granada, Columbus anchored at an island off the coast of America thereby ushering another territorial expansion: the Conquest of America. The Conquistadors who undertook this task were descendants of those men who had been involved in the Reconquest, and came in the main from Castile and Extremadura. Such deeds as they undertook – the interminable journeys through all kinds of inhospitable terrain, the battles where they were heavily outnumbered – surely were fit for an epic treatment. Surprisingly perhaps, only one poem of this kind was written in the sixteenth century, *La Araucana* by Alonso de Ercilla (1533–94), a work that has lived in the shadow of the most famous secondary epic poem to have been written in the Iberian Peninsula: the *Lusiads* of the Portuguese poet Camões – a celebration of the overseas discoveries by his fellow-countrymen.

Ercilla's poem is also a literary epic, as befits a Renaissance poet who had as a model not only the classical precursor of the *Aeneid* but recent Italian examples, notably Boiardo's *Orlando Innamorato* and Ariosto's continuation, *Orlando Furioso*. These later poems are often referred to as 'romantic' or 'chivalric' epic, and their impact on Ercilla, who regarded Ariosto as the new Virgil, is undoubted. As Arthur Terry has pointed out, Ercilla saw no essential difference between romance epic and heroic epic, though what Ercilla takes from Ariosto is not so much romance material as 'a narrative voice which can comment on the action in ways which directly involve the reader, often with Ariosto's own sense of ironic distancing'.[5] The poem avoids reference to the pagan and supernatural, and in this respect has an affinity with the *Poema de mío Cid*, sometimes praised for its realism and moderation.

What modern commentators have found attractive about Ercilla is his even-handedness. He does not idealize the Conquistadors, reserving his greatest admiration for the bravery of the Araucanian Indians of Chile in defence of their liberty. In the invocation, with which the literary epic conventionally opens, the allusion to 'el valor, los hechos, las proezas' ('the courage, the deeds, the achievements') of the Spaniards is succeeded by a greater tribute to the defiant enemy:

> Cosas diré también harto notables
> de gente que a ningún rey obedecen,
> temerarias empresas memorables
> que celebrarse con razón merecen,
> raras industrias, términos loables
> que más los españoles engrandecen
> pues no es el vencedor más estimado
> de aquello en que el vencido es reputado.[6]

> I shall also relate things that are truly remarkable, of people who do not obey a king, bold and memorable enterprises that properly deserve to be commemorated, wondrous deeds, laudable ends that bring greater credit

to the Spaniards, for the high reputation of the vanquished enhances the victor's worth.

In this, Ercilla comes nearer to the kind of idealization present in the Moorish ballad of the Golden Age (to be discussed in Chapter 4), with its depiction of the enemy as a chivalric opponent, than to the Counter Reformation intolerance of otherness, evident in a poem that Francisco de Aldana addressed to Philip II on the dangers facing Spain in the 1570s. Accordingly Ercilla's poem lacks a grand vision despite its massive proportions: 37 cantos and 15,000 lines. Ercilla was, however, first and foremost a soldier, and his descriptions of battles and atrocities have a commendably downbeat note when set alongside the rhetoric and glorification of a poem like Herrera's on the Battle of Lepanto. Ercilla's poem, however, is not just a war diary accommodating the conventions of the literary epic. If it does not possess the mythologizing power of the *Poema de mío Cid* it still communicates a sense of history, a momentousness of event and, inevitably, of place. Such features are evident in cantos 26 and 27. The first of these describes the defeat of the Araucanians followed by the summary execution of their leaders. The stoical demeanour of one of these, by the name of Galbarino, provokes the poet's sympathy and admiration. Indeed at one point so moved is he by the brave Indian's words – as so often with Ercilla envisaged with an eloquence that would not have disgraced a sixteenth-century courtier – that he intervenes in a vain attempt to save his life. The account of the horrors of war is then succeeded by a passage that stretches over the remainder of canto 26 and the whole of the following one. The narrator encounters an aged Araucanian, a wise man by the name of Fitón. He asserts that he could avenge himself upon the Spanish invaders but chooses instead to allow events to take their course as it has been ordained that the Araucanian people should be punished and that the good fortune presently enjoyed by their enemy is ephemeral. He next leads the narrator into a large and beautiful garden, that is a replica of the idyllic natural setting of Renaissance pastoral:

> hoja no discrepaba de otra un punto,
> haciendo cuadro o círculo hermoso,
> en medio un claro estanque, do las fuentes
> murmurando enviaban sus corrientes.
>
> (II, p. 218)

> not a single leaf was out of shape with others, forming a square or a beautiful circle, and in the middle was a bright pond, to where the murmuring fountains sent their streams.

In this retreat the old man reveals to the narrator with the aid of a globe a comprehensive vision of the known world. For the most part it is little more than an encyclopaedic listing of places in Asia, Europe and Africa (though, unsurprisingly, he is especially detailed about the Iberian Peninsula) and, finally, America, culminating in a description of the territories of the Araucanians, effectively what would become Chile. Whereas the earlier sections, however, were a plain enumeration of the known world, the climax is a more emotive evocation of the new lands: the mountains, deserts, seas and straits as yet unnamed. Here the poetry articulates a sense of discovery and appears to take possession as securely in linguistic novelty as had Ercilla's fellow-soldiers through military conquest:

> 'Vees las manchas de tierras tan cubiertas
> que pueden ser apenas divisadas:
> son las que nunca han sido descubiertas
> ni de estranjeros pies jamás pisadas,
> las cuales estarán siempre encubiertas
> y de aquellos celajes ocupadas
> hasta que Dios permita que parezcan
> porque más sus secretos se engrandezcan.'
>
> (II, p. 233)

> 'You see the marks on the earth so covered that they can hardly be made out: they are those that have never been discovered nor trodden upon by foreign feet, and they will always remain hidden and visited by those clouds until God allows them to appear so that their secrets can be rendered greater.'

Ultimately, however, true to his epoch, Ercilla interprets the new-found land as essentially an additional detail in the great scheme of things – in the pre-Copernican cosmology of planetary movements:

> 'Y como vees en forma verdadera
> de la tierra la gran circunferencia,
> pudieras entender, si tiempo hubiera,
> de los celestes cuerpos la excelencia,
> la máquina y concierto de la esfera,
> la virtud de los astros y influencia,
> varias revoluciones, movimientos,
> los cursos naturales y violentos.'
>
> (II, pp. 233–4)

> 'And as you see the great circumference of the land in its true shape, you could understand, if there were time, the excellence of the celestial bodies, the operation and the order of the sphere, the virtue and influence of the stars, their varied revolutions and movements, the natural and violent circulations.'

Four centuries after completing *La Araucana* Ercilla appears in another work on a scale as vast as his own, a poem about America in general and Chile in particular: Pablo Neruda's *Canto general*. Ercilla figures in a section entitled 'Los conquistadores' and he is singled out by Neruda for his humanity as well as his poetic gifts. The section that Neruda devotes to his predecessor strangely contains that same note of warning and augury as had been voiced by Fitón in *La Araucana*:

> En vano, en vano,
> sangre por los ramajes de cristal salpicado,
> en vano por las noches del puma
> el desafiante paso del soldado,
> los órdenes,
> los pasos
> del herido.
> Todo vuelve al silencio coronado de plumas
> en donde un rey remoto devora enredaderas.[7]

> In vain, in vain, blood spattered on the crystal branches, in vain the defiant procession of soldiers along the night of the puma, the orders, the footsteps of the wounded one. Everything returns to the silence crowned with feathers where a remote king devours creepers.

And just as the venerable magician in *La Araucana* had engaged in the naming of places so Neruda in the first canto of his own poem, 'La lámpara en la tierra' ('The lamp on the earth'), turns to the physical appearance of the South American continent. If the old man's recital, however, eventually achieves the effect of an incantation through naming, Neruda's meditation is rooted in indecipherability. Indeed he looks to a place and a time *before* names, to 'las tierras sin nombres y sin números' ('the lands without names and numbers'):

> En el fondo de América sin nombre
> estaba Arauco entre las aguas
> vertiginosas, apartado
> por todo el frío del planeta.
>
> (p. 123)

> In the depth of nameless America was Arauco among the vertiginous waters, isolated by the whole of the planet's cold.

He even seeks a new language as he invokes the exotically named Bío Bío, a Chilean river:

> Pero háblame, Bío Bío,
> son tus palabras en mi boca
> las que resbalan, tú me diste
> el lenguaje, el canto nocturno
> mezclado con lluvia y follaje.
>
> (p. 115)

> But speak to me, Bio Bio, it is your words that slip in my mouth, you gave me the language, the night song mixed with rain and foliage.

Neruda is disingenuous, however. The conception of a new language for what has not yet been described – whether rivers, trees, birds or beasts – is at most what it has ever been: a matter of neologism. Neruda claimed that Hispano-American poetry, such as his own and that of César Vallejo (1895–1937), was different from that of modern Spain because the precursors were not the same. While Lorca and his contemporaries had behind them the poets of Spain's Golden Age, Neruda believed that for South American poets such an inheritance was insignificant because 'everything has been painted in Europe, everything has been sung in Europe. But not in America.'[8] Yet even in the first section with its emphasis on a continent in the making, Neruda's language betrays less a primitive splendour than a sophisticated delicacy – a joy of metaphor that offers unmistakable echoes of Góngora. To speak of the ripening corn as 'una lanza terminada en fuego' ('a lance that ends in fire') (p. 108) may appear to be an elemental evocation of the source of early man's food, but it is the kind of extravagant visualisation characteristic of baroque poets. Even more reminiscent of the Gongorist manner are passages like the opening of the second part of the first section describing the fauna:

> Era el crepúsculo de la iguana.
>
> Desde la arcoirisada crestería
> su lengua como un dardo
> se hundía en la verdura,
> el hormiguero monacal pisaba
> con melodioso pie la selva,
> el guanaco fino como el oxígeno
> en las anchas alturas pardas
> iba calzando botas de oro

> It was the twilight of the iguana. From its rainbowed cresting, its tongue like a dart sank into the greenery, the monastic anteater trod the jungle floor with melodious foot, the guanaco as refined as oxygen was wearing golden boots in the high brown plains

Phrases like 'melodioso pie' ('melodious foot') and the depiction of the 'guanaco' (a species of llama) with its feet shod with gold are inspired by the kind of metaphorical imagination we encounter in seventeenth-century Spanish poets. Typical of Góngora in particular is the tendency to confuse the animate and non-animate. Thus the toucan is 'una adorable / caja de frutas barnizadas' ('an adorable box of varnished fruit') (p. 111), and in another passage Neruda envisages the material world in human terms:

Madre de los metales, te quemaron,
te mordieron, te martirizaron,
te corroyeron, te pudrieron
más tarde, cuando los ídolos
ya no pudieron defenderte.
Lianas trepando hacia el cabello
de la noche selvática   (p. 116)

Mother of metals, they burnt you, they bit you, they martyred you, they
eroded you, they putrefied you later, when the idols could no longer
defend you. Lianas creeping towards the hair of the jungle night

Passages such as the following in Góngora's *Soledad primera*, where the division between the human and vegetable worlds is blurred, come readily to mind:

Del verde margen otra [zagala] las mejores
rosas traslada y lilios al cabello,
o por lo matizado o por lo bello,
si Aurora no con rayos, Sol con flores . . .
Tantas al fin, el arroyuelo, y tantas
montañesas da el prado.[9]

From the green bank another [peasant girl] transfers the best roses and
lilies to her hair, which in its subtle texture or its beauty is if not a dawn
with rays of sun then a Sun with flowers . . . So many mountain girls are
finally yielded by the stream and the meadow.

Appropriately when the coming of man is mentioned in the final part of the first section of *Canto general* it is envisaged in terms of emergence from the very substance of the land:

Como la copa de la arcilla era
la raza mineral, el hombre
hecho de piedras y de atmósfera,
limpio como los cántaros, sonoro.
                 (p. 119)

Like the crown of clay was the mineral race, man made of stones and
atmosphere, clean as the pitchers, sonorous.

Moreover, when Neruda describes the brutality of the Conquest in the third section the mode of description directly parallels the terms in which he had envisaged the creation of the continent:

Los hijos de la arcilla vieron rota
su sonrisa, golpeada
su frágil estatura de venados,

y aun en la muerte no entendían.
Fueron amarrados y heridos,
fueron quemados y abrasados,
fueron mordidos y enterrados.

(p. 145)

The sons of clay saw their smile destroyed, their fragile stature of deer
struck down, and even in their deaths they did not understand. They were
bound and wounded, burnt and scorched, bitten and buried.

The opening section mimics the Book of Genesis in its gradual unfolding
of creation, culminating in the emergence of man in the sixth and final part,
precisely paralleling the biblical account according to which God created
male and female on the sixth day. Biblical echoes do not of themselves make
for an epic poem, however, and the disparate character of *Canto general* with
its mix of recent Latin American history and ancient civilizations, propagan-
distic denunciation and lyrical evocation, global politics and autobiography,
makes it a difficult work to get into perspective. It lacks both the linear
thrust of the *Poema de mío Cid* and the concentrated clash of the Old and
the New World in *La Araucana*, and so one may be tempted to concede that
it is, as the editor of the edition from which I quote claims, encyclopaedic
rather than epic in nature. To deny the poem its epic qualities, however,
would impoverish our understanding. These qualities are not merely dependent upon the sheer scale of the work, daunting though that is: an epic in
cinematographic terms invested with a kind of populism such as we find in
the work of the Mexican Muralists. *Canto general*, however, radiates a poetic
awareness of place and identity in a way that recalls the 'true' epic. The first
five sections comprise a largely chronological account of the formation of
the continent, the pre-Columbian civilizations, the Conquest, resistance,
and finally the people's struggle for freedom in more recent times, concluding with a denunciation of González Videla, the President (or, as Neruda
would have it, 'traitor') of Chile.

In the later sections the attention shifts more to Neruda himself. The
tenth section, 'El fugitivo' ('The fugitive'), describes his flight into exile
while the final one, 'Yo soy' ('I am'), relates events in his life from his
earliest recollections. His journey to exile, his life and his song become a
metonymy of the history and struggles of the continent. Lines from the
final part of the last, autobiographical section enunciate this in simple but
profound terms:

Libro común de un hombre, pan abierto
es esta geografía de mi canto,
y una comunidad de labradores

alguna vez recogerá su fuego,
y sembrará sus llamas y sus hojas
otra vez en la nave de la tierra.   (p. 629)

This geography of my song is the common book of a man, broken bread, and a community of farmers will some day gather their fire, and sow their flames and their leaves once more in the earth's ship.

In this writing-in of the self, though, Neruda follows the example of Ercilla, who is a protagonist as well as a narrator. For instance in the account of the defeat of the Araucanians that precedes the appearance of the wise man, Fitón, it is Ercilla himself who leads the attack when those about him falter. His own name figures in the text when his fellow-soldiers appeal to him for inspiration.

However fair-minded Ercilla may appear alongside his contemporaries though, he could not elicit more than a nod of recognition for his decency from Neruda, a Communist writing in the early years of the Cold War, whose continent was subjected to the self-interested intervention of the United States. The concept of heroism in *Canto general* is envisaged as resistance, and if the ethos of epic implies colonization through the desire for discovery then Neruda's poem is best understood as the inversion of epic. Consequently, on the one hand there is a denial of history through the assertion of timeless values represented in the common man. The last poem in the eighth section has the same title as the whole section – 'La tierra se llama Juan' ('The land is called Juan') – and celebrates the survival of the persecuted. In Neruda's sharp rhetoric such an assertion becomes a tribute to the human spirit that, as at the start of the poem, appears to grow and acquire strength from the very earth:

Detrás de los libertadores estaba Juan
trabajando, pescando y combatiendo,
en su trabajo de carpintería o en su mina mojada.
Sus manos han arado la tierra y han medido
los caminos.

Sus huesos están en todas partes.
Pero vive. Regresó de la tierra. Ha nacido.
Ha nacido de nuevo como una planta eterna.

(p. 436)

Behind the liberators was Juan, working, fishing and fighting, in his carpenter's shop or in his damp mine. His hands have ploughed the land and measured the paths. His bones are everywhere. But he lives. He returned from the earth. He has been born. He has been born again like an eternal plant.

On the the other hand there is a sinking back into history, a movement that is even more anti-epic in its regressive thrust. The most famous section of *Canto general* is the second, a description of Macchu Picchu, the Inca civilization in the heights of the Peruvian Andes, undiscovered until the start of the twentieth century. This, however, is not merely a set-piece description, an evocation of a past time. It is a journey from present to past, an ascent that is metaphorical as well as literal, hence the injunctions at the start of the eighth and final parts: 'Sube conmigo, amor americano' ('Rise with me, American love') (p. 134); 'Sube a nacer conmigo, hermano' ('Rise to be born with me, brother') (p. 140). Indeed the first five poems are not concerned with the Inca site but with the poet's own experience. As Neruda's translator John Felstiner puts it: 'the beginning of *Alturas de Macchu Picchu* is pervaded by loneliness, thwarted passion, disintegrative forces, and death'.[10] Even as Macchu Picchu comes into sight, however, and the vision becomes grander and the atmosphere more rarefied, Neruda looks beyond the 'confused splendour', beyond the majestic impression of the condor in flight, and sees:

> el antiguo ser, servidor, el dormido
> en los campos, veo un cuerpo, mil cuerpos, un hombre, mil mujeres,
> bajo la racha negra, negros de lluvia y noche,
> con la piedra pesada de la estatua:
> Juan Cortapiedras, hijo de Wiracocha,
> Juan Comefrío, hijo de estrella verde,
> Juan Piesdescalzos, nieto de la turquesa,
> sube a nacer conmigo, hermano.   (p. 140)

> the ancient one, a slave, the one sleeping in the fields, I see one body, a thousand bodies, one man, a thousand women, under a black gust of wind, blackened by rain and night, with the heavy stone of the statue; John Stonebreaker, son of Wiracocha, John Coldeater, son of the green star, John Barefoot, grandson of the turquoise, rise to be born with me, brother.

'Alturas de Macchu Picchu' has at least what could be described as the epic *vision* – a sweep and a sensation of discovery, that here, as elsewhere in *Canto general*, involves self-discovery. It is not a complex matter as it mainly entails an initial emotional uncertainty and later thematic shifts. Just how important such an experience is, however, for the creation of a dynamic process becomes evident when Neruda's conception of Macchu Picchu is compared to a poem written ten years later, also based on an ancient American civilization: Octavio Paz's *Piedra de sol*. The poem consists of 584 lines, one for each day in the Aztec calendar, while by repeating the opening lines of the poem at the end Paz suggests the cyclical nature of time. These

lines depict a serene Spring landscape, one that would not be out of place
in a European pastoral:

> un sauce de cristal, un chopo de agua,
> un alto surtidor que el viento arquea,
> un árbol bien plantado mas danzante,
> un caminar de río que se curva,
> avanza, retrocede, da un rodeo
> y llega siempre[11]

> a willow of crystal, a poplar of water, a high fountain arched by the wind,
> a well-planted but dancing tree, the course of a river that meanders,
> progresses, returns, diverges and always arrives

The two terms of the title – stone and sun – suggest the centrality of
human sacrifice in the Aztec religion, but Paz's poem lacks the elemental
force of Neruda's 'Alturas de Macchu Picchu'. This is not merely because
it is essentially a meditative and occasionally philosophic poem but because
the poet is far less preoccupied with the primitive basis of the work. The
present-day reader may well view it as a curiously eclectic exercise in which
are blended such diverse strands as the influence of T. S. Eliot (the focus on
the moment in time and the incorporation of personal anecdote) and an
anticipation of the 'Make love, not war' slogan of the 1960s, as in a passage
that alludes to the Spanish Civil War:

> Madrid 1937,
> en la Plaza del Ángel las mujeres
> cosían y cantaban con sus hijos,
> después sonó la alarma y hubo gritos,
> casas arrodilladas en el polvo,
> torres hendidas, frentes escupidas
> y el huracán de los motores, fijo:
> los dos se desnudaron y se amaron
> por defender nuestra porción eterna,
> nuestra ración de tiempo y paraíso...
> los dos se desnudaron y besaron
> porque las desnudeces enlazadas
> saltan el tiempo y son invulnerables.
>
> (p. 106)

> Madrid 1937, in the Square of the Angel the women were sewing and
> singing with their children, then the alarm sounded and there were cries,
> houses kneeling in the dust, split towers, spat foreheads and the hurricane
> of the engines, fixed: the two undressed and made love to each other to
> defend our eternal portion of land, our ration of time and paradise... the
> two undressed and kissed because entwined nakednesses leap over time
> and are invulnerable.

Beside Neruda's compelling understanding of Macchu Picchu, Paz's adaptation of the mysteries of identity implicit in the Aztec ritual to a poetry of statement and assertion is unconvincing and forced:

> nunca la vida es nuestra, es de los otros,
> la vida no es de nadie, todos somos
> la vida – pan de sol para los otros,
> los otros todos que nosotros somos –,
> soy otro cuando soy, los actos míos
> son más míos si son también de todos.
>
> (p. 113)

> life is never ours, it belongs to others, life is nobody's, we are all life –
> bread of sun for the others, all the others that we are – I am another when
> I am, my acts are more mine if they also belong to others.

Twentieth-century sensitivities understandably recoiled before the idea of epic. The horror of total war and the adverse reaction to European colonization were hardly conducive to the success of the genre. We prefer our heroes to be ancient rather than modern, somehow domesticated either by the sheer passage of time or by their conversion into literary types. The epic vision, however, can still affect us at a deeper level. It can at the very least function negatively – reminding us of what we are not, what we no longer are. Such is the impression provided by the poem entitled 'A orillas del Duero' ('On the banks of the Duero') from Antonio Machado's *Campos de Castilla*. His evocation of a time when Spain was, according to one point of view, greater, significantly alludes both to the Cid and the Conquistadors:

> Castilla no es aquella tan generosa un día,
> cuando Myo Cid Rodrigo el de Vivar volvía,
> ufano de su nueva fortuna y su opulencia,
> a regalar a Alfonso los huertos de Valencia;
> o que, tras la aventura que acreditó sus bríos,
> pedía la conquista de los inmensos ríos
> indianos a la corte, la madre de soldados,
> guerreros y adalides que han de tornar, cargados
> de plata y oro, a España, en regios galeones,
> para la presa cuervos, para la lid leones.[12]

> Castile is not that generous place that it was once when Rodrigo, my Cid,
> from Vivar, returned, proud of his new fortune and wealth, to reward
> Alfonso with the fields of Valencia; or the place that after the venture that
> was a credit to its valour asked the court for the conquest of the immense
> rivers of America, [Castile] the mother of soldiers, warriors and leaders
> who are to return in royal galleons, laden with silver and gold, to Spain,
> like ravens in the pursuit, like lions in combat.

Such a conception is as regressive as Neruda's in 'Alturas de Macchu Picchu' although it is not nearly as energizing as the Chilean poet's journey of discovery. It would, however, be an error to judge either the poem or the poet as reactionary on the basis of these lines. It betrays exasperation rather than nostalgia; indeed the two-line refrain that recurs in the middle of the poem is sharply decisive in the manner of a moralist:

> Castilla miserable, ayer dominadora,
> envuelta en sus andrajos, desprecia cuanto ignora.
>
> (p. 102)

> Wretched Castile, yesterday so dominant, now wrapped in its rags, it scorns all that it does not know.

Moreover, this is a poem that moves abruptly between the two extremes of historical events and their attendant fluctuations and the unchanging pattern of humble lives integrated into the natural rhythms of generation and season:

> Veía el horizonte cerrado por colinas
> obscuras, coronadas de robles y de encinas;
> desnudos peñascales, algún humilde prado
> donde el merino pace y el toro, arrodillado
> sobre la hierba, rumia; las márgenes del río
> lucir sus verdes álamos al claro sol de estío,
> y, silenciosamente, lejanos pasajeros,
> ¡tan diminutos! – carros, jinetes y arrieros –
> cruzar el largo puente   (p. 102)

> I saw the horizon closed with dark hills, crowned with oaks and ilexes; bare crags, a humble meadow where the merino sheep grazes and the bull, kneeling on the grass, ruminates; the river banks displaying their green poplars in the bright Summer sun and people passing by silently in the distance, so tiny! – carts, horsemen and muleteers – crossing the long bridge

Machado's contemporary Miguel de Unamuno (1864–1936) would have recognized such a description as an instance of *intrahistoria* – the ceaseless flow of unremarkable lives that collectively endure beyond or, to use his own term, *within* history. In Unamuno's striking metaphor they are the underlying movement of the sea while the deeds of history are but the waves that form and then dissolve. One recalls in this tension Neruda's reaching beyond the Inca monuments to discover the lives and celebrate the toil of countless generations of 'Juans'.

Dissatisfaction with place and nation is another anti-epic keynote of twentieth-century literature. For many Spaniards, the middle decades of the twentieth century, in particular, were a time of sorrow and impotence. The austerity and the repression of the Franco years left a deep imprint, frequently conducive to the same kind of sardonic commentary as colours 'A orillas del Duero'. 'Apología y petición' ('Apology and plea') by Jaime Gil de Biedma (1929–90) is remarkable for its directness and the choice of form. His poem is a sestina, a rarely used form that originated in the work of the Provençal troubadours but which has been used in many languages down the centuries. Its six-line stanzas end with the same six words, though never in the same order, while a final short stanza of three lines uses all six words by placing three of them in the middle of each line. Although the form is highly contrived and rigorous this does not necessarily result in an artificial utterance. On the contrary; the effect is to highlight through repetition the key ideas and thereby establish a pattern of sound-bites. Indeed the danger is that the poem could appear too plain and heavy-handed. A good sestina will be alive to the possibility of morphological variation – changing the function of words as they are repeated. Thus the colloquial use of 'demonios' in the phrase in the second line of the opening stanza will not be used in the same way on subsequent appearances:

> ¿Y qué decir de nuestra madre España,
> este país de todos los demonios
> en donde el mal gobierno, la pobreza
> no son, sin más, pobreza y mal gobierno
> sino un estado místico del hombre,
> la absolución final de nuestra historia?[13]

> And what is there to say of our mother Spain, this accursed land where bad government and poverty are not, it goes without saying, poverty and bad government but a mystical condition of man, the final absolution of our history?

The cutting edge here is supplied by the ironic appropriation of patriotic and religious concepts ('nuestra madre España'; 'estado místico'; 'absolución final'). Moreover the six key words – 'España', 'demonios', 'pobreza', 'gobierno', 'hombre', 'historia' – not only sustain and define the poem's subject but suggest an insistent subliminal message as we unconsciously make the syntactical connection: *Spain*, and its *government* in particular, are associated with *evil* ('demonios') and *poverty*, and the *inhabitants* ('hombre') are the victims of her *history*. The poem develops these ideas imaginatively. The sardonic note of the first line is echoed by the opening of the third stanza: 'Nuestra famosa inmemorial pobreza' ('Our famous, immemorial poverty'). The bitter tone manifests itself in a determined assault upon the mystique of poverty as an accident and the interpretation of history as a matter of destiny. Eventually, in the last of the six-line stanzas the poet turns to blunt statement and home truth in order to demolish the tyranny of fatalism:

> Porque quiero creer que no hay demonios.
> Son hombres los que pagan al gobierno,
> los empresarios de la falsa historia,
> son hombres quienes han vendido al hombre,
> los que le han convertido a la pobreza
> y secuestrado la salud de España.

> Because I want to believe that there are no devils. It is men who pay the government, the entrepreneurs of false history, it is men who have sold out man, they who have converted him to poverty and kidnapped the health of Spain.

Gil de Biedma's poem has therefore an important intertextual aspect: it emerges as a response to the conception of Spain as a homeland invoked as an elevated abstraction, such as characterized the mediocre poetry produced by Nationalist writers during and after the Civil War. As Natalia Calamai has shown, this tendency to the abstract co-existed with the invocation of old ideals, as in lines such as the following from an anthology of poetry written in support of Franco's rebellion:

> Una España yo quiero igual que aquella España
> que hace doscientos años se nos quedó dormida . . .
> Una Espãna perfecta y generosa, compendio
> de constantes trabajos y supremas conquistas.[14]

> I want a Spain like that Spain that has been dead for two hundred years. . . . A perfect and generous Spain, an amalgam of ceaseless work and supreme conquest.

This is the Spain that is evoked in Machado's 'A orillas del Duero', albeit in a more sophisticated connection, and attacked by Gil de Biedma.

'Apología y petición' is the kind of poem likely to be produced by what has been termed an 'internal exile' – that is, a disaffected writer who operates within the constraints of expression imposed or implied by the regime with which he/she is at odds. The alternatives were, starkly, either to be silent or to leave Spain. The true exile's vision of homeland is likely to be mellower than that of the internal exile's if only because memory in absence is more conducive to nostalgia than is the impotent witnessing of events. Like many fellow artists, Luis Cernuda left Spain in 1936 never to return. In his poem entitled 'Un español habla de su tierra' ('A Spaniard speaks of his land'), written in the early years of his exile, the two tendencies – recollection and resentment – alternate. The opening stanzas are concisely pictorial:

> Las playas, parameras
> Al rubio sol durmiendo,
> Los oteros, las vegas
> En paz, a solas, lejos;
>
> Los castillos, ermitas,
> Cortijos y conventos,
> La vida con la historia,
> Tan dulces al recuerdo[15]

> The beaches and moorlands sleeping in the blond sun, the hillocks, the meadows, in peace, alone, distant; the castles, hermitages, mansions and convents, life with history, so sweet for recollection

In this wistful remembrance the notion of history, unlike in Gil de Biedma, is positive. Through the evocation of the landscapes and buildings of Spain – the objects of the poet's yearning – the history of the land becomes real and precious. Immediately following, however, is a stanza that seethes with bitterness:

> Ellos, los vencedores
> Caínes sempiternos,
> De todo me arrancaron.
> Me dejan el destierro.

> They, the victors, eternal Cains, snatched everything away from me. They leave me exile.

The victors of the Civil War – a war between brothers as it has often been called – are like the fratricidal Cain. Because of them, the poet asserts, the very name of Spain 'poisons his dreams', even though he is instinctively drawn to it as a physical reality now lost. He concludes pessimistically with the observation that by the time that Spain is rid of 'their' baleful influence it will be too late as he will by then be dead:

> Un día, tú ya libre
> De la mentira de ellos,
> Me buscarás. Entonces
> ¿Qué ha de decir un muerto?

> One day, when eventually you are free of their lies, you will seek me out. But what can a dead man say then?

In this and in other poems on exile Cernuda questions both the notions that love of a place implies patriotism and that patriotism entails obedience to a political system. Such an attitude is in keeping with the twentieth century's more individual understanding of what both epic and nationhood suggest. It is at a far remove from the anti-anarchic ethos of the *Poema de mío Cid* and the unquestioning, if unusually compassionate, mentality of the Conquistador narrator of *La Araucana*. Indeed, landscapes also become personalized: not only observed through the eye of the beholder but defined in terms of the beholder. Thus the reader who comes across a poem entitled 'Castilla' by Guillermo Carnero is required to adjust any expectations that may have been aroused by the title with its promise of a focus on landscape and, specifically, by a knowledge of what kind of poem such a title would have suggested to Carnero's precursors from the Generation of 1898. The poem comes from a collection entitled *Dibujos de la muerte* ('Sketches of death'), which was initially considered a purely aesthetic work and compared unfavourably by some critics to the directness of the social poets of the 1950s. As Trevor Dadson has shown, however, despite his penchant for 'complicated and arcane cultural references', several of Carnero's poems suggest 'a deliberate and clever attack through a reappropriation of those very symbols and myths appropriated by Franco thirty years previously'.[16] What is significant about 'Castilla' is the denial of reader expectations. It is not a celebration of Castile, and only an evocation inasmuch as it relates to the self that is inscribed in the poem. It offers, then, a sharp contrast to both those poems that trade on abstractions and those that depict place. For the focus in Carnero's poem is not a landscape or a building but the individual; the point of reference is, in fact, the speaker's body, by which the town walls and the parched lands of Castile are measured:

> No sé dónde extiende mi cuerpo.
> No sé hasta cuándo cayera el más lejano cuerpo de muralla; no sé
> hasta qué altura yacen los sillares entre las serpientes o lenguas del sol,
> entre la alucinada tierra, bajo ese cráter polvoriento y callado,
> bajo los cuarteados terrones de ese cielo de arcilla.
> Tampoco sé hasta dónde se extiende la tierra; quizás
> un horizonte redondo.[17]

> I don't know where my body extends. I don't know until when the most distant body of wall should have fallen; I don't know to what height the ashlars stand between the snakes or tongues of sun, in the hallucinated land, under that dusty and silent crater, under the cut clods of that clay sky. Neither do I know to where the land extends; perhaps a round horizon.

Carnero briefly evokes the same vision of the martial past of Castile as had preoccupied Machado in 'A orillas del Duero':

> Me han despertado voces y ladridos lejanos
> y chocar de armaduras y de yelmos y hachas
> y de pieles rasgadas por la luz de la espuela.

> I have been woken by voices and barking in the distance and the clash of
> armour and helmets and axes and skins torn by the light of the spur.

The dominant image is that of walls. The primary significance is that of
fortification but with an added association of imprisonment:

> Conozco muchos nombres de murallas.
> Murallas para mirar la noche (murallas lamidas por los dedos escamosos
>   del sol)
> murallas para tocar esqueletos y plumas de pájaros; murallas
> para gritarlas contra otras murallas.

> I know many names of walls. Walls to look at the night (walls licked by the
> scaly fingers of the sun) walls for touching skeletons and birds' feathers;
> walls that are for shouting against other walls.

The poet's body, however, as wide as a river, attempts to break loose from
both the monumentality and the restriction of the walls, the epitome of
Castile. I say 'attempts' because lines from near the end suggest that this may
not be achieved:

> Y otra vez al galope, matando,
> descuartizando telas y andamiajes y máscaras
> y levantando muros y andamiajes y telas
> y máscaras.

> And once more at a gallop, killing, tearing apart cloths and scaffolding
> and masks and raising walls and scaffolding and cloths and masks.

Other than the obvious contradiction, the repetition here is expressive of
an energy being drained, of a force somehow crippled.

My final illustration is aptly both a rejection and an affirmation (in that
order) of the epic vision of homeland. Jorge Luis Borges (1899–1986) wrote
his 'Oda escrita en 1966' for the 150th anniversary of the Argentine con-
federation at Tucumán in 1816. The horseman referred to in the opening
is San Martín, whose equestrian statue stands in the square in Buenos Aires
that bears his name:

> Nadie es la patria. Ni siquiera el jinete
> Que, alto en el alba de una plaza desierta,
> Rige un corcel de bronce por el tiempo,
> Ni los otros que miran desde el mármol,
> Ni los que prodigaron su bélica ceniza
> Por los campos de América
> O dejaron un verso o una hazaña
> O la memoria de una vida cabal
> En el justo ejercicio de los días.
> Nadie es la patria. Ni siquiera los símbolos.[18]

> No-one is the homeland. Not even the rider who on high at dawn in an empty square controls a bronze steed through time, nor the others who look from the marble, nor those who squandered their martial ash on the lands of America or left a verse or a deed or the memory of a life fulfilled in the proper exercise of their days. Nobody is the homeland. Not even the symbols.

This is a resonantly negative conception of patriotism. The majesty of the imagery and the splendour of the rhetoric cannot disguise the scepticism that is encapsulated in the oxymoron 'bélica ceniza' ('martial ash'). There is an unmistakable evocation of epic here in the combination of deed, word and destiny; indeed the phrase 'campos de América' ('lands of America') suggests the Conquistadors rather than the nineteenth-century liberators.

The second stanza begins with lines that convey the essence of heroic as well as literary epic as it lists what could be regarded as hallmarks of the genre. If it is *La Araucana* that is echoed in the first stanza then now it is the *Poema de mío Cid*:

> Nadie es la patria. Ni siquiera el tiempo
> Cargado de batallas, de espadas y de éxodos
> Y de la lenta población de regiones
> Que lindan con la aurora y el ocaso

> Nobody is the homeland. Not even time laden with battles, swords, endless exodus and the slow peopling of regions that border on dawn and sunset

By now we are aware that the denial of nationhood as a manifestation of the individual is nonetheless communicated in a tone and in terms that are ringingly affirmative. All of this prepares us for a statement of what a homeland *is*: 'un acto perpetuo / Como el perpetuo mundo' ('a perpetual act / Like the perpetual world'). Nationhood is not realized in the individual deed but through collective memory, the perpetuation of an initial act:

> Nadie es la patria, pero todos debemos
> Ser dignos del antiguo juramento
> Que prestaron aquellos caballeros
> De ser lo que ignoraban, argentinos.

> Nobody is the homeland, but we all must be worthy of that ancient oath sworn by those gentlemen, to be something that they did not know, to be Argentines.

Borges, who disliked Neruda, would not have relished the comparison, but the conclusion of his poem echoes that solidarity of past and future, of man and destiny, and of individual life and shared history, that informs some of the intense moments in *Canto general*. In both poets there is an understanding of heroic aspiration and significant place that, though modern in its idea, is nonetheless resonant with the impulses of the epic genre:

> Somos el porvenir de esos varones,
> La justificación de aquellos muertos;
> Nuestro deber es la gloriosa carga
> Que a nuestra sombra legan esas sombras
> Que debemos salvar.
>
> Nadie es la patria, pero todos lo somos.
> Arda en mi pecho y en el vuestro, incesante,
> Ese límpido fuego misterioso.

We are the future of these men, the justification of those who are dead; our duty is the glorious burden bequeathed to our shadow by those shadows that we must save. Nobody is the homeland, but we are all the homeland. May that clean, mysterious fire burn ceaselessly in my breast and in yours.

Chapter 4

The ballad and the poetry of tales

Even on the basis of those few poems considered in the previous chapter, epic, evidently, is not so much a story as a narrative that is made up of a number of stories. Indeed such 'tales within the tale' are often referred to as episodes or incidents. These designations are not merely a convenient term for locating specific events within the poem; they also indicate how these episodes were subject to isolation and extraction, the most important consequence of which was the creation of a further poetic form: the ballad or, to use the Spanish term, the *romance*. As Colin Smith has pointed out: 'Many of the early ballads in a number of countries are of a semi-epic kind, drawn either from historical epics or based upon new events and real persons.'[1]

The relationship of the Spanish ballad to the epic is undoubted but complex. The many ballads on Fernán González, a tenth-century count who secured the independence of Castile from the kings of Asturias-Leon, derive from a fourteenth-century chronicle which itself drew on a lost epic poem. Rather than the independence of Castile, however, it is Fernán González's disputes with the kings of Leon and Navarre with which these poems are concerned. In similar fashion, many of the ballads on the Cid owe little to the thirteenth-century epic poem. When the ballads were composed in the fifteenth century the epic poem had long since ceased to be performed, with the result that episodes from the earlier poem were subjected to substantial rewriting. Thus King Búcar's expedition to reconquer Valencia (lines 2311–428 in the *Poema de mío Cid*) is re-worked as an essentially sentimental story. Indeed several *romances* do not invoke the epic on the Cid at all. It is the later, more sensational, *Mocedades de Rodrigo* that supplies the source for the ballads about the Cid in his youth. These are fictional, and present a strikingly different picture of the Cid from the mature and measured figure of the *Poema*. Whereas the hero of the epic reveals himself as unswervingly loyal to his King despite the injustice of his banishment, the Cid of the ballads emerges on occasion as disrespectful and boorish. One of the legends relates how the Cid killed Count Lozano, the father of his betrothed, in a duel because the Count had insulted the Cid's father. One ballad ('Cabalga Diego Laínez') relates how the Cid and his father have an audience with

the King at Burgos. When the Cid overhears one of the courtiers say that
it was he, the Cid, who had killed the Count, he responds angrily and in-
temperately ('con alta y soberbia voz'), threatening to do the same to him.
He is reluctant to kiss the King's hand, only doing so on his father's bidding
and then with bad grace:

> Todos se apearon juntos
> para al rey besar la mano;
> Rodrigo se quedó solo
> encima de su caballo.
> Entonces habló su padre,
> bien oiréis lo que ha hablado:
> 'Apeáos vos, mi hijo,
> besaréis al rey la mano,
> porque él es vuestro señor
> vos, hijo, sois su vasallo.'
> Desque Rodrigo esto oyó
> sintióse más agraviado;
> las palabras que responde
> son de hombre muy enojado:
> 'Si otro me lo dijera
> ya me lo hubiera pagado;
> mas por mandarlo vos, padre,
> yo lo haré de buen grado.'[2]

> They all dismounted together to kiss the King's hand; Rodrigo remained
> alone on his horse. Then his father spoke, and you shall hear what he
> spoke: 'Dismount, my son, and kiss the King's hand, because he is your
> master, and you, son, are his vassal.' When Rodrigo heard this, he felt
> more aggrieved; his response was that of an enraged man: 'If another had
> told me that, he would have paid for it; but as it is you who order me,
> father, I will do it willingly.'

Such fictional, even coarse, traits are symptomatic of the *romance*'s suitability for pure entertainment. It has to be remembered that the ballad
was originally, and is still potentially, a song. Even as a poem, however, it
possesses formal and metrical features that are conducive to familiarity and
memorability. It typically has a strong stress on the seventh and penultimate
syllable, and has other subsidiary stresses placed in a variety of ways earlier in
the line. In the opening of Lorca's 'Muerte de Antoñito el Camborio' the
stress in each of the lines falls on the first and fourth syllables as well as on
the seventh. This evenly spaced pattern makes for a smooth yet rapid beat,
one that could facilitate quick memorizing:

> Voces de muerte sonaron
> cerca del Guadalquivir.

Voces antiguas que cercan
voz de clavel varonil.[3]

Voices of death resounded near the Guadalquivir. Ancient voices that
surround a voice of manly carnation.

Stories circulated about how illiterate soldiers on the Republican side in
the Civil War were able to learn Lorca's ballads by heart. Centuries earlier,
Juan de Valdés, a theorist on language, had observed how the *romance* metre
seemed to be the most natural for the Spanish language: 'porque en ellos
me contenta aquel su hilo de dezir que va continuado y llano, tanto que
pienso que los llaman *romances* porque son muy castos en su romance'[4]
('because I am pleased by that thread of narrative that they possess, which
flows smoothly and evenly, so much so that I fancy that they call them
romances because they are so unspoilt in their own [Romance] speech').

Indeed the ballad has been through the ages the most versatile of poetic
forms. Moreover it has been functional in ways that go beyond pure literary
considerations. In particular the link of the *romance* with performance and
popular entertainment has always been a strong one. Thus, when in Lorca's
play *La zapatera prodigiosa* (*The Shoemaker's Prodigious Wife*) the henpecked
husband returns home disguised as a puppet-master to put on a show that
reflects his own condition, the form in which the performance is cast is a
romance. One of the commonest modes of popular diffusion of the ballad
up until the nineteenth century, however, was the *romance de ciegos* ('blind
men's ballad'). The blind man was not only a performer but also a seller
of ballads in loose-leaf publications called *pliegos sueltos* – a single sheet
printed on both sides and folded twice. Such figures were a common sight
especially in the south of Spain and were converted into a literary type
or commonplace. Although varied in content, drawing on themes from the
traditional ballad and the literary canon, especially the theatre, their tendency
to over-statement through the exaggeration of emotion and the quest for
the lurid detail led to critical neglect. The two leading authorities on the
Spanish ballad in the twentieth century – Marcelino Menéndez Pelayo and
Ramón Menéndez Pidal – paid scant attention to them. While it would
be hard, however, to make a case for them on purely literary grounds they
are important as a cultural phenomenon, and cannot be overlooked for an
understanding of the ballads of such poets as Zorrilla, Antonio Machado
and Lorca. The fascination of these and other poets with crime, violence,
the supernatural and the sensational relates to the readiness of the *romances
de ciegos* – responding to popular taste and demand – to glorify such figures
as the outlaw and the bandit. One of these entitled 'Juan Portela' narrates
the bloody exploits of the eponymous hero whose first crimes were directly
related to his rejection in love. Such was his fury and thirst for vengeance

that he enters the home of the woman who has spurned him and kills both
her and her husband:

> Con mi trabuco, yo entré
> a la casa que habitaban,
> y a su marido encontré,
> que los dos cenando estaban,
> venganza determiné.
> –Vengo a quitarte la vida
> delante de tu marido,
> y pagaré con la mía
> si acaso soy atrevido.[5]

> With my blunderbuss I entered the house in which they lived, and I found
> her husband, because the two of them were having dinner, and I resolved
> to avenge myself. 'I've come to take away your life in front of your
> husband, and I will pay with my own if I am daring.'

In another ballad, 'Los bandidos de Toledo' ('The Bandits of Toledo'), a
young man's bravery so attracts the attention of a group of bandits who attack
him that they invite him to become their leader. It is characteristic of the
romance de ciegos that we are given no indication why he should have decided
apparently on a mere whim to embark on a life of crime. Indeed the very
opening of the poem tells us that he had been summoned by the king, so it is
not as though he had an obvious affinity to the criminal class. Evidently the
heroic qualities of the protagonist, underlined by the author, equipped him
ideally if not uniquely for such an existence. The initial exchanges between
the bandits and their new leader are incongruously courteous as though in
deference to the hero's social status:

> Todos le dicen; amigo,
> no temas ni desconsueles,
> que todos desesperados
> vivimos de aquesta suerte;
> si quieres estar seguro,
> aquí con nosotros quedes,
> serás nuestro capitán
> y muy respetado siempre.
> El les dice: caballeros,
> de tanta lucida gente
> no podré ser la cabeza;
> igual estaré obediente.[6]

> They all tell him: 'Friend, don't be afraid or disheartened, because we all
> live in this desperate condition; if you want to be sure, stay here with us,
> and be our leader, for you will be highly respected always.' He replies:
> 'Gentlemen, I cannot be the leader of such illustrious people; I shall be
> obedient like you.'

Such a portrait emerges as a degenerate version of the Romantic hero, the kind epitomized in Espronceda's pirate:

> Que es mi barco mi tesoro
> que es mi Dios la libertad,
> mi ley la fuerza y el viento,
> mi única patria la mar.[7]

> For my treasure is my ship, my God is freedom, my laws violence and the wind, my only homeland, the sea.

There is nothing as socially subversive as this, though, about the *romances de ciegos* despite their taste for the lurid. Patriotic events, such as the naval victory over the forces of the Ottoman Empire at Lepanto in 1571, were also suitable material for poems, as it was deeds in which the poets of the *romances de ciegos* were interested, and in the choice and presentation of these they were as undiscriminating as the tabloid press of our own day.

The association of *romance* with narration and, because of its strongly oral pedigree, declamation made it the most popular medium for the thousands of poems produced on both sides during the Spanish Civil War. Indeed it is slightly surprising that only just over a half of the surviving compositions of that conflict should have been in that form. The comparatively large number of sonnets indicates, however, that many of the writers were attempting a more learned or elevated style, presumably to dignify the cause or the message. For the call-to-arms, however, the ballad proved supreme, as Miguel Hernández (1910–42), a highly gifted and versatile poet, realized. His poem 'Vientos del pueblo me llevan' ('Winds of the people carry me along') is a fine example of the declamatory ballad. It is characterized by anaphora and enumeration, simple rhetorical devices that are entirely appropriate for a defiant and stirring poem:

> ¿Quién habló de echar un yugo
> sobre el cuello de esta raza?
> ¿Quién ha puesto al huracán
> jamás ni yugos ni trabas,
> ni quién al rayo detuvo
> prisionero en una jaula?

> Asturianos de braveza,
> vascos de piedra blindada,
> valencianos de alegría
> y castellanos del alma,
> labrados como la tierra
> y airosos como las alas . . .
> vais de la vida a la muerte
> vais de la nada a la nada:

> yugos os quieren poner
> gentes de la hierba mala,
> yugos que habéis de dejar
> rotos sobre sus espaldas.[8]

> Who spoke of placing a yoke on the neck of this race? Who has ever
> placed yokes or shackles on the hurricane, and who has held the ray of
> light as a prisoner in a cage? Fierce Asturians, stone-hard Basques, joyous
> Valencians, and soulful Castilians, made like the earth and proud as
> wings ... you all go from life to death, from nothingness to nothingness:
> the rabble want to place yokes upon you, yokes that you will leave broken
> on their shoulders.

Such an enumerative device can be traced back to the old ballad, like the
one that describes a Moorish commander named Reduán going into battle
at Jaén in 1407:

> Reduán pide mil hombres,
> el rey cinco mil le daba.
> Por esa puerta de Elvira
> sale muy gran cabalgada:
> ¡Cuánto del hidalgo moro!
> ¡Cuánta de la yegua baya!
> ¡Cuánta de la lanza en puño!
> ¡Cuánta de la adarga blanca!
> ¡Cuánta de marlota verde!
> ¡Cuánta aljuba de escarlata!...
> Toda es gente valerosa
> y experta para batalla.[9]

> Reduán asked for a thousand men, the king gave him five thousand.
> Through the gate of Elvira a large force left on horseback: How many
> Moorish noblemen! How many cream-coloured mares! How many lances
> at the ready! How many white shields! How many green gowns! How
> many scarlet cloaks! ... All are men of valour and skilled in battle.

From what we have seen of the *romances* thus far, two traits emerge: a
connection with real events, however tenuous (for only a minority of ballads
are entirely fictional); and a desire for colourful effect. Both these features
appealed to Spanish poets of the Romantic era, though the popularity of the
ballad from the 1820s was also due to nationalistic considerations – the desire
to reassert a sense of Spanish identity after a period of French cultural and,
albeit briefly, political domination. Although the ballad has been cultivated
continuously over many centuries, its prestige has fluctuated. In the first half
of the fifteenth century, when they were starting to be written down, the
romances were regarded as a low poetic form as in the summary dismissal of
the Marqués de Santillana in his survey of the poetry of the day: 'Infimos
son aquéllos que sin ningún orden, regla nin cuento façen estos romances e

cantares, de que las gentes de baxa e servil condiçión se alegran'(In the lowest
category are those poets who with no sense of form, regulation or structure
compose these ballads and songs in which people of low and humble status
take delight).[10] As a result of court patronage, however, by the end of that
century, ballads were being included in the *cancioneros* ('song-books'). In
the later sixteenth and seventeenth centuries the *romance* was an attractive
form for all the major Spanish poets. They not only extended its range but
endowed it with a sophistication that makes it at times as subtle and difficult
as poems written in the newer, Italianate, style as, for example, with the
late works of Góngora. The ballad fell from grace in the eighteenth century
when the preference was for French models in accordance with neo-classical
taste. The second revaluation occurred after the Peninsular War when the
assertion of patriotic values coincided with Romantic ideals about a poetry
of the people. The leading figure in this revival was the Duque de Rivas, an
aristocrat who had been wounded in battle against the French. His *Romances
históricos* are partly an exaltation of Spain's past, though shot through with
the Romantics' fascination for the dark side of history. This is evident in
the choice of figures such as the thirteenth-century king of Castile, Pedro
el Cruel:

> Síguele el rey con los ojos,
> que estuvieran en su puesto
> de un basilisco en la frente,
> según eran de siniestros;
> y de satánica risa,
> dando la expresión al gesto,
> salió detrás del alcalde
> a pasos largos y lentos.[11]

> The king followed him with his eyes which could have been placed on the
> head of a basilisk so sinister were they; and with a satanic laugh,
> transferring his expression into movement, he followed the gaoler out
> with long, slow paces.

For his view of Philip II Rivas makes use of a legend whereby the King was
involved in the murder of Juan de Escobedo and the downfall of Antonio
Pérez. Rivas's portrait of the king is that of an introverted and sinister individual, one that has become very much the stereotype:

> Melancólico era el uno,
> de edad cascada y marchita,
> macilento, enjuto, grave,
> rostro como de ictericia,
> ojos siniestros, que a veces
> de una hiena parecían,
> otras, vagos, indecisos,

y de apagadas pupilas.
Hondas arrugas, señales
de meditación continua,
huellas de ardientes pasiones
mostraba en frente y mejillas.

(p. 148)

One of them was melancholy, worn and withered with age, lean, gaunt
and solemn, whose face had the signs of jaundice, sinister eyes, which
occasionally seemed those of a hyena, and that, at other times, were
vague, uncertain, and with lifeless pupils. His brow and cheeks revealed
deep wrinkles, the indications of constant meditation and the traces of
burning desires.

For Rivas, too, the ballad form seemed inevitably associated with the
macabre and the supernatural. His poem on the religious crisis experienced by the Marquis of Lombay, who withdrew from the world after the
death of the wife of Charles V and who was canonized as St Francis Borgia
after his death, is a case in point. For much of the poem it appears that the
protagonist is prey to dark, even malevolent, forces, hardly indicative of one
about to embark on the religious life:

En estado miserable
su espíritu estaba puesto,
y era infeliz en las dichas,
luchando consigo mesmo,
entre pasiones, virtudes,
obligaciones, deseos,
infernales sugestiones
y celestiales preceptos.

(p. 195)

His spirit had sunk into a wretched state, and he was malcontent in his
happiness, struggling with himself, between passion, virtue, duty, desire,
hellish suggestions and heavenly precepts.

The ballad was also employed in longer poems of the Romantic era,
sometimes as one among a mix of verse-forms. This polymetrical conception
had been a distinguishing feature of Spanish drama of the sixteenth and
seventeenth centuries, where the ballad metre was reserved for passages
that related events – 'las narraciones piden romances' ('narrations require
ballads'), as Lope de Vega put it. It is also as we saw in the Introduction,
the *romance* form that is used for the evocative night-scene at the start of
Espronceda's *El estudiante de Salamanca*.

It is with José Zorrilla (1817–93) that the Romantic ballad attains its peak
as a poem of the sensational and supernatural. Though a less interesting

poet ideologically than Rivas or Espronceda, Zorrilla was a highly accomplished technician and his fluency as a versifier sometimes masks his narrative achievement. His stories are unfailingly exciting, notably his legend *A buen juez, mejor testigo* ('For a good judge, a better witness'), a work that has an affinity with *El estudiante de Salamanca*. It tells of a young woman, Inés, who is abandoned by her lover, a soldier named Diego Martínez. She summons the statue of Christ as a witness of the promise of marriage that he has broken. In the fifth section of the poem Zorrilla makes considerable use of dialogue for the scene where Inés attempts to convince the judge of the justice of her cause:

> –Mujer, ¿qué quieres?
> –Quiero justicia, señor.
> –¿De qué?
>   –De una prenda hurtada.
> –¿Qué prenda?
>   –Mi corazón.
> –¿Tú le diste?
>   –Le presté.
> –¿Y no te le han vuelto?
>   –No.
> –¿Tienes testigos?
>   –Ninguno.
> –¿Y promesa?
>   –Sí, ¡por Dios!,
> que al partirse de Toledo
> un juramento empeñó.
> –¿Quién es él?
>   –Diego Martínez.
> –¿Noble?
>   –Y capitán, señor.[12]

'Woman, what do you want?' 'I want justice, sir.' 'Because of what?' 'Because of a stolen object.' 'Which object?' 'My heart.' 'Did you give it?' 'I lent it.' 'And it has not been returned to you?' 'No.' 'Do you have witnesses?' 'None.' 'And a promise?' 'Yes, most certainly! For when he left Toledo he gave me his word.' 'Who is he?' 'Diego Martínez.' 'Is he a nobleman?' 'And a captain, sir.'

The old ballad had also made use of direct speech but such rapid-fire exchanges are unusual, a sign of Zorrilla's virtuosity. It may be observed, too, how the abruptness and *staccato* effect are enhanced by the employment of an *agudo* rhyme (on *ó*).

Although the ballad, like other literary forms, adapts to the characteristics or dictates of a particular era, it is evident that it owes much to certain enduring and unchanging traits. Let us consider two such features, one thematic and one stylistic. We have already seen from the *romances de ciegos*, insofar as they veer towards the criminal and the anti-social, a fascination with what could be termed 'otherness'. One of the sub-genres of the *romance viejo* was the frontier ballad, the so-called *romance fronterizo*. These poems are rooted in historical events and were probably first composed by minstrels attached to Christian armies engaged in the reconquest of the Peninsula from the Moors. They are far removed, however, from the bias and propaganda of the Civil War ballads. Indeed, their ability to look at matters from the Moorish standpoint is such that it was once believed that they must have been translations of Arabic originals. A favourite *romance* with Golden Age musicians was a poem that presaged the fall of Granada by reference to the loss of Alhama. The opening supplies a vivid picture of the alarm experienced by the Moors, underlined by the simple pathos of the refrain:

> Paseábase el rey moro
> por la ciudad de Granada,
> desde la puerta de Elvira
> hasta la de Vivarambla.
> (¡Ay de mi Alhama!)
> Cartas le fueron venidas
> que Alhama era ganada;
> las cartas echó en el fuego
> y al mensajero matara.
> (¡Ay de mi Alhama!)[13]

> The Moorish king was walking through the city of Granada, from the gate of Elvira to the one of Vivarambla. (Alas for my Alhama!) Letters came to him stating that Alhama had been captured; he threw the letters in the fire and killed the messenger. (Alas for my Alhama!)

Moorish life also figured, however, in ballads that had nothing to do with warfare. One of the most delightful and amusing is one in which a Moorish girl describes how she was deceived by a Christian into allowing him entry to her house. He spoke in Arabic and pretended to be the girl's uncle fleeing from the law. Like the best ballads (and unlike the *romances de ciegos*) it is understated, posing more questions than it answers. It captures with great delicacy the conflict between the girl's shyness and her overwhelming curiosity:

> '¿Cómo te abriré, mezquina,
> que no sé quién te serás?'
> 'Yo soy el moro Mazote,
> hermano de la tu madre;
> que un cristiano dejo muerto,
> tras mí venía el alcalde;
> si no me abres tú, mi vida,

aquí me verás matar.'
Cuando esto oí, cuitada,
comencéme a levantar;
vistiérame una almejía
no hallando mi brial,
fuérame para la puerta
y abríla de par en par.[14]

'How can I, vulnerable as I am, open for you if I don't know who you are?' 'I am the Moor Mazote, your mother's brother; I've just left a Christian for dead, and the law is after me; if you don't open for me, my life, here you will see me killed.' When I heard this, poor thing, I began to get up; I flung a cloak over myself as I couldn't find my tunic, I went to the door and flung it wide open.

Such a poem could be labelled a *romance morisco*, and it is the predecessor of an important category of ballads much in vogue in the late sixteenth and early seventeenth centuries. By this time the exotic element had been tempered by the superimposition of the conventions of Italianate poetry so that at the opening of one of Lope de Vega's Moorish ballads it is only the incorporation of the protagonist's Arabic name, Zaide, that prevents it being read as a typical late Renaissance love poem:

Gallardo pasea Zaide
puerta y calle de su dama,
que desea en gran manera
ver su imagen y adorarla
porque se vido sin ella
en una ausencia muy larga.[15]

Zaide walks elegantly in the street and by the gate of his lady, as he deeply desires to see her image and adore her because he has been without her, absent for a long time.

What is distinctive about Lope's Moorish ballads, as with others he wrote, is the way in which he incorporates autobiographical elements into stock amatory situations and attitudes, notably his disgrace and internal exile occasioned by his stormy love-affair with Elena Osorio and his libellous attacks on her family.

The association of the ballad with otherness and with minorities has extended also to its mode of diffusion. Notable in this respect is the way in which the *romance* has continued to be cultivated by the Sephardim, the descendants of Jews who were expelled from Spain in the wake of a decree of 1492. The old ballad is perhaps the most important cultural possession of the Sephardic Jews, especially those who settled in North Africa and the lands of the former Ottoman Empire. Scholarly interest in these works has been encouraged by the fact that the majority of the Sephardic ballads pre-date the fateful year of 1492 and that in some cases they are the unique source of some versions of well-known ballads.

Although cultivated in South and Central America, the ballad has not flourished there as much as one might have expected. Its influence, however, is certainly evident in a distinctive Spanish American sub-genre that appeared in the nineteenth century: the gaucho ballad. Gaucho songs and what we can conveniently designate gaucho poetry flourished for the same reasons as did the *romance* in Spain. The harshness of life on the Argentinian pampas, the emphasis on deeds and bravery, and the cult of the anti-hero or 'gaucho malo', led to a kind of composition that parallels the *romances de ciegos*. Moreover the performer himself became an admired figure: as quick in his improvisation as the gaucho was quick on his feet. Such singers, or *payadores*, competed with each other in improvisation contests, the subject-matter often being of a simple philosophic nature.

More than with the oral ballads of Spain, however, the gaucho songs tended to satire. It is protest nourished on grievance that informs the most famous of all gaucho poems and, by common consent, the finest Spanish American poem of the nineteenth century, *Martín Fierro* by José Hernández (1834–86). The hero is a *payador* who is sent to fight the Indians at the frontier but is so incensed at his treatment – he is beaten for daring to ask for his pay – that he becomes an outlaw and eventually joins the Indians. In the sequel, published after the first part had proved a runaway success, much of the narrative is concerned with the tribulations experienced by Martín Fierro's sons. The elder son had spent years in prison for a crime he did not commit, while the second had been put in the charge of a horse-thief who had schooled him in the ways of crime. At the end, aptly, Martín Fierro is challenged to a *payada* or song-contest in which answers have to be improvised to questions. He wins, the family separates again, and the poem ends.

Although the *romance* form predominates in gaucho poetry, Hernández employs a distinctive variant:

> Aquí me pongo a cantar
> al compás de la vigüela,
> que el hombre que lo desvela
> una pena extraordinaria,
> como la ave solitaria
> con el cantar se consuela.[16]

> Come gather around as I tune my guitar / And I'll tell you a sorrowful tale, / Of the life that I've led and the tears that I've shed / And the nights without sleep on the trail. / Like the lonely bird on the open plain / My song is a refuge from pain.[17]

This is the opening stanza of the poem, a conventional self-introduction by the singer. Crucially, though, it is a stanza rhyming ABBCCB, an unusual form, the invention of which is credited to Hernández. The later Argentinian poet Leopoldo Lugones suggested that the six lines of the stanza correspond to the six strings of the guitar. At a purely poetic level, however, what Hernández does is to develop further the preference of gaucho poets for the four-line stanza, rhyming ABCB. In the specific case of *Martín Fierro* the six-line stanza pattern is appropriate for constructing a long poem with an epic feel; in that respect, rather than the guitar it is the eight-line stanza or *octava real* of the Renaissance epic, for example Ercilla's *La Araucana*, that is invoked, although the shorter, octosyllabic, line is more pacy than the ponderous and dignified hendecasyllable.

In Hernández's hands this stanza form becomes wieldy. It is weighty enough for such passages as the one where the eponymous hero explains his philosophy of life with an aphoristic swagger:

> Soy gaucho, y entiéndanlo
> como mi lengua lo esplica:
> para mí la tierra es chica
> y pudiera ser mayor;
> ni la víbora me pica
> ni quema mi frente el sol.
>
> (p. 56)

> I'm a born and bred gaucho, a son of the plains, / I call the great pampa my home, / But the earth's a small place to a man of race / Who likes to be moving along. / There's nothing can harm me by day or by night, / The sun doesn't burn me, the snake doesn't bite.

There are echoes here of Espronceda's pirate, of the fearlessness and independence of the Romantic hero. Hernández varies his metrical patterns rather more in the sequel, including the incorporation of *romance* proper, than he does in the first part where he is content to adhere to the six-line stanza form. The exception is, however, highly significant. It occurs in the part of the narrative that describes how Martín Fierro, the worse for drink, gets into a fight with a negro over a girl. For this episode Hernández reverts to the more conventional gaucho verse-form (ABCB) as though this were more appropriate for the degeneracy and lawlessness of his hero's behaviour, appalling in word as well as deed. Firstly he insults the negro:

> 'A los blancos hizo Dios,
> a los mulatos San Pedro,
> a los negros hizo el diablo
> para tizón del infierno.'

Había estao juntando rabia
el moreno dende ajuera;
en lo oscuro le brillaban
los ojos como linterna.

Lo conocí retobao,
me acerqué y le dije presto:
'Por . . . rudo . . . que un hombre sea
nunca se enoja por esto.'

Corcovió el de los tamangos
y creyéndose muy fijo:
–'Más *porrudo* serás vos,
gaucho rotoso', me dijo.

(p. 99)

'God made the white man first of all, / Saint Peter the brown, I've heard tell. / But the devil made men as black as coal / To stoke the fires in hell.' / You could feel her man's anger mounting / As he stood looking into the room, / there was no way he could hide his rage, / his eyes blazed like lamps in the gloom. / I sidled up alongside him, / I knew he was seeing red, / 'I never hold back', I told him, / 'From calling a spade a spade.' / His muscles grew tense and he stiffened, / He was ready to spring I could tell, / 'I'd rather be black than yellow, / Gaucho swine! You can go to hell!'

The fight-scene is remarkably protracted. The initial exchanges are in the manner of a bar-room brawl as Martín Fierro cracks his opponent over the head with a bottle of gin, but, ominously observing how there is nothing like danger to sober up someone who is drunk, Martín has recourse to his knife and ruthlessly cuts down the negro:

Por fin en una topada
en el cuchillo lo alcé,
y como un saco de güesos
contra el cerco lo largué.

Tiró unas cuantas patadas
y ya cantó pa el carnero.
Nunca me puedo olvidar
de la agonía de aquel negro.

(p. 102)

In one last jab I got him / And opened his ribs with my blade, / Then I lifted him up like a sack of bones / And smashed him against the stockade. / I'll never forget what I saw and heard / As he twisted and turned on the ground, / The flailing legs were his final move, / The rattle of death his last sound.

The conclusion is chillingly matter-of-fact:

> Limpié el facón en los pastos,
> desaté mi redomón,
> monté despacio y salí
> al tronco pa el cañadón.
>
> Despué supe que al finao
> ni siquiera lo velaron,
> y retobao en un cuero
> sin resarle lo enterraron.
>
> (p. 103)

> I cleaned my knife against my boots, / Unhitched my horse, mounted slow, / Turned my back on the scene of the crime. / And galloped away to lie low. / They wrapped him in hide I later heard / And somebody dug him a hole, / But nobody bothered to give him a wake / And nobody prayed for his soul.

Not even Martín's prick of conscience, by way of an afterthought, succeeds in eliminating our shock at the randomness of the violent deed, as gratuitous and sensational as any *romance de ciegos*:

> Yo tengo intención a veces,
> para que no pene tanto,
> de sacar allí los güesos
> y echarlos al camposanto.
>
> (p. 104)

> So maybe one day I'll go back there / And give him his final release, / I'll bury his bones in hallowed ground / So his soul can rest in peace.

Finally let us consider a stylistic feature that is present in *romances* of all periods – what is perhaps the most salient feature of ballad narrative: *fragmentismo*. This arises from the tendency of the old ballad to have abrupt openings or conclusions, thereby supplying an air of mystery and open-endedness. *Fragmentismo* comes about in various ways: (i) from a resort to ellipsis, especially where the background of the story is well known; (ii) as a result of accidental abridgement in the transmission of the ballad; and (iii) as a consequence of deliberate curtailment where there was more than one version of the piece. By their very nature, ballads could exist in several competing versions, and often it was quite simply the length of the poem that was responsible for the variation. As Colin Smith has pointed out, judicious cutting can often be the making of a ballad; where we have access to two versions it is nearly always the shorter that impresses us because of its elusive quality.[18]

Such is the case with the so-called *Romance del prisionero* ('Ballad of the prisoner'). Its shorter version is a genuinely lyrical utterance, comprising the prisoner's lament. With the coming of Spring he contrasts his plight with the lot of those who enjoy freedom and love. His sole consolation had been the song of a bird at dawn but he loses this when it is killed. In its shorter version the ballad concludes with the prisoner cursing the archer who shot the bird:

> 'Que por mayo era, por mayo
> cuando hace la calor,
> cuando los trigos encañan
> y están los campos en flor,
> cuando canta la calandria
> y responde el ruiseñor,
> cuando los enamorados
> van a servir al amor;
> sino yo, triste, cuitado,
> que vivo en esta prisión,
> que ni sé cuándo es de día
> ni cuándo las noches son,
> sino por una avecilla
> que me cantaba al albor.
> Matómela un ballestero,
> ¡déle Dios mal galardón!'[19]

> 'It was in the month of May when the warmth returns, when the wheat ripens and the fields are in flower, when the lark sings and the nightingale replies, when lovers start to serve love; but not so for me, sad and wretched as I am, who lives in this prison, who does not know when it is day or when it is night, except for the little bird that sang to me at dawn. An archer killed him; may God reward him as he deserves!'

The poem also exists, however, in a longer version of forty lines. It continues beyond the end of the text printed above to supply additional details: the name of the prisoner's wife, his hope that she can help him to escape, and the happy resolution whereby the king orders his release. As Colin Smith, however, puts it succinctly: 'In this state the ballad is nothing special'.[20]

That the ballad thrives on a tension created by suspense and non-resolution is well exemplified by one of a type common throughout Europe, based on the infidelity of an unhappy wife. A Spanish ballad of this type begins with a dialogue between the wife and her lover. He compliments her on her beauty and she expresses her loathing of her husband. The husband, however, returns unexpectedly and, suspicious, interrogates his wife about her behaviour and the signs of another's presence. At first she attempts to explain away such incriminating evidence as the horse in the yard and the armour scattered in the hall, but she eventually realizes the futility of deceit. The poem ends dramatically:

'¿Cuyas son aquellas armas
que están en el corredor?'
'Señor, eran de mi hermano,
y hoy os las envió.'
'¿Cuya es aquella lanza,
desde aquí la veo yo?'
'¡Tomadla, conde, tomadla,
matadme con ella vos,
que aquesta muerte, buen conde,
bien os la merezco yo!'

(p. 198)

'Whose armour is that in the hall?' 'Sir, it is my brother's, for today he sent it to you.' 'Whose is that lance that I see from here?' 'Take it, count, take it and kill me with it, for such a death, good count, I well deserve.'

We are denied a resolution. Does the husband kill his wife, does he forgive her or is she saved by her hidden lover? These are, however, artificial questions as the ballad, despite its open-ended quality, is sufficiently complete as a poetic tableau not to require their articulation. The reader is likely to accept the poem as it stands without experiencing the kind of curiosity that would lead to such questions.

The hallmarks of *fragmentismo* are present too in a number of the ballads of Góngora, writing in the heyday of the *romance nuevo*. For the *romance morisco* beginning 'Entre los sueltos caballos', as with many poems belonging to the older genre, there are different versions. Once again the length of the poem is the crucial issue: in one manuscript the poem is seventy-two lines long, but this is dwarfed by another version which is forty lines longer. This discrepancy is between a comprehensive narrative and one that is as open-ended as the old ballad just considered. In Góngora's poem, a Moorish captain is taken prisoner by his Christian counterpart. The latter is surprised at the melancholy demeanour and 'ardent sighs' of one who had fought so bravely and asks why he acts this way. The Moor responds with an account of how he had unsuccessfully courted a noble Moorish girl over many years. No sooner had she started to show signs of yielding, however, than he found himself captured in battle. The Chacón manuscript ends with the Moor addressing his captor:

Apenas vide trocada
la dureza de esta sierpe,
cuando tú me cautivaste:
¡mira si es bien que lamente![21]

No sooner did I see the harshness of this serpent change than you captured me. How right, then, that I should lament!

We get to know nothing in this version of the Christian captain's reaction nor of any other outcome, and as a result it ends in a way that would be entirely appropriate for the old ballad. In the longer version, however, the effect of *fragmentismo* is lost. The additional material relates how the Christian, moved by the Moor's lament, decides to free him.

The opening of the poem (in both versions) has something of the abrupt quality of the older genre:

> Entre los sueltos caballos
> de los vencidos Cenetes,
> que por el campo buscaban
> entre la sangre lo verde,
> aquel español de Orán
> un suelto caballo prende,
> por sus relinchos lozano,
> y por sus cernejas fuerte.
>
> (p. 143)

> Among the loose horses of the vanquished Zenetas [a Berber tribe] seeking greenness amid the blood on the battlefield, that Spaniard of Oran seizes a stray horse, one who seems sprightly by his neighing, and strong by his fetlocks.

We start, as so often, *in medias res*, with a recourse to cross-referencing: the allusion to 'aquel español de Orán' is a probable reference to another ballad, 'Servía en Orán al Rey' ('In Oran there served the king'), which relates an event immediately prior to the battle where presumably the lovesick Moor was taken prisoner. The other ballad describes how the Christian captain ('un español con dos lanzas' ('a Spaniard with two lances')) reluctantly takes leave of his mistress, a Moorish girl ('una gallarda africana' ('an elegant African girl')), when summoned by the call to arms. Such an intertextual device harks back to the practice in those old ballads that derived from epic material where there was a presumption that the audience would be in possession of essential details. This dispenses with the need for explanation and thereby contributes to the paciness of the narrative. Thus *fragmentismo* is also a consequence of an assumption of prior knowledge of events, so that the mere citing of a name, either of person or place, is sufficient.

A process of this kind occurs in another of Góngora's ballads, perhaps his most famous, entitled 'Angélica y Medoro'. It is based on an epic poem, though, unlike the *romances viejos*, on a literary, not heroic, epic, Ariosto's *Orlando furioso*. Góngora's poem recounts how Angélica, a princess of Cathay, comes across Medoro, a wounded Saracen, in a battlefield. Until this point Angélica has been a cold-hearted beauty, disdainful of all her suitors, including Ariosto's eponymous hero. She immediately falls in love with the wounded Moor, however, and nurses him back to health. The lovers enjoy a brief idyll in the beauty of nature, but their joy is to be threatened as the dark conclusion of the poem makes clear:

> Choza, pues, tálamo y lecho,
> cortesanos labradores,
> aires, campos, fuentes, vegas,
> cuevas, troncos, aves, flores,
> fresnos, chopos, montes, valles,
> contestes de estos amores,
> el cielo os guarde, si puede,
> de las locuras del Conde.
>
> (p. 286)

> So, hut, marriage bed and couch, courteous peasants, breezes, fields, fountains, meadows, caves, treetrunks, birds and flowers, ash trees, poplars, hills and valleys, witnesses of this love, may Heaven save you, if it can, from the madness of the count.

After concisely enumerating by way of invocation many of the scenes presented in the course of the poem, Góngora warns of the 'madness of the Count', an allusion to Orlando's jealous rage and the destruction he would wreak on the countryside. Modern readers are less likely to be aware of the significance of the allusion than Góngora's contemporaries, but even so they will sense the terror of the single, final line that so clouds the carefree eroticism of the poem. Again, as with the best of the earlier ballads, what makes for the starkly ominous close is the insinuation rather than the enunciation of connected details – a trademark of *fragmentismo*.

Góngora's adherence to such traits of the old ballad, however, was untypical of his age. On the one hand, the range of the subject-matter of ballads was broadening considerably as with the vogue for satirical and burlesque compositions, notably in the work of Góngora's contemporary and rival, Francisco de Quevedo. Moreover, the distinction in approach and content between the ballad as a characteristically indigenous genre and the newer forms associated with the advent of the Italianate style in the sixteenth century was disappearing. Lope de Vega's ballads to Filis are less indebted to the older forms than are Góngora's even though elsewhere in his poetry, as we shall see, he was an adept pseudo-folklorist. The ballads to Filis, it is true, possess an occasional rustic air and local colour, but on the whole they appear more akin to the Petrarchan *canzone* than to the *romance viejo*, especially in the settings where the lover's lament is played out against a pastoral backdrop.[22] Even the autobiographical touches of some of these ballads are comparable to the Italianate *canzone*, as witness Garcilaso's *Canción tercera*.[23] While Lope's ballads are not lacking in a dramatic quality, it is not generated by the same means as in the older forms – principally *fragmentismo* – but by the rhetoric and conventions of the courtly Petrarchist conception of love.

The *romance* for Spanish Romantic poets – Rivas, Espronceda and Zorrilla – is, as we have seen, a medium for Romantic story-telling. The tendency to mystery, suspense and horror has more in common with the narratives of Edgar Allan Poe than with the *romance viejo*. In one respect, however, Rivas's historical ballads possess a structural quality that harks back to the *romance viejo*. Nearly all of them are divided into parts, each entitled 'romance'; in effect we could say that each ballad (or macro-ballad) contained a number of micro-ballads. This procedure is comparable to the presence in the old ballad tradition of series or networks of poems on single figures such as Rodrigo, the last of the Visigothic kings, or the Cid. Rivas's micro-ballads are admittedly more in the nature of parts of a whole than the *romances viejos* concerned with the same figure, but his concept of narrative and his penchant for visual set-pieces and cameos give the impression of the detachable unit.

A similar method is in operation in a poem that dates from the early twentieth century: Antonio Machado's *La tierra de Alvargonzález* (1912). Machado came from a family steeped in traditional popular poetry: his father was a renowned collector of folk-songs and a writer on traditional *canciones* and *romances*, while his great-uncle Agustín Durán was the leading authority of his day on the ballad, and the compiler of the monumental *Romancero general* (1828–51). Indeed, *La tierra de Alvargonzález* has several of the trademarks of the old ballad, unlike the *romance* of the eighteenth and nineteenth centuries. To start with, it was based on a real-life event, and as Machado wrote a prose account as well as a poem it could be said to exist in different versions. Furthermore, as with Rivas's ballads, the poem is divided into various sub-ballads bearing titles; in the preface to the 1917 edition of *Campos de Castilla*, in which the poem is included, Machado refers to his poem as 'mis romances' ('my ballads'), while these are further divided into numbered sections. The incorporation of such elements as dreams and omens is also a characteristic of the old form.

The poem also contains a significant instance of *fragmentismo*. To appreciate this fully it will be necessary to summarize the events of the poem up until the place it occurs. Alvargonzález is a successful farmer with three sons. The first two – Juan and Martín – will inherit the father's land while the youngest, Miguel, is destined for the Church. The two older brothers both marry and soon long to own the land which will be theirs after the father's death. Meantime, the youngest son abandons the Church and leaves for the Indies. One day in Autumn Alvargonzález sets off into the countryside. Near a fountain he falls asleep and has a dream that ends with the vision that his sons are killing him – a nightmare that proves to be true as dream and reality coincide. The sons throw his body into a deep lake and there is no evidence of a crime other than the discovery of the father's cloak nearby. Juan and Martín are not implicated; shortly afterwards, an itinerant pedlar is arrested, and the mother dies of grief. Now the sons have the lands to themselves, but soon all kinds of misfortune befall them: the land proves barren, the crops fail. One Winter night as they are huddled around the fire there is a knock at the door; it is Miguel, the youngest brother, who has made his fortune and returned home from the Indies. He notices the weak fire, but is told that there is no more wood. Then the ghost of the father opens the door and comes in with a bundle of wood on his shoulder. True to the tradition of the suspenseful irresolution of the genre Machado dramatically breaks off the narrative at this point without any mention of the reaction of the older brothers as we might have expected. I cite the passage leading up to and including this moment of horror:

> Los tres hermanos contemplan
> el triste hogar en silencio;
> y con la noche cerrada
> arrecia el frío y el viento.
> –Hermanos, ¿no tenéis leña?–
> dice Miguel.
>
> –No tenemos–
> responde el mayor.
>
> Un hombre,
> milagrosamente, ha abierto
> la gruesa puerta cerrada
> con doble barra de hierro.
> El hombre que ha entrado tiene
> el rostro del padre muerto.
> Un halo de luz dorada
> orla sus blancos cabellos.
> Lleva un haz de leña al hombro
> y empuña un hacha de hierro.[24]

The three brothers look at the sad hearth silently; and as night closes in the cold and the wind intensify. 'Brothers, have you no wood?' asks Miguel. 'We have none', replies the older one. A man, by some miracle, has opened the heavy door secured with a double wooden bar. The man who has entered has the face of the dead father. His white hair is surrounded by a halo of golden light. He has a bundle of wood on his shoulder and he grasps an iron axe.

Following this there is immediately a new section, or, following the poet's own definition, another ballad ('El indiano') which relates how Miguel buys a portion of land from his brothers. The effect is one of a truncation akin to *fragmentismo*.

Finally, a subtle recourse to *fragmentismo* is also discernible in the most celebrated ballad collection of modern times, Lorca's *Romancero gitano*. Critics have drawn attention to this trait but perhaps overlooked its significance for the way in which we read and interpret the text. Proof of this is the urge among several commentators to 'read in' meanings, to force the text to yield more, against the grain. Such has been the fate of the best-known of the ballads, 'Romance sonámbulo' ('Sleepwalking ballad'). Most conspicuously of all the set, it operates by a juxtaposition of different scenes and the alternation of voices: the unattributable 'yo' of the opening lines that become the poem's refrain and the interlocutors who speak in urgent and anguished tones throughout. We partly deduce, partly surmise, that one of the protagonists is a wounded smuggler pursued by the Civil Guard. He seeks refuge at the house of a woman with whom he is in love and speaks with her father. We also discover, or at least we suspect, that the girl has died, presumably by killing herself. The clearest indication of this – if anything is clear in the poem – comes in the description of her floating on top of a water-tank. I quote from this point to the end of the poem to illustrate what will by now be recognized as a classic ballad ending:

> Sobre el rostro del aljibe,
> se mecía la gitana.
> Verde carne, pelo verde,
> con ojos de fría plata.
> Un carámbano de luna
> la sostiene sobre el agua.
> La noche se puso íntima
> como una pequeña plaza.
> Guardias civiles borrachos
> en la puerta golpeaban.
> Verde que te quiero verde.
> Verde viento. Verdes ramas.
> El barco sobre la mar.
> Y el caballo en la montaña.[25]

On the surface of the water-tank the gipsy-girl was rocking. Green flesh, green hair, with eyes of cold silver. An icicle of moon supports her upon the water. Night became intimate like a little square. Drunken Civil Guards were knocking at the door. Green, how much I love you, green. Green wind. Green branches. The ship on the sea. And the horse on the mountain.

The plot of the poem, such as it is, is unresolved, and we are left with as many questions as with the ballad about the unfaithful wife.[26] They are, too, equally invalid questions: with a text which is so evidently open-ended it would be perverse to demand solutions. One might also note in passing that the lines contain a variety of verb-tense that is a characteristic of the old form. In particular the use of the imperfect for the penultimate verb, referring to the Civil Guards knocking on the door, intensifies the poem's 'non-completion'.

In another *romance* from the same collection Lorca reveals a conscious awareness of the essentially fragmentary nature of the genre. It occurs in a poem that Robert Havard labels 'the joker in the pack', not least because it is not in regular ballad form.[27] It is one of the sub-group of three *romances históricos* entitled 'Burla de don Pedro a caballo' ('Jest of Don Pedro on horseback'). The identity of Don Pedro has taxed commentators, but more intriguing than this are the implications of the poem's sub-title 'Romance con lagunas'. The poem is interspersed with three such 'lagunas', which has a double meaning in Spanish: both 'lagoon' and 'lacuna'. The pun is evident in the line that opens all three passages: 'Bajo el agua' ('Beneath the water'). This not only evokes the setting of a lagoon, but hints at something submerged or unexpressed. In a sense this perhaps serves as a warning against a decoding interpretation of this ballad, but it is also the very embodiment of *fragmentismo*, an instance of how the silences in poetry are often as eloquent as the words. On such occasions, the *romance*, perhaps because of its roots in performance, makes as many demands upon the reader as any poetic form, whether popular or artistic.

Chapter 5

Songs and sonnets – popular and learned poetry

Throughout the last chapter the dual character of the *romances* was evident: they were primarily tales but often associated with song or, indeed, performance. Just as they are the precursors of sophisticated narrative poems, so folk-songs that are not primarily narrative in nature are the forerunners of lyric poetry. It is true that much modern poetry is unrecognizable as a derivative of folk-song, overlaid as it is with successive layers of learning. Nonetheless many poets writing in Spanish in the last 500 years have sought variously to mimic and echo the characteristics of the so-called 'poesía popular'.

'Popular' is what translators would call a false friend. Although for convenience we might render it by the same word in English it is more accurately understood as something like 'of the people' or 'belonging to the people'. As with the *romances*, the earliest 'poesía popular' – the traditional lyric – consisted of anonymous pieces that were set down in words and music in the heyday of the *cancioneros*, in the late fifteenth and early sixteenth centuries. Although a handful are among the most familiar of Spanish songs, most have come down as brief lyric poems, highly regarded by scholars for their literary quality. One of the best-known as a song purely and simply is a piece first published in the middle of the sixteenth century:

> De los álamos vengo, madre,
> de ver cómo los menea el aire.
>
> De los álamos de Sevilla,
> de ver a mi linda amiga,
> de ver cómo los menea el aire.
>
> De los álamos vengo, madre,
> de ver cómo los menea el aire.[1]

> I come from the poplars, mother, to see how the breeze shakes them. From the poplars of Seville, from seeing my pretty girlfriend, to see how the breeze shakes them. I come from the poplars, mother, to see how the breeze shakes them.

Indeed a phrase from the tune was incorporated into Manuel de Falla's *Harpsichord Concerto*. As a poem it is characteristic, both in form – the *villancico* – and subject-matter, of the early lyric. It contains a refrain or *estribillo* that serves as a frame and which is glossed in the intervening section. As a consequence the poem is not only short but, because of the repetition, limited in in its material. This, however, renders the early lyric concise and allusive. Its capacity for evocation is certainly in part due to an adherence to the conventions of early Peninsular folk-song. As a consequence a song became interesting or enjoyable not because of striking originality but as a result of arousing expectations that appealed to the listeners' taste for the familiar.

One can, even in the brief poem quoted above, identify three elements that are a hallmark of many such songs: (i) the description of nature; (ii) the presence of love, for which nature serves as an appropriate setting; (iii) the recourse to the mother as a confidante. In one respect, however, the song is unusual. The speaker is evidently male as he has just returned from seeing his 'linda amiga', whereas the norm is for the speaker confiding in the mother to be a girl. Such songs were common throughout the Iberian Peninsula. A snatch of a song that survives as a *kharja* (see Introduction) outlines in just a few words the familiar situation:

> ¿Qué faré, mamma?
> Meu *al-habib* est ad yana.[2]

> What shall I do, mother? My lover is at the door.

The largest corpus of poetry that has a female speaker belongs, however, not to Spanish but to Portuguese literature. Such *cantigas d'amigo* are not, correctly speaking, 'poesía popular' but the compositions of named and known poets including, most famously, a Portuguese king, Don Dinis. They were written during the thirteenth and fourteenth centuries and belong to the tradition of women's song that is a European as well as Iberian phenomenon. Together with the more clearly Provençal-inspired love and satirical poetry, they comprise the Galician-Portuguese lyric, which was influential even beyond the frontiers of Galicia and Portugal in the Middle Ages. Indeed a highly distinctive formal feature of the *cantiga d'amigo* is utilized in a Spanish poem from the *Cancionero musical de Palacio*:

> Al alba venid, buen amigo,
> al alba venid.
> Amigo, el que yo más quería,
> venid al alba del día.

> (Amigo, el que yo más quería,
> venid a la luz del día).
> Amigo, el que yo más amaba,
> venid a la luz del alba.

Venid a la luz del día,
non trayáis compañía.

Venid a la luz del alba,
non tragáis gran compañía.[3]

Come at dawn, my fine lover, come at dawn. Lover, he whom I loved the
most, come at day's dawning. (Lover, he whom I loved the most, come at
daybreak). Lover, he for whom I had the greatest love, come at the light of
dawn. Come at daybreak, and don't bring any company. Come at the
light of dawn, and don't bring much company.

The poem is a mild variant of the *canción paralelística* ('parallelistic song'),
which is characterized by alternating assonance (í-a and a-a) in a process
of overlapping repetition whereby the second line of a couplet becomes
the first of the one after next. This produces a slow-moving development,
and almost certainly has its origin in a song that would have accompanied
a dance. One could envisage each assonantal pattern relating to a specific
group of dancers, either male and female, or individual and several.

This song of a girl yearning to meet her lover belongs to an important
sub-genre of the Spanish and European traditional lyric: the dawn song.
There were two varieties – the *alba*, in which the lovers part at dawn, and
the *alborada*, as with the poem cited above, which refers to a dawn meeting
or reunion. Although such poems were conventional even by the time they
came to be set down, and we may now be tempted to prize them purely for
their atmospheric and symbolic significance, they had their roots in the daily
realities of life. Thus when there are references to lovers meeting at fountains
it is quite legitimate to think in terms of a standard idyllic setting and a symbol
of fertility. There is a more mundane aspect, however, to the meeting, as one
unusually narrative poem from the *Cancionero d'Évora* suggests. This graphic
but delicate poem of a girl losing her virginity (symbolized by the broken
pitcher) speaks for itself. One may note again the presence of the mother,
though not this time as confidante:

Enviárame mi madre
por agua a la fuente fría:
vengo del amor herida.

Fui por agua a tal sazón
que corrió mi triste hado,
traigo el cántaro quebrado
y partido el corazón;
de dolor y gran pasión
vengo toda espavorida,
y vengo del amor herida.

Dejo el cántaro quebrado,
vengo sin agua corrida;
mi libertad es perdida
y el corazón cativado.
¡Ay, qué caro me ha costado
del agua de la fuente fría,
pues de amores vengo herida!⁴

My mother sent me for water to the cold fountain; I return, wounded by love. I went for water and it so happened that misfortune befell me, as I brought back a shattered pitcher and a broken heart; I return in complete trepidation from sorrow and great passion, and I come back wounded by love. I left the broken pitcher, I return without running water; I have lost my freedom and my heart is enslaved. O how costly for me was the water in the cold fountain, since I return wounded by love.

Local pilgrimages also provided opportunities for lovers to meet, and this social custom is the basis for a whole sub-category of the Galician-Portuguese lyric: the *cantiga de romaria*. Like other sub-genres it passed into Spanish songs. The following poem from Barbieri's *Cancionero musical* combines elements of the *cantiga de romaria* and the *alba*. I cite the opening:

So el encina, encina,
so el encina.

Yo me iba, mi madre,
a la romeria,
por ir más devota
fui sin compañía.
So el encina.

Por ir más devota
fui sin compañía,
tomé otro camino,
dejé el que tenía.
[So el encina.]

[Tomé otro camino,
dejé el que tenía;]
halléme perdida
en una montiña.⁵

Beneath the oak, the oak, beneath the oak. I was going, mother, to the shrine, and to be more devout I went alone. Beneath the oak. To be more devout I went alone, I took another path, I left the one I was following. [Beneath the oak.] [I took another path, I left the one I was following;] I found myself lost on the mountain.

Once more there are atmospheric and symbolic resonances: the oak tree as the place where love is fulfilled and the image of the girl losing her way. It is no surprise therefore that later in the poem she should awake at midnight to find herself 'en los brazos / del que más quería' ('in the arms of he whom I most loved'), only for the lovers to be separated at the coming of dawn.

As well as planned meetings, the early lyric contained songs that celebrated chance encounters. Once more, such songs – *serranillas*, or what in French is termed a *pastourelle* – were common to many countries and frequently involved a meeting between social unequals: a nobleman and a peasant girl. These songs often had inconclusive endings, rather in the manner of some *romances*, as with the following poem by Santillana:

> Después que nací,
> no ví tal serrana
> como esta mañana.
>
> Allá en la vegüela,
> a Mata 'l Espino,
> en ese camino
> que va a Loçoyuela,
> de guissa la vy
> que me fizo gana
> la fruta temprana.
>
> Garnacha traía
> de oro, presada
> con broncha dorada,
> que bien relucía.
> A ella volví
> diziendo: 'Loçana,
> ¿e soys vos villana?'
>
> 'Sí, soy, cavallero;
> si por mí lo avedes,
> deçit ¿qué queredes?
> fablat verdadero.'
> Yo le dixe assí:
> 'Juro por Santana
> que no soys villana.'[6]

Since I was born I have never seen such a peasant girl as the one I saw this morning. There in the meadow at Mata el Espino, on the road that goes to Loçoyuela, and seeing her made me yearn for the early fruit. She wore a gold blouse, decorated with a golden fastener that shone brightly. I turned to her and said: 'My pretty one, are you a country girl?' 'Yes, I am, sir knight; if you take me for so, say, what do you want? Speak the truth.' I answered thus: 'I swear by Santana that you are not a country girl.'

The poem contains many of the characteristic elements of the encounter poem as well as an unusual self-reference in the final sentence. Such poems are light in tone with an air of implied eroticism appropriate to seduction. They are notable for the variety of response possible through the incorporation of direct speech, enabling the girl to articulate replies that range from innocence to irony.

Perhaps one of the best indications of the versatility and popularity of a convention is its suitability for parodic treatment. Thus, a century before Santillana's delicate *serranilla*, there appeared in the *Libro de buen amor* by Juan Ruiz, the Archpriest of Hita, a very different kind of encounter poem. Drawing on the wild-woman folklore of the Middle Ages, the Archpriest depicted four *serranas* of fearsome aspect. These grotesque *pastourelles* form only a tiny part of a long and varied work, which contains a bewildering number of poetic genres, forms and styles. It includes a strong religious component, but its main concern – as implied by the title – and its unifying features are explorations of aspects of love, which become, indeed, in places a quest for love to which the *serranas* make a small but memorable contribution. The parodic nature of these adventures is anticipated by Juan Ruiz's irreverent allusion to Paul's *Epistle to the Thessalonians*: 'Provar todas las cosas el Apóstol lo manda' ('The Apostle commands us to experience all things'). What the hapless protagonist experiences, however, is in fact an inversion of all that was pleasing about the encounter poem. Thus in the meeting with the fourth *serrana*, dawn is not, as we might have expected, a magical time. It is perishingly cold:

> Cerca la Tablada,
> la sierra passada,
> fallé me con Alda
> a la madrugada.
>
> En cima del puerto,
> coidé me ser muerto
> de nieve e de frío,
> e dese rroçío
> e de grand elada.[7]

> Near Tablada, having left the mountain, I came across Alda at dawn. At the summit of the pass I believed I would die of the snow and the cold, of that ice and the severe frost.

More drastically the woman he encounters is exceptionally ugly – a negation of the physical beauty and innocence of the girl in the *serranilla*:

> Avía la cabeça mucho grande sin guisa;
> cabellos chicos, negros, más que corneja lysa;

ojos fondos, bermejos, poco e mal devisa;
mayor es que de yegua la patada do pisa.

Las orejas mayores que de añal burrico;
el su pecueço negro, ancho, velloso, chico;
las narizes muy gordas, luengas, de çarapico;
bevería en pocos días cabdal de buhón rrico.

Su boca de a lana, e los rrostros muy gordos.
(p. 322)

Her head was very big and shapeless; her hair was short, black and sleeker
than a crow's; her eyes were deep-set and red, and she was short-sighted;
her footsteps were larger than a mare's. Her ears were bigger than a
yearling donkey; her neck was black, wide, hairy and short; her nose was
very fat and long, like a curlew's bill; she would have drunk a large puddle
in a few days. She had the mouth of a hound, and a face that was
uncommonly fat.

By contrast with the shyness and timidity of the peasant girl in the encounter
poem, the Archpriest's Alda is bold and demands gifts:

'Pues dam una çinta
bermeja, bien tynta,
e buena camisa,
fecha a mi guisa
con su collarada.'
(p. 327)

'So give me a belt, one that's red, well dyed, and a fine blouse with a
collar cut to my size.'

The vitality of the traditional lyric is such that its resonances are not
limited to the Middle Ages or Renaissance. Thus just as Juan Ruiz writing
in the fourteenth century seeks to parody the encounter genre so Lorca, six
centuries later, supplies his own variant:

Arbolé arbolé
seco y verdé.

La niña del bello rostro
está cogiendo aceituna.
El viento, galán de torres,
la prende por la cintura.
Pasaron cuatro jinetes,
sobre jacas andaluzas
con trajes de azul y verde,
con largas capas obscuras.
'Vente a Córdoba, muchacha.'

La niña no los escucha.
Pasaron tres torerrillos
delgaditos de cintura,
con trajes color naranja
y espadas de plata antigua.
'Vente a Sevilla, muchacha.'
La niña no los escucha.
Cuando la tarde se puso
morada, con luz difusa,
pasó un joven que llevaba
rosas y mirtos de luna.
'Vente a Granada, muchacha.'
Y la niña no lo escucha.
La niña del bello rostro
sigue cogiendo aceituna,
con el brazo gris del viento
ceñido por la cintura.

Arbolé arbolé
seco y verdé.[8]

Tree, tree, dry and green. The girl with the pretty face is collecting olives.
The wind, the suitor of towers, seizes her by the waist. Four horsemen
pass by on Andalusian ponies, with suits of blue and green, with long dark
capes. 'Come to Cordoba, lass.' The girl does not listen to them. Three
slim-waisted *toreros* passed, with orange-coloured suits and swords of old
silver. 'Come to Seville, lass.' The girl does not listen to them. When the
afternoon became deep red, with vague light, a young man passed
carrying roses and moon myrtles. 'Come to Granada, lass.' And the girl
does not listen to him. The girl with the pretty face continues to gather
olives, with the grey arm of the wind tight around her waist. Tree, tree,
dry and green.

Though a far gentler realization than the poem from the *Libro de buen amor*,
it has a subtle bitterness achieved by defamiliarization, that is by simultaneously invoking and questioning a topic or convention. There is evidence
of folk-song not only in the *romance* form but also in the final syllable stress
in the framing refrain, created by the addition of an accented vowel to the
word 'árbol' and the displacement of the stress in 'verde'. The narrative is
unfolded as a reducing counting-song in which the variation in the descriptions of the suitors is succeeded on each occasion by an identically worded
proposal and response. It appears then as a poem made from repeated
patterns and formulae, consistent with the different verses of a song. In
two respects, however, the balance is disrupted. Most obvious is the elision
in the reducing counting-song: from four to three, then not to two but
directly to one. This is not so significant in itself but it is symptomatic of

another discrepancy. The first two groups of suitors – the four horsemen and the three *toreros* – are characterized as conventionally colourful and in keeping with what a listener to such a sung tale would expect to hear. The final approach to the girl, however, where we note the jump from three to one, contrasts sharply with the preceding ones. In place of the strikingly dressed and swaggering suitors is a sole melancholy youth with his roses and myrtle. Although myrtle has been interpreted as a symbol of loneliness, we do not require this random kind of decoding to appreciate the disruption, the ultimate lack of harmony in the song.

I have chosen two parodies of the encounter genre widely separated in time to indicate how central the traditional lyric is to Spanish poetry, and how it has influenced what could be termed 'learned' or 'artistic' poetry – what in Spanish is described as 'poesía culta'. Let us now consider three periods when folk-songs or popular songs were especially important. The earliest of these comprises a long stretch of time: rather more than a hundred years beginning from the time of the Catholic Kings, Ferdinand and Isabella. 'Poesía popular' had been dismissed by Santillana in his treatise on poetry from the middle of the fifteenth century. The musicians at the court of the Catholic Kings, however, betrayed a fascination with *villancicos* and *romances*. An indication of the success of this kind of poetry is the fact that Portuguese poets of the sixteenth century cultivated the Spanish *villancico*, a reversal of the linguistic practice of earlier centuries when the Galician-Portuguese lyric was cultivated by poets of Castile such as Alfonso X. Both Sá de Miranda and Camões, the two leading sixteenth-century Portuguese poets, wrote *villancicos*, though arguably the freshest and most memorable are those of Gil Vicente (1456?–1537), a playwright whose surviving *villancicos* come from both his Spanish and Portuguese plays. Vicente's knowledge of 'poesía popular' was considerable, as the majority of his pieces in this form are either transcriptions of or improvisations upon existing models. One of the best-known betrays Vicente's Portuguese nationality in its incorporation of a parallelistic technique:

> En la huerta nace la rosa:
> quiérome ir allá
> por mirar al ruiseñor
> cómo cantabá.
>
> Por las riberas del río
> limones coge la virgo.
> Quiérome ir allá
> por mirar al ruiseñor
> cómo cantabá.

Limones cogía la virgo
para dar al su amigo.[9]

The rose is born in the garden; I want to go there to see the nightingale
and how it sings. Along the banks of the river the maiden gathers lemons.
I want to go there to see the nightingale and how it sings. The maiden was
gathering lemons to give to her lover.

Around a century later Spain's most prolific playwright Lope de Vega was
also producing *villancicos* for the stage. Indeed Lope's recreations characteristically cover a wide range of subjects: work-songs, encounter poems, May
songs, dawn songs. His version of a well-known refrain reflecting a folk
ceremony from Valencia, where he lived in internal exile for some years,
betrays the authentic vigour and enjoyment of the traditional song and its
association with folk-custom:

Naranjitas me tira la niña
en Valencia por Navidad,
pues a fe que si se las tiro
que se le han de volver azár.
A una máscara salí
y paréme a su ventana;
amaneció su mañana
y el sol en sus ojos vi.[10]

The girl throws oranges at me in Valencia at Christmas-time, and in faith
if I throw them back they will turn into orange blossom for her. I went out
to a masked ball and I stopped at her window; her morning dawned and I
saw the sun in her eyes.

I have already commented on the revival of the ballad in the early nineteenth century principally through the efforts of the Duque de Rivas. A
related feature was the idealized notion of a people or community as a
collective creative talent. Such a notion was a hallmark of early European
Romanticism, enjoying a particular vogue in Germany as a result of the theories of Herder. A Spanish admirer of Heine, the leading German Romantic
poet, outlined the idea of the people as poet in emphatically enthusiastic
terms:

El pueblo ha sido, y será siempre, el gran poeta de todas las edades y de
todas las naciones.
Nadie mejor que él sabe sintetizar en sus obras las creencias, las
aspiraciones y el sentimiento de una época.[11]

The people have been, and always will be, the great poet of all ages and all
nations. No-one better than they can synthesize in their works the beliefs,
aspirations and feeling of an epoch.

Bécquer's eulogy comes from a review of a work by a lesser contemporary, Augusto Ferrán. A translator of Heine, Ferrán is important for his brief lyrics or *coplas* whose form coincidentally approximates to the *leider* of the German poet. The combination of the direct manner of Heine with the intensity and local colour of the Andalusian *cantar* is evident in many of the four-line poems from Bécquer's *Rimas*. His *coplas*, however, reveal a surprising variety of manner. Some are disarmingly simple:

> Por una mirada, un mundo;
> por una sonrisa, un cielo;
> por un beso . . . ¡yo no sé
> que te diera por un beso![12]

> For a glimpse, a world; for a smile, a sky; for a kiss . . . I don't know what I'd give you for a kiss.

Some are more precious, as with the pseudo-baroque twentieth *rima* that recalls the love poetry of Quevedo:

> Sabe si alguna vez tus labios rojos
> quema invisible atmósfera abrasada,
> que el alma que hablar puede con los ojos
> también puede besar con la mirada.
> (p. 123)

> Know if on some occasion the scorched atmosphere invisibly burns your red lips that the soul that can speak with the eyes can also kiss with the glance.

In others, Bécquer adopts, as he sometimes does in his longer poems, a disconcertingly colloquial manner that appears deliberately to eschew the lyric sweetness that is the predominant mood of his collection:

> ¡No me admiró tu olvido! Aunque de un día
> me admiró tu cariño mucho más,
> porque lo que hay en mí vale algo,
> eso . . . no lo pudistes sospechar.
> (p. 133)

> It did not surprise me that you forgot me! But your one-day love surprised me a lot more, because what there is in me is worth something, and that . . . you could not suspect.

A final instance of the intrusion of popular elements into poetry written in Spanish relates to the rise of protest movements in recent decades. The protest song is an international phenomenon whose essential requirement is a cause, usually one that is minoritarian, marginalized or unconventional.

Though protest songs can flourish in democratic societies, as they did with the Civil Rights and anti-Vietnam-War movements in the 1960s, they more commonly emerge in countries where there is repression. The most notable instance in Spain was the *Nova cançó* ('New song'), the Catalan-language song where political grievance was sharpened by a linguistic factor: the supression of Catalan as an official language during the Franco regime.

It is in South America, however, where the protest song in Spanish has had greatest impact. Even a cursory knowledge of the history of that continent in the twentieth century indicates that political circumstances were highly conducive to the growth of the genre. Right-wing authoritarian regimes imposed themselves upon populations that were largely illiterate. Protest songs thus supplied a necessary recreational as well as political function and they had their roots in traditional folk-song. The leading authority on the Spanish American protest song, Robert Pring-Mill, has pointed out how the modern song grew out of the folk tradition in two distinct but overlapping phases.[13] The earlier tendency initially involved compilation by singers normally from humble backgrounds who later went on to write original songs with an increasing measure of overt social commitment. A leading exponent was the Chilean Violeta Parra (1917–67), from a poor family of Mapuche descent, the Mapuches being the Araucanian tribes that held out longest against the Spanish in the sixteenth century. The second phase, which involved such singers as Violeta's children, Isabel and Ángel, embraced political causes more avowedly. Performers had also become more aware of the importance of the mass media and international interest in their causes. Thus another Chilean singer, Víctor Jara (1938–73), executed shortly after the Pinochet coup, set out to imitate such singers as Bob Dylan and Pete Seeger, albeit in Latin American terms. Jara's militant 'Plegaria a un labrador' has all the hallmarks of a protest poem:

> Levántate / y mira la montaña
> de donde viene
> el viento, el sol y el agua,
> Tú que manejas / el curso de los ríos,
> tú que sembraste / el vuelo de tu alma,
> levántate / y mírate las manos,
> para crecer / y estréchala a tu hermano,
> juntos iremos
> unidos en la sangre,
> Hoy es el tiempo / que puede ser mañana.
>
> Líbranos de aquel que nos domina
> en tu miseria,

tráenos tu reino de justicia
e igualdad...

Hágase por fin tu voluntad
aquí en la tierra,
danos tu fuerza y tu valor
al combatir.[14]

Arise and lift your eyes to the mountains whence comes the wind, the sun
and the water. You who govern the course of the rivers, you who sowed
the seeds of your soul's flight, arise and look at your hands, to grow, and
clasp your brother's hand, together we shall advance united in our blood.
Today is the time that can forge tomorrow. Free us of the man who
dominates us in our want, bring us your kingdom of justice and
equality... May your will be done here on earth, give us your strength
and courage when we fight.

The directness of the tone – tending to the plea or the exhortation – is
obvious enough, but the simplicity of the language should not blind us to two
carefully worked features. Firstly there is a rhetorical figuration reminding us
that oral poetry, perhaps even more than the written form, needs to be alive
to the rise and fall within sentences, as Lorca, one of the great performers of
his own poetry, knew when he wrote some of the more declamatory poems
of his *Poeta en Nueva York*. Anaphora in itself as in lines 4 and 5 of Jara's
'Plegaria' is not enough – what is also required is the precise balancing of
long and short phrases reflecting (or quite simply constituting) the spoken
word. Then there is a judicious employment of imagery. Jara, like many
singers who operate in such a socio-political context, realizes the peculiar
potency of biblical overtones, whether the audience are believers or not.
The opening word echoes Christ's injunctions to the man sick with palsy,
while much of the rest of the poem is pervaded by diction and phrases that
derive from the Lord's Prayer. In like manner, the Peruvian freedom-fighter
Javier Heraud (1942–63) evokes the daily bread from the same prayer as a
political right:

El cielo es nuestro.
Nuestro el pan de cada día.
Hemos sembrado y cosechado
el trigo y la tierra,
son nuestros
y para siempre nos
pertenecen
el mar,
las montañas
y los pájaros.[15]

> Heaven is ours. Ours the daily bread, for we have sown and harvested the
> grain and the earth, and the sea, the mountain and the birds are ours too
> and belong to us for ever.

Pring-Mill reminds us that as well as possessing popular roots, protest poems
'have a long and many-stranded literary-cum-rhetorical tradition behind
them, which has not only its conventional modes of viewing events but
also its conventional techniques for representing what the poet's seeing eye
selects'.[16] Indeed it could be argued that the heightened awareness of the
audience for such a genre demands a greater adherence to conventions than
poetry designed for silent individual reading. Furthermore the apparent
artlessness of these lyrics and the way in which they implicitly or directly
shun the complexity of learned or (to put it in tendentious terms) elitist
poetry are no less conventional. Throughout the ages poets of even the
most uncompromisingly intellectual bent have claimed that their verses
are peculiarly heart-felt because they write more simply than their fellows.
Poets who boast about their departure from the norm because they
think their work is natural and the genuine article, however, are in fact
following a well-established poetic convention, one that dates back to the
Middle Ages.

   This is perhaps one reason why the relationship between the popular and
the artistic in Spanish poetry is more often than not a source of productive
tension rather than mere confrontation. Another reason may be because, as
Octavio Paz has observed in a critique of the work of Antonio Machado
and Juan Ramón Jiménez (1881–1958), 'poesía popular' is not the same as
the spoken language, if only for the simple reason that it is song and not
speech.[17] As a consequence, it could be argued that Spanish poetry is further
removed from everyday speech than is English poetry. The dismissal of
certain kinds of poetry on the grounds of form or metre, such as we saw with
Santillana, is therefore unusual. Indeed when a major revolution occurred
with the importation of the Italianate style in the early sixteenth century
and the consequent neglect of indigenous forms, the reaction was motivated
not by a popular versus learned consideration but by patriotism. Cristóbal
de Castillejo (1492?–1550), the author of a satirical poem attacking the
formal innovations of Boscán and Garcilaso, was a poet who served both the
Catholic Kings and the Archduke Ferdinand, ruler of Bohemia and Hungary.
His own poetry, in the tradition of courtly or *cancionero* poetry of the fifteenth
century, is fully as 'learned' as that introduced by the Italianate pioneers.

   In the broadest sense this revolution involved a new way of looking at
experience, one that owed nearly everything to Italian Humanism. Such
visions were manifested in the development in Spanish of such genres or
sub-genres as the pastoral, cultivated in prose as well as poetry. Indeed the

three Eclogues of Garcilaso are perhaps the most important poetic works in Spanish in the first half of the sixteenth century. It is in metre and form, however, that the most radical and enduring changes occurred. The adoption of the hendecasyllable line supplied Spanish with another standard line-length alongside the octosyllabic *romance* metre. Poetic structures and what could be termed the way of thinking in a poem also changed. While *cancionero* poetry operated by a process of repetition and accumulation, the Italianate form encouraged a more dynamic movement. If we compare part of a composition in praise of the lady by Hugo de Urries from the *Cancionero general* (1511) with the opening of Garcilaso's first *Canción* we notice how static the former appears beside the argumentative thrust of the later work:

> Estrema gracia tenedes,
> e muy noble condición;
> los buenos vuestros facedes
> e los malos atraedes
> a conocer la razón;
> vos sois la pura virtut,
> vos sois la graciosidat.[18]

You are endowed with supreme grace and nobility; you make the good your own and you draw the wicked towards a knowledge of reason; you are pure virtue, you are beauty.

> Si a la región desierta, inhabitable
> por el hervor del sol demasïado
> y sequedad d'aquella arena ardiente,
> o a la que por el hielo congelado
> y rigurosa nieve es intratable,
> del todo inhabitada de la gente,
> por algún accidente
> o caso de fortuna desastrada
> me fuésedes llevada[19]

If you were to be borne away from me by some chance event or great misfortune to the deserted region, uninhabitable through the excessive heat of the sun and the dryness of that burning sand, or to that place which is frozen over with ice and inaccessible because of the snow, and where no people dwell

There is a change too in the syntactical realization: the predominantly short sense-units and the end-stopped lines of the Urries poem contrast with the discursive manner of Garcilaso. Garcilaso's *canción* is a Spanish equivalent of the Petrarchan *canzone*, sometimes designated as a longer lyrical form to distinguish it from the shorter, and the commonest, Renaissance lyrical form: the sonnet.

Sonnets were not unknown in Spain before Boscán and Garcilaso but they had not enjoyed any lasting success. If the *canción* demanded precision in the development of an argument then the sonnet, by dint of its brevity, also required concision and a greater attention to the interaction of form and content. Thus the fourteen-line Petrarchan sonnet was conceived in terms of an octave and a sestet, and, in a further division, as two quatrains and two tercets. The allocation of rhymes comprised an unvarying pattern (ABBA ABBA) for the octave and a flexible distribution of two or three additional rhymes (CD or CDE) for the sestet. In the development of an argument, however, the four-fold division is more apparent, as with the following sonnet by Garcilaso:

> En tanto que de rosa y d'azucena
> se muestra la color en vuestro gesto,
> y que vuestro mirar ardiente, honesto,
> con clara luz la tempestad serena;
> y en tanto que'l cabello, qu'en la vena
> del oro s'escogió, con vuelo presto
> por el hermoso cuello blanco, enhiesto,
> el viento mueve, esparce y desordena:
> coged de vuestra alegre primavera
> el dulce fruto antes que'l tiempo airado
> cubra de nieve la hermosa cumbre.
> Marchitará la rosa el viento helado,
> todo lo mudará la edad ligera
> por no hacer mudanza en su costumbre.[20]

While the colour of the rose and the lily are displayed in your face, and your passionate, chaste, glance soothes the storm with its bright light; and while the wind moves, scatters and disperses your hair, which was chosen in the finest seam of gold, into disarray about your beautiful, white and straight neck: pluck the sweet fruit of your happy Springtime before angry time covers the beautiful summit with snow. The icy wind will cause the rose to wither, and fickle time will change everything so as not to have to change its customary ways.

This is a type of poem known as *carpe diem* (literally: 'seize the day') as the poet, for his own erotic purposes, urges the woman he addresses to return his love. The quatrains describe her beauty in conventional terms. Living as she does on borrowed time, the woman is urged to make the most of her youth, the Springtime of her life. To underscore this warning the eulogy is ominously qualified by the conjunction 'en tanto que' ('while'), repeated at the start of the second quatrain as if to specify the sonnet's structural hinges. Both the tercets make a distinctive addition to the poem's argument with the result that it seems to gather pace as it nears the end. The first contains the *carpe diem* exhortation ('coged') while the second bleakly states what will befall the rose – a symbol of the lady's beauty – and concludes ironically with a play on the words 'mudar' and 'mudanza': time changes all because that is of its essence, for to do otherwise time itself would need to change.

When Góngora wrote a sonnet on the same theme more than half a century later the vogue of the sonnet was such that poets were increasingly compelled to seek variation or enrichment. One way of achieving this was lexical: by neologism or extravagant metaphor. Góngora himself, as we have already noted, was the principal exponent of such practices. In his *carpe diem* sonnet of 1582, however, he is less concerned with lexical fireworks than with the structural implications of the form. At first sight his sonnet is closely connected to Garcilaso's, especially in the way in which the ominous conjunction (now 'mientras') is highlighted:

> Mientras por competir con tu cabello
> oro bruñido al sol relumbra en vano;
> mientras con menosprecio en medio el llano
> mira tu blanca frente el lilio bello;
>
> mientras a cada labio, por cogello,
> siguen más ojos que al clavel temprano,
> y mientras triunfa con desdén lozano
> del luciente cristal tu gentil cuello,
>
> goza cuello, cabello, labio y frente,
> antes que lo que fue en tu edad dorada
> oro, lilio, clavel, cristal luciente,
>
> no sólo en plata o víola troncada
> se vuelva, más tú y ello juntamente
> en tierra, en humo, en polvo, en sombra, en nada.[21]

> While, to compete with your hair, the sun, burnished gold, gleams in vain, while your white forehead looks contemptuously at the beautiful lily in the middle of the plain; while more eyes follow each of your lips, to catch it, than follow the early carnation, and while your delicate neck triumphs over gleaming crystal with gentle disdain, enjoy, neck, hair, lip and forehead, before what was in your golden age gold, lily, carnation, gleaming crystal, not only turns to silver or plucked violet, but you and it together are turned to earth, smoke, dust, shadow, nothing.

As with Garcilaso, Góngora's governing metaphor is the blooming and fading of flowers. The tercets, however, supply a significant divergence from the precursor text. For a start, Góngora is more preoccupied with the symmetry of the sonnet than is Garcilaso. Where the earlier sonnet ends with the development of an argument the later one concludes with the development – effectively the disruption – of the pattern of lexical components that constitute the sonnet's principal structural motor. The lady's beauty is conveyed through the focus on four elements ('cabello'; 'frente'; 'labio'; 'cuello'), as is the related aspect of the natural world ('sol'; 'lilio'; 'clavel'; 'cristal'). These, however, are presented in the tercets in ways that deviate from the pattern established in the quatrains. Although the sequence that is broken in line 9 is restored in line 11 this is only a temporary restoration for there are further disruptions in the final tercet. These are achieved by a numerical adjustment: the concept of four that had dominated in the quatrains yields firstly to two ('plata o vïola'; 'tú y ello'), and finally to five. This last change is highly dramatic. On the one hand there is a false expectation: we might have assumed as we read the final line that we would have been reverting to the earlier four-fold pattern. Moreover, the fifth and extra term – the last word of the poem – is the most emphatic of negative words ('nada'). Here is not decay, as with Garcilaso, but disintegration. What is more, Góngora'a acute awareness of symmetry has enabled us to experience such disruption not only as a theme we extract from the poem on reflection or analysis but as a sensation that occurs in the very act of reading, we could almost say of *seeing*, the sonnet.

It would be an error to think of the occurrences of classical and asymmetrical sonnets purely in terms of chronology and literary history. Modern and contemporary poets are as capable of writing classical sonnets as a Golden Age poet like Góngora is of composing one that is deviant in its structure. Indeed in his later sonnets, Góngora separates syntax and structure quite drastically so that sentences end in mid-line and new points in the argument are introduced in mid-stanza.[22] The following sonnet entitled 'Blind Pew' by Borges, however, offers us as regular and standard a form as could be desired:

> Lejos del mar y de la hermosa guerra,
> que así el amor lo que ha perdido alaba,
> el bucanero ciego fatigaba
> los terrosos caminos de Inglaterra.
>
> Ladrado por los perros de las granjas,
> pifia de los muchachos del poblado,
> dormía un achacoso y agrietado
> sueño en el negro polvo de las zanjas.
>
> Sabía que en remotas playas de oro
> era suyo un recóndito tesoro
> y esto aliviaba su contraria suerte;

> a ti también, en otras playas de oro,
> te aguarda incorruptible tu tesoro:
> la vasta y vaga y necesaria muerte.[23]

Far from the sea and the beauty of war, for so love praises what it has lost, the blind bucanneer wandered wearily throughout the muddy roads of England. Barked at by dogs in the farms, shouted at by the boys in the villages, he slept a painful and broken sleep in the black dust of the ditches. He knew that on golden beaches far away a hidden treasure was his, and this alleviated his unhappy lot; there awaits you too, on other golden beaches, your incorruptible treasure: the immense and vague and necessary death.

The name alluded to in the title is a character from *Treasure Island*, a novel by one of Borges's favourite writers, Robert Louis Stevenson. Each of the four parts of the sonnet makes a distinctive contribution to the whole. The first quatrain outlines the situation of the blind beggar and pirate, the second expands on this by focusing on the wretchedness of his life. As with Garcilaso's *carpe diem* sonnet there is a double shift in the tercets: from actions to thought and from image (the blind beggar's thoughts of buried treasure) to referent (the treasure that is death).[24] The irony of the closing line provides that kind of ultimate surprise that a good sonnet will keep up its sleeve.

Classical though this sonnet is in its form and structure, however, it is in no sense a pastiche. The same cannot be said for the following sonnet by the contemporary Spanish poet, Fernando de Villena (1956–):

> Cuando, tras tanto pretender en vano,
> vuelvo a mi soledad cansado y triste,
> dudo, señora, de si en vos existe
> alma piadosa y corazón humano;
>
> cuando de Amor juzgo el poder tirano
> y mi pecho en sus redes se resiste,
> es tan alto el sentir, que noche viste,
> es tan fiero el dolor que tigre hircano;
>
> cuando, en fin, mi razón cuitada advierte
> que esta cárcel jamás tendrá salida
> ni es posible mudar desdén tan fuerte,
>
> vengo a dar toda lucha por perdida,
> hallo la vida con sabor de muerte,
> pido a la muerte me conceda vida.[25]

When after I have wooed so much in vain I return weary and sad to my solitude, I doubt, my lady, if there dwells in you a soul that pities and a heart that is human; when I judge the tyrannous power of Love and my breast resists in its nets, so lofty is my feeling, clothed in night, so harsh is the pain, caused by the Hircanian tiger; when at last my troubled reason warns me that this prison will never have a way out nor is it possible to change a scorn that is so strong, I conclude that any struggle is a lost cause, I discover that life has the taste of death, and I ask death to concede me life.

It is apt that this sonnet should follow one by Borges as it recalls one of the Argentinian's short stories, 'Pierre Menard, autor del Quijote' ('Pierre Menard, author of the Quixote'), which comprises a discussion of the work of a fictional writer, whose most daring achievement is to have copied Cervantes's great novel word-by-word. But, Borges argues, Menard's is not the same work. For a start the language is perceived as different: Menard's is archaic while that of Cervantes was appropriate for its day. Then there is the matter of ideology, whereby what passes as an acceptable truth in the earlier version is inappropriate or even shocking when repeated. Villena does not go so far as to copy a sonnet as such. His lexicon, imagery and phraseology, however, are those of a sixteenth-century poet writing to an inaccessible beloved: the abject lover reproaching the lady for her cruelty and comparing her, as countless Renaissance sonneteers did, to a Hircanian tiger (lines 1–4, 8); the imagery of entrapment and imprisonment (lines 6, 10); and the reversibility of the concepts of life and death by a play on their literal and metaphorical significance (lines 13–14). Villena has written a large number of such sonnets and it is a moot point if they are mere exercises or something more profound: the cultivation of archaism to demonstrate the invalidity of a poetic tradition. This is an issue to which I shall return in the following chapter.

Where modern sonneteers most conspicuously differ from their Renaissance predecessors, however, is perhaps in a readiness to adopt a casual or colloquial manner even while adhering to the basic formal requirements of the sonnet. The opening quatrain of a sonnet by the Peruvian poet César Vallejo is, by comparison with Villena, disconcertingly down-beat, adhering to the patterns of speech rather than of song:

Enfrente a la Comedia Francesa, está el Café
de la Regencia; en él hay una pieza
recóndita, con una butaca y una mesa.
Cuando entro, el polvo inmóvil se ha puesto ya de pie.

Entre mis labios hechos de jebe, la pavesa
de un cigarrillo humea, y en el humo se ve
dos humos intensivos, el tórax del Café
y en el tórax, un óxido profundo de tristeza.

Importa que el otoño se injerte en los otoños,
importa que el otoño se integre de retoños,
la nube, de semestres; de pómulos, la arruga.

Importa oler a loco postulando
¡qué cálida es la nieve, qué fugaz la tortuga,
el cómo qué sencillo, qué fulminante el cuándo!²⁶

Opposite the Comédie Française is the Regency Café; in it there is a
hidden room, with an easy chair and a table. When I go in, the still dust
has already got to its feet. Between my rubber lips, the stub of a cigarette
smoulders, and in the smoke two intensive smokes can be seen, the thorax
of the Café and, in the thorax, a profound oxide of sadness. It is
important that the Autumn be grafted onto Autumns, it is important that
the Autumn be integrated into young shoots, the cloud, with half-years;
the wrinkle into the cheekbones. It is important to smell like a madman
who postulates how hot the snow is, how fleeting the tortoise, how simple
the how, how overwhelming the when!

The location of the reference to the poet in the last line of the first quatrain supplies another divergence from the classical model. We might have
expected that new material in the form of this incorporation would have
occurred in a new structural component, that is the second quatrain. If
the sonnet is unorthodox initially, however, it increasingly reverts more to
the standard type. Despite the enjambements, the second quatrain lacks the
prosaic and casual air of the first. The repetitions ('humea . . . humo . . . humos'; 'tórax . . . tórax') together with a more elevated diction incline towards
the monumental manner that is a hallmark of the baroque sonnet. This process is taken a stage further in the tercets. Here we encounter anaphora (the
repetitions of 'importa' and the exclamation 'qué'), enumeration and a sophisticated rhetorical device known as chiasmus in the inversion that creates
a mirror effect (AB:BA) in line 11 where a simple paralleling effect would
have rendered the line as 'la nube, de semestres; la arruga, de pómulos'. In
the tercets there is a rhyme scheme whereas assonance had been used for the
quatrains. The other formal irregularity comprises the variation of the line
length. The hendecasyllable is only used for two of the sonnet's lines, the
remainder comprising mainly fourteen-syllable lines. Yet while we register
this as an irregularity we ought not to overlook the fact that such a line
length – conceived as two groups of seven syllables – was a standard line for
Medieval verse, for the *cuaderna vía*. Vallejo's sonnet is characteristic of much
twentieth-century poetry in the way in which order and chaos combine.
The attempt to impose a meaning on reality and everyday life – unavailing it
would appear from the nonsensical formulations of the second tercet – is en-
coded in the structure as well as the words of the poem; or, to put it another
way, with the best poetry the division of manner and matter is inappropriate.

The disconcerting leaps and illogical connections of this sonnet render
it what many would consider a 'difficult' poem. In a discussion of popular
and learned poetry it would be tempting to conclude that the former is easy

to understand while the latter is relatively difficult. Even within the limited scope of this examination, however, it is evident that such a neat distinction would not be valid. Just as there are poems belonging to or arising from the oral tradition that are mysterious and evade analysis, so there are countless poems of a learned nature which are instantly accessible. Such difficulties as learned poetry possesses can moreover be readily defined: the problem is understanding either what is *said* or what is *meant*.

The poetry of the baroque era offers the best example of the former difficulty. Góngora sought not only to invest Spanish poetry with the characteristics of Latin but also to make his poetry incomprehensible to the many: 'hacerme escuro a los ignorantes, que es la distinción de los hombres doctos, hablar de manera que a ellos les parezca griego' ('to make myself obscure to the ignorant, for it is a distinguishing feature of wise men, to speak in such a way that it appears Greek to them').[27] Góngora was merely following the current of his times, but as he was the most successful poet to write in this manner it was his name that was attached to such uncompromisingly difficult poetry. Just as *culterano* was coined as a pejorative term – by analogy with *luterano* – so *gongorismo* was often used as a dismissive rather than merely descriptive label. It is not merely the choice of word that challenges the reader, a difficulty that is nonetheless more acute for the modern reader unable to seize, as would his seventeenth-century counterpart, the fleeting mythological allusion. A larger problem in understanding what is being said arises from syntactical rather than semantic factors. While individual lexical details can be isolated and eventually resolved, it is less easy to come to terms with Góngora's convoluted sentence-structures. Not only are his sentences frequently long – straddling many lines of verse and riddled with delaying parentheses – they deviate sharply from normal word-order in order to make Spanish seem more like Latin. Hyperbaton, as such a dislocation is designated, is to an extent present in much Spanish poetry, given the flexibility and licence afforded by the genre, but with Góngora it is taken to an extreme. A passage from his *Fábula de Polifemo y Galatea* offers a good example of the kind of demands made upon the reader:

> Donde espumoso el mar sicilïano
> el pie argenta de plata al Lilibeo
> (bóveda o de las fraguas de Vulcano,
> o tumba de los huesos de Tifeo),
> pálidas señas cenizoso un llano
> – cuando no del sacrílego deseo –
> del duro oficio da[28]

> Where the foamy Sicilian sea gives a sheen of silver to Lilybaeum's foot (either a vault for Vulcan's forge, or a tomb for the bones of Typhon), a

> plain covered in ash gives pale signs – if not of the sacrilegious desire –
> then of the harsh toil

This is effectively the opening of the poem, as the preceding stanzas had comprised the dedication. The parenthesis, including an 'either-or' phrase, almost immediately softens up the reader before the violent dislocation of the main clause which (taking away the portion of parenthesis) is a 'transcription' of 'un llano cenizoso da pálidas señas del duro oficio'. The disruption arises from the position of the adjective (preceding the article), the object (preceding the subject) and the verb (following both object and subject). Yet somehow we register the import and perhaps the sense of these lines even before fully understanding them by parsing. There is an electric quality about such poetry: it has an impact *before* we understand. The concluding phrase, in particular, communicates a menace that is a keynote of the whole poem. The abrupt ending of the rambling sentence with a monosyllable completes an emphatic alliteration: 'deseo – / del duro oficio da'. When poetry can trigger such responses it has gone beyond technique, and its surface difficulty and apparent inaccessibility are not as forbidding.

The difficulty of modern poetry, however, is often understanding not what is said but what is meant. The opening of a poem from Alberti's *Sobre los ángeles* is a case in point:

> Yo te arrojé de mi cuerpo,
> yo, con un carbón ardiendo.
>
> –Vete.
>
> Madrugada.
> La luz, muerta en las esquinas
> y en las casas.
> Los hombres y las mujeres
> ya no estaban.
>
> –Vete.
>
> Quedó mi cuerpo vacío,
> negro saco, a la ventana.
>
> Se fue.
>
> Se fue, doblando las calles.
> Mi cuerpo anduvo, sin nadie.[29]

> I threw you out of my body, yes, with a burning coal. 'Go away.' Dawn. The light, dead at the street corners and in the houses. The men and the women were no longer there. 'Go away.' My body remained empty, a

> black sack, at the window. It went away. It went away, crossing along the streets. My body walked on, without anyone.

These lines have none of the difficulties of Góngora's *Polifemo*. The diction is plain; the sentences are short; there are no syntactical disruptions. Most readers, however, would readily conclude that it is 'difficult' poetry. A major cause of this difficulty is the tendency for such poetry to lack a logical or even merely sequential development, either because successive sentences or sense-units do not obviously connect or because of a lack of sufficient detail. Thus we feel compelled to make assumptions that may or may not be confirmed. We presume, for example, that the pronoun 'te' in line 1 is the soul, because body and soul are commonly presented as opposites. We further assume that the command in line 3 is the body addressing the soul and that the men and women are absent from the houses, just as the soul is from the body. Our reasoning, however, may well be challenged by the ending. It is not clear if the subject of 'se fue' is the body, referred to in the adjacent lines, or the soul, because 'se fue' is very much the action we would expect in response to the command to go away. To repeat what was implied in Chapter 2, fulfilling the need to choose is the course of action in which the tidying analyst rather than the experiencing reader will engage. If we decide against choosing and against the single meaning, however, this does not imply that we have not confronted the problem of the poem's sense. Indeed because we do not feel obliged to resolve what has been identified as a problem it may be that our perception is more acute, more certain.

Chapter 6

Love poetry

The sonnet, as we have seen, is an immensely adaptable and versatile form. Not the least of its strengths is the opportunity it affords poets for striking a balance between conforming to certain norms and deviating from them. So powerful, however, is what could be termed the *idea* of the sonnet that whenever the form is used, however loosely, the classical notion is inescapably evoked, together with expectations of what kind of poem it will be. While a sonnet's subject-matter can be as wide-ranging as any kind of poetry it is especially associated with love poetry. Indeed it could be safely said that it is the vehicle *par excellence* of amatory verse down the ages.

Even though the connection of sonnet and love poetry is not confined to any particular period it was the sixteenth century that was its heyday. It has been calculated that over a quarter of a million sonnets were written in Europe during this century. However approximate that statistic may be, it should nonetheless serve as a formidable warning against reading poetry as autobiography. Writing about Renaissance literature, A. J. Krailsheimer observes that 'originality in the sense of doing something new, and sincerity, in a simple autobiographical sense, are irrelevant concepts'.[1] We have already seen in Chapter 1 the dangers inherent in such an approach with Garcilaso's poetry. A similar wrong-headedness has also been manifested by commentators on Quevedo's sonnets to Lisi, although more recently critics have been content to accept the name of Lisi as essentially a fiction. This is not tantamount to admitting that the poetry is lacking in conviction or credibility; rather, it is an acknowledgement that the name and the figure might embody a blend of imagination and biography, and that they are the product of the experience of reading as well as of life. Indeed one can reasonably assert that the poet's acquaintance with Petrarch's *Canzoniere* is, as far as we can ascertain, more important than the existence of any single woman whom Quevedo would have represented as Lisi.

The poems to Lisi constitute a rare, if not unique, example of a sonnet sequence in Spanish. Such coherent collections of poems about a single woman, modelled directly or indirectly on Petrarch's sequence, were nonetheless very common in other European literatures of the sixteenth century. Such collections had a number of features in common: a poem or poems that described the impact of the poet's first sight of the beloved, descriptions of her beauty, accounts of her activities, and other ideas such as the poet's absence from his lady and his envying an object that the lady possessed or which would have been in close contact with her person. Although Spanish poets composed poems on all these topics, by either accident or design they have come down to us as individual poems rather than as parts of an organic whole. The following sonnet from Quevedo's poems to Lisi is a rare Spanish example of an anniversary sonnet. The lover marks the tenth anniversary of his first meeting with the beloved:

> Diez años de mi vida se ha llevado
> en veloz fuga y sorda el sol ardiente,
> después que en tus dos ojos vi el Oriente,
> Lísida, en hermosura duplicado.
>
> Diez años en mis venas he guardado
> el dulce fuego que alimento, ausente,
> de mi sangre. Diez años en mi mente
> con imperio tus luces han reinado.
>
> Basta ver una vez grande hermosura;
> que, una vez vista, eternamente enciende,
> y en l'alma impresa eternamente dura.
>
> Llama que a la inmortal vida trasciende,
> ni teme con el cuerpo sepultura,
> ni el tiempo la marchita ni la ofende.[2]

> Ten years of my life have been borne away in rapid and noiseless flight by the burning sun since I saw the Orient, in your two eyes, Lisi, in doubled beauty. For ten years I have kept in my veins the sweet fire that, in my absence, I nourish on my blood. For ten years your lights have reigned imperiously over my mind. It is enough to see great beauty once, for once seen, it burns eternally and lasts forever, imprinted in the soul. The flame that extends to immortal life does not fear the tomb with the body, nor does time wither or burn it.

Such a poem can only achieve its full effect in the context of a poetic sequence. We can admittedly appreciate the mood of sustained devotion from the quasi-incantatory repetitions of the very phrase — 'diez años' — that identifies the poem type. We lose, however, that ability to make cross-references, especially of imagery, that inevitably occurs when we come across a sonnet in a developing and interconnected set of poems. Thus when the poet refers to the 'dulce fuego' 'en mis venas' ('sweet fire' 'in my veins') we are more likely to be alert to the peculiarly physical character of the poet's experience if we have also read several other sonnets where there is a similar understanding of the effects of love. There is, however, an even more important way in which the reader achieves a more complete understanding of the sonnet in its context. In the tercets, as so often, there is a shift: from the affirmation of the value of time as a sign of the extent of the lover's devotion to the transcendental realization that a single glimpse of such beauty would have sufficed. The single moment ('una vez') would have supplied something that the ten years by their very nature could not, that is, the intimation of eternity. Consequently the poet–lover moves from the temporal plain of the anniversary to the realm of a love that endures beyond death. This is in fact a topic of a kind that we find in a number of Shakespeare's sonnets and it is immediately developed in the next poem in the Lisi cycle, the sonnet beginning 'Cerrar podrá mis ojos', considered in Chapter 2. As we have already seen, its hollow assertiveness ultimately challenges the vision of eternal love, but what we will not have experienced unless we have also read the preceding sonnet in its place in the cycle is a dynamic process of change between the two sonnets: time superseded by eternity in the first, and then the value of eternity, established at the end of the first of these sonnets, undermined by the false logic of the second. Such interrelationships are what give the sonnet sequence its distinctive, even unique, quality.

The dearth of Petrarchan cycles in Spanish literature does not, however, mean that poets were any less taken with the Petrarchan manner. The revolution that was responsible for the rise to prominence of the sonnet also ushered in a new way of writing. In a nutshell, whereas the *cancionero* poets of the fifteenth century had traded in abstraction, as in the passage from the *Cancionero general* quoted in the previous chapter (see p. 122), the new poets followed Petrarch and his like-minded successors in their liberal use of terms drawn from the natural world. These served both as a backdrop and for the creation of metaphors related to the experience of love. 'Creation' is perhaps an inappropriate designation, as the images were invariably commonplace analogies. Thus the lady's beauty was described in a codified fashion in accordance with what Petrarch had systematized. Her hair was gold; her cheeks, roses; her teeth, pearls; her lips, rubies; her eyes, suns or stars; her neck, ivory or alabaster. In like manner the lover's reactions were also prescribed: his passion was a flame or a fire, his suffering and his tears were rivers or fountains. By a witty development, the snow or ice that represented the lady's beauty by allusion to the whiteness of her skin could also stand for her disdain and cruelty, and in the harsh world of the lover the laws of nature were reversed: (his) fire could not melt (her) snow.

The love poems of the *Cancionero general* envisage the experience in a disembodied manner. They articulate the essence of the amatory experience: it is as though the lovers figure in a vacuum. Together with its distinctive stylistic traits such poetry acquires an intensity of expression; not for nothing does one critic consider it endowed with 'an obsessive intensity which can still startle'.[3] It is, however, in some ways at least, a world apart from a sonnet like the following by Fernando de Herrera, the leading Spanish Petrarchist of the second half of the sixteenth century:

> Serena Luz, en quien presente espira
> divino amor, qu'enciende i junto enfrena
> el noble pecho qu'en mortal cadena
> al alto Olimpo levantars' aspira;
>
> ricos cercos dorados, do se mira
> tesoro celestial d'eterna vena;
> armonía d'ángelica sirena
> qu'entre las perlas i el coral respira:
>
> ¿Cuál nueva maravilla, cuál exemplo
> de la inmortal grandeza nos descubre
> aquessa sombra del hermoso velo?
>
> Que yo en essa belleza que contemplo,
> aunqu'a mi flaca vista ofende i cubre,
> la inmensa busco i voi siguiendo al cielo.[4]

Serene Luz, in whose presence is exhaled divine love, that kindles and at the same time checks the noble breast that in its mortal chains aspires to rise up to the heights of Olympus; rich golden circles, where is seen the celestial treasure mined from an eternal seam; the harmony of an angelic siren which is breathed between the pearls and the coral: what new wonder, what example of immortal greatness does this shadow of the harmonious veil reveal to us? For although my fragile sight offends and blurs this beauty that I contemplate, I seek the immense [beauty] and I am seeking it up to the heavens.

The first point to make is that a poem like this is no less conventional or stylized than those in the *Cancionero general*. In no sense is it more 'real' or 'human', but it does have an awareness of the world of things as well as of emotions. Not that this world of things makes it less idealistic. On the contrary, consistent with the philosophy of Italian Neoplatonists, Herrera interpreted the world of objects, specifically the lady's beauty, as a sign or a shadow of a higher reality. Thus the commonplaces of Petrarchism acquire an added significance. The lady's physical presence is described in time-honoured fashion: her hair as gold (line 5), her teeth as pearls and her lips as coral (line 8). This earthly beauty, however, hints at a greater one; significantly the pseudonym for the lady, employed here and elsewhere, is Luz ('light'). The poet–lover is inspired to look beyond the *apparent* beauty or, in terms of the Platonic philosophy invoked here, to look upwards (lines 3–4, 12–14). The link between the real and the ideal is effected in the metaphors of the second quatrain. The golden ringlets of the lady's hair remind the poet of the circling planets, hence the treasure is heavenly (line 6) and consequently inexhaustible – 'd'eterna vena' ('of eternal seam'). In the cosmogonic theory to which Herrera, like all Renaissance poets, subscribed, the circling planets each emitted a musical note that taken together formed the music of the spheres, of which the lady's voice is a reflection (lines 7–8).

The examples of love poetry I have supplied hitherto presuppose a concept of love as decorous and unfulfilled. More broadly, the idea of love as unfulfilled desire could be considered the standard situation in love poetry, deriving from the innovative poetry produced at the Provençal courts in the twelfth and thirteenth centuries. This so-called 'courtly' love ethos established certain norms that with slight amendment and addition largely determined the content of love poetry and the attitude of love poets down to the present day. It envisages Woman as a superior being, an ideal that the poet longs to possess but which he acknowledges with good (occasionally less than good) grace he cannot. It is important, however, to note two details in this flimsy summary of courtly love ideology. In the first place the poet's love may be unfulfilled, but it is not chaste in its intent: courtly love is physical desire even if the lover seldom achieves consummation. Secondly, however much she may be idealized, Woman is an *object*, while the poet–lover, thematically as well as grammatically, is the *subject*. Both these observations are important in an exploration of how Spanish love poetry has functioned at different periods.

Cancionero poetry was long held to be inferior and insipid. The most influential Spanish critics of the start of the twentieth century wanted to consign it to the dustbin of literature. More recent investigations, however, have suggested that the poetry may possess a veiled eroticism.[5] The abstract and unspecific terminology of the Castilian courtly poem lends itself readily to hidden meaning, euphemism and the *double entendre*. Words like 'bien' ('good'), 'mal' ('evil'), 'vida' ('life'), 'muerte' ('death'), 'pena' ('pain'), 'fe' ('faith') are prone to mean more than we might suspect if only for the reason that the limited vocabulary of the *cancionero* lyric implies that nouns necessarily have to cover a wider semantic field. Such a practice is not only ingenious – it is devious. It may derive from Medieval and Renaissance poetic riddles that seem to be unambiguously obscene until the moment of solution when their innocent nature is unexpectedly revealed – an issue I shall explore in Chapter 8.

We should not imagine that the attribution of secondary obscene meanings to seemingly standard amatory laments is the work of later interpreters. In several cases the additional erotic significance was well known, as with the use of the word 'death' in amatory contexts for the orgasm. More important, however, than the attempt to identify whether certain words were innocent or not at each occurrence is an awareness of the erotic resonance and tension that the employment of this diction implies. It is worth noting too that the premiss of those poems in which these terms appear is love as frustrated desire, a condition conducive to a covert eroticism. While it would clearly be gross and grotesque to read every Renaissance love poem as a code for indecency, it is by the same token an error to dismiss these poems as vapid expressions of chaste emotions.

Even those who have studied Spanish love poetry of the Golden Age in some depth may be surprised by the quantity of clandestine and porno-graphic – in a word, 'underground' – poetry. The modern imagination and modern tastes may query the use of such terms but they are convenient for distinguishing such poetry from the conventional and canonic amatory production of the day. Even though this poetry is marginalized and largely the work of anonymous poets, however, its relationship to the decorous mainstream is a surprisingly close one. For a start it is certain that 're-spectable' poets were also the authors of obscene verses. More significantly, the thematic as well as the stylistic divide between the acceptable and the indecent was seldom clear-cut – not surprising if we think of the potentially ambiguous nature of *cancionero* verse.

The following sonnet from the *Jardín de Venus* ('Garden of Venus'), one of the most important collections of pornographic poetry of the Golden Age, dating from around the middle of the sixteenth century, is a case in point:

> Tu cabello me enlaza ¡ay mi señora!,
> y tu hermosa frente me enternece,
> la lumbre de tus ojos me escurece,
> y tu nariz me enciende de hora en hora.
>
> Tu pequeñuela boca me enamora,
> tu cuello un alabastro me parece,
> tus pechos leche que ya mengua y crece,
> y en medio están dos bultos de una aurora.
>
> Tu vientre llano y liso, allí es mi gloria;
> tus blancas piernas, donde vivo y muero;
> tu pie chiquito, donde pierdo el seso.
>
> Mas adonde me falta la memoria,
> y no sé comparallo como quiero,
> es en lo que es mejor que todo eso.[6]

Your hair ensnares me, O my lady! and your beautiful forehead moves me, the light in your eyes makes me dark, and your nose arouses me constantly. I am in love with your small mouth, your neck seems to me like alabaster, your breasts, milk that falls and rises, and they are two bulks in the midst of a dawn. In your belly, flat and smooth, there lies my glory; your white legs are where I live and die; your tiny foot is where I become mad with love. But where my memory fails me, and where I cannot compare it with anything as I wish is in that [part of you] which is better than all of this.

The sub-genre is instantly recognizable: it is a portrait poem along the lines of Petrarch's description of Laura or Quevedo's of Lisi. Indeed the sonnet conforms with the respectable model also in detail until around mid-point. There is the Petrarchan itemization or fragmentation of the lady's beauty, including some standard metaphors: the lady's hair snaring the lover, her neck compared to alabaster. While the portrait sonnet, however, could occasionally refer to the upper part of the lady's body, including therefore the breasts, to proceed downwards was unthinkable. Yet even though this sonnet clearly breaks the unwritten rules in the first tercet (note yet again the recourse to a thematic shift at a pivotal structural point) it does so with a clear awareness of the conventions of 'respectable' poetry. For a start, while the woman's belly, legs and feet are mentioned directly, her private parts are alluded to in a coy and circumlocutious manner. Moreover, the poet incorporates into the most explicit part of the sonnet the kind of abstract terminology that is common in *cancionero* poetry: 'gloria' ('glory'); 'vivo y muero' ('I live and die'). Such terms may be more erotically charged than usual here, but they are unmistakably the currency of mainstream Petrarchism.

There is evidence too that the movement between obscene and decorous poetry was not all one way. Let us consider in this connection part of an anonymous poem from the end of the sixteenth century:

> *Ya empieza a deletrear*
> *Perico, el del bachiller,*
> *porque, en sabiendo leer,*
> *dice que ha de predicar.*
> Donde vee hermosas damas
> da liciones, aunque aprende
> y con sus letras enciende
> en sus pechos vivas llamas;
> y quiere sobre las camas
> dar liciones y tomar,
> *porque, en sabiendo leer,*
> *dice que ha de predicar*...
> Y trae consigo la pluma,
> que quiere escribir primero,
> y echa tinta en el tintero
> de lo que della rezuma.[7]

Now Perico, the student, begins to spell it out, because, as he knows how to read, he says that he has to give sermons. Wherever he sees lovely ladies

he gives lessons, although he is himself learning, and with his letters he
kindles living flames in their breasts; and he wishes to give the lesson and
do it on the bed, because as he knows how to read, he says that he has to
give sermons . . . And he brings along his pen because he wants to write
first, and dips it into the inkwell so that it oozes forth.

The obscene significance of the act of writing and the phallic pen are obvious. The poem is unremarkable for its type. It is neither particularly ingenious nor unduly pornographic, merely a laboured working-out of an
obscene metaphor. If it seems a jaded composition, however, it may be because it is repeating a well-worn analogy, rather like a dirty story that has
been re-told too often. Certainly the same analogy occurs in another poem
from that era, Aldana's 'Epístola a una dama cuyo principio falta' ('Letter to
a lady, the start of which is missing'), a very different kind of composition
from the smutty trifle just quoted. Indeed its adherence to the *cancionero*
manner in diction and phraseology lends it an unusually austere air. The
opening lines outline the poet's subjection to the will of his lady, whom he
labels 'enemy', a common Petrarchan hyperbole:

> ¡Ay dura ley de amor que así me obliga
> a no tener más voluntad de aquella
> que me ordena el rigor de mi enemiga![8]

> O harsh law of love which obliges me thus to have no will other than that
> ordained for me by the severity of my enemy.

In the course of the 142 lines of the poem, however, there is a gradual movement from abject surrender to subtle defiance. The use of legal-sounding
phraseology and the cultivation of casuistry contribute to this incipient rebelliousness. At one point the poet observes that, although ordered by his
lady not to write to her, if he were to do so it would only be to tell her that
he will comply with her command:

> pues si te escribo, es sólo por decirte
> que ella obedecerá cuanto quisieres,
> y no por ofenderte ni escribirte.
>
> (p. 133)

> since if I write to you it is only to tell you that it [my soul] will obey you in
> all that you would wish, and not to offend you nor to write to you.

The contradiction is perhaps only apparent. It seems likely that 'escribo'
in the first line has a literal meaning, while 'escribirte' in the third has the
same obscene association as it did in the anonymous poem, especially as it
is juxtaposed with the idea of giving offence. Indeed it could be argued
that these lines are *only* comprehensible if we are prepared to accept the
existence of two levels of meaning. It is not fanciful therefore to suggest

that a phrase at the end of the poem – 'Quédese, pues, aquí mi dolorosa / y baja pluma' ('So may my sorrowful and lowly pen remain here') – also has a secondary significance where 'pluma' is obviously a phallic symbol. Of course it would be absurd to read every line as an erotic code but there can be no doubt that words such as 'escribir' ('write') and 'pluma' ('pen') have the resonance of the *double entendre*, crucially because the poem so clearly articulates defiance and challenge. That it contains a secondary *intent* – the endeavour to overcome the obstacles of the lady's hostility – is beyond doubt.

The note of aggression that the poem embodies may seem surprising for a poetics based on the courtly love premiss of the superior lady and the unworthy suitor. The idealization of the woman in the courtly Petrarchan lyric, however, is as nothing when compared to the self-aggrandizement of the poet–lover. It is he who has the advantage of being the subject as opposed to the object, and as such in control of words and language. The ethos of Petrarchism was consonant with the anthropocentric vision of the Renaissance: man was at the centre of things – the legitimate focus of curiosity. The idealization of woman entailed not only stereotyping and a measure of dehumanization: it also implied disembodiment as in the portrait sonnet. In one important respect, then, the Petrarchan approach shares common ground with the pornographic imagination, and so we should not be surprised at how the author of a collection like the *Jardín de Venus* could simultaneously engage with idealization and indecency.

The survival of Petrarchism in form and ideology more or less down to the present day is a complex phenomenon and perhaps one that has not been adequately explained.[9] It would be glib to make the claim that is sometimes made for courtly love that it epitomizes some universal truth about the relationship of men and women, for it undoubtedly contains notions that have dated – that have become repellent or ludicrous. It is perhaps its idealizing tendency that is the key to its versatility and its success, albeit in a negative way. It invites contradiction and parody, as when Shakespeare begins a sonnet with the observation that his mistress's eyes are, after all, nothing like the sun, or when Quevedo mocks the idea of the sustained devotion enshrined in the anniversary sonnet, rudely distorting the magical ten years of acquaintanceship with Lisi in this cynical sonnet entitled 'A un hombre casado y pobre' ('To a married and poor man'):

> Diez años en su suegra estuvo preso,
> a doncella, y sin sueldo, condenado;
> padeció so el poder de su cuñado;
> tuvo un hijo no más, tonto y travieso.[10]

> For ten years he was imprisoned in his mother-in-law, condemned to a maidservant and without wages; he suffered under the power of his brother-in-law; he had just the one son, and he was a mischievous idiot.

One of the characteristics of Romanticism was a fascination with the Medieval world and chivalric ideas. It was not surprising therefore that the poets of the time should adopt, however superficially, the ethos and the phraseology of Petrarchism; it suited their lofty concept of poetry and fitted the image of woman as muse. Both these features are present in the works of Bécquer. His description of the ideal beloved in one of his *rimas* is firmly rooted in Petrarchan soil, in both its detail and its development:

> Es tu mejilla temprana
> rosa de escarcha cubierta,
> en que el carmín de los pétalos
> se ve al través de las perlas . . .
> Es tu boca de rubíes
> purpúrea granada abierta
> que en el estío convida
> a apagar la sed con ella . . .
> Es tu frente que corona
> crespo el oro en ancha trenza,
> nevada cumbre en que el día
> su postrera luz refleja.[11]

> Your cheek is the early rose covered in frost, where the carmine of the petals can be seen through the pearls . . . Your mouth is a purple pomegranate that has been opened to reveal rubies, that invites one in Summer to slake one's thirst in it . . . Your forehead, crowned in abundant tresses by curls of gold, is a snowy peak where the day reflects its fading light.

Perhaps his most famous poem is one whose attention to the details of the natural world and delicate realization of pathetic fallacy contribute to a piece that is the very epitome of Romantic poetry:

> Volverán las oscuras golondrinas
> en tu balcón sus nidos a colgar,
> y otra vez con el ala a sus cristales
> jugando llamarán.

> Pero aquéllas que el vuelo refrenaban
> tu hermosura y mi dicha a contemplar,
> aquéllas que aprendieron nuestros nombres . . .
> ésas . . . ¡no volverán!

> Volverán las tupidas madreselvas
> de tu jardín las tapias a escalar,
> y otra vez a la tarde aún más hermosas
> sus flores se abrirán.

> Pero aquellas cuajadas de rocío
> cuyas gotas mirábamos temblar

y caer como lágrimas del día . . .
ésas . . . ¡no volverán!

Volverán del amor en tus oídos
las palabras ardientes a sonar,
tu corazón de su profundo sueño
tal vez despertará.

Pero mudo y absorto y de rodillas
como se adora a Dios ante su altar,
como yo te he querido . . . desengáñate,
así . . . ¡no te querrán!   (p. 144)

The dark swallows will return to hang their nests on your balcony, and,
once more, as they play, to knock with their wings on the window-panes;
but those that stopped flying to contemplate your beauty and my joy,
those who learnt our names . . . they . . . will not return! The thick
honeysuckles of your garden will return to climb the walls, and once again
will open their flowers, even more beautifully, in the evening; but those
curdled with dew, whose drops we witnessed trembling and falling, like
day's tears . . . they . . . will not return! Passionate words of love will once
more sound in your ears; perhaps your heart will awake from its deep
sleep; but silent, rapt and kneeling, as one worships God before His altar,
as I have loved you . . . do not fool yourself: you will not be loved like
that!

This poem is far from being the sentimental fancy that it has popularly been
supposed to be. It is sinewy rather than sugary. It establishes a structural
symmetry in the first five stanzas through the alternation of 'volverán' and
'no volverán' at strategic points, only to destroy it in the final line where
in place of the the expected verb we have the emphatic 'no te querrán',
as though spat rather than spoken. The shift in the final stanza from the
intensity of love as devotion to the bitterness of love as jealousy is arrestingly
poignant.

Bécquer's ideal woman was more ethereal than anything envisaged by Renaissance Petrarchists. In his *rima* XI (previously considered in Chapter 2),
he rejects the physical manifestation – including the Petrarchist blonde
strereotype – in favour of something that is pure spirit:

–Yo soy un sueño, un imposible
vano fantasma de niebla y luz;
soy incorpórea, soy intangible:
no puedo amarte.
–¡Oh, ven; ven tú!   (p. 113)

'I am a dream, an impossible being, a vain phantasm of mist and light; I
am incorporeal, I am intangible: I cannot love you.' 'O come; do come!'

In some ways this poem is a *reductio ad absurdum* of the metaphysics of the absent and unattainable beloved. Compared to this, the first poem of Neruda's earliest collection, *Veinte poemas de amor y una canción desesperada* (*Twenty Love Poems and a Song of Despair*), seems like a hymn to the carnal presence and the imposing sexuality of Woman:

> Cuerpo de mujer, blancas colinas, muslos blancos,
> te pareces al mundo en tu actitud de entrega.
> Mi cuerpo de labriego salvaje te socava
> y hace saltar el hijo del fondo de la tierra.
>
> Fui solo como un túnel. De mí huian los pájaros
> y en mí la noche entraba su invasión poderosa.
> Para sobrevivirme te forjé como un arma,
> como una flecha en mi arco, como una piedra en mi honda.
>
> Pero cae la hora de la venganza, y te amo.
> Cuerpo de piel, de musgo, de leche ávida y firme.
> Ah los vasos del pecho! Ah los ojos de ausencia!
> Ah las rosas del pubis! Ah tu voz lenta y triste!
>
> Cuerpo de mujer mía, persistiré en tu gracia.
> Mi sed, mi ansia sin límite, mi camino indeciso!
> Oscuros cauces donde la sed eterna sigue,
> y la fatiga sigue, y el dolor infinito.[12]

> Body of woman, white hills, white thighs, you are like the world in your pose of surrender. My wild farmer body excavates you and makes the child jump from the depth of the earth. I was alone like a tunnel. The birds flew away from me, and night came into me in a powerful invasion. To survive I forged you like a weapon, like an arrow on my bow, like a stone in my sling. But the hour of vengeance arrives and I love you. Body of skin, moss, of avid, firm milk. Ah, the cups of the breast! Ah, the eyes of absence! Ah, the roses of the pubis! Ah, your slow, sad voice! Body of woman of mine, I shall persist in your gracefulness. My thirst, my limitless anxiety, my uncertain path! Dark channels where my eternal thirst flows, and my weariness follows, and infinite pain.

In several respects, however, this poem falls squarely within the tradition of male poets writing about women. The female addressee is passive whereas the poet–lover is creative, industrious according to the images in lines 3 and 7. Woman is conceived as the work of man, designed for his benefit. And even though the initial physical realization is enhanced by the sexual focus in the third stanza the close of the poem reverts to the melancholy egocentricity of Petrarchan poetry. This is not merely a matter of mood. It is conveyed by turns of phrase that could have been lifted directly from a poet such as Quevedo: 'mi ansia sin límite' ('my limitless anxiety'), 'mi camino indeciso' ('my uncertain path'), 'la sed eterna' ('eternal thirst'), 'el dolor infinito' ('infinite pain').

If, however, we imagine that Neruda's is the dominant voice in Spanish love poetry of his age and that the Romantic poet with his head in the clouds has been ousted by a new earthy directness, we would be mistaken. A decade after *Veinte poemas*, Pedro Salinas published *La voz a ti debida*, the title of which was discussed in Chapter 2 (see p. 46). In some places Salinas outdoes Bécquer, so incorporeal is his envisaging of the woman he seeks:

> Sí, por detrás de las gentes
> te busco.
> No en tu nombre, si lo dicen,
> no en tu imagen, si la pintan.
> Detrás, detrás, más allá.
>
> Por detrás de ti te busco.
> No en tu espejo, no en tu letra,
> ni en tu alma.
> Detrás, más allá.
>
> También detrás, más atrás
> de mí te busco. No eres
> lo que yo siento de ti . . .
>
> Por encontrarte, dejar
> de vivir en ti, y en mí,
> y en los otros.
> Vivir ya detrás de todo,
> al otro lado de todo,
> –por encontrarte–,
> como si fuese morir.[13]

> Yes, I seek you beyond people. Not in your name, if they say it, not in your image, if they paint it. Beyond, beyond, further away. I seek you beyond you. Not in your mirror, not in your handwriting, nor in your soul. Beyond, further away. I also seek you beyond, further away than me. You are not what I feel of you . . . To find you, I would cease to live in you, and in me, and in others. To live now beyond everything, on the other side of everything – to find you – as if it were to die.

The woman is beyond image, beyond name, beyond spirit and even beyond the impression the poet has of her. Here repetition, especially because of the plainness of the diction, is inflation: the quest for the ultimate in 'beyond-ness' appears forced when couched in such matter-of-fact terms. As a consequence the echoes of the poetry of San Juan de la Cruz at the end seem less an emotional *dénouement* and more a solution of how to follow the extreme of 'beyond-ness', that is through the invocation of the death-in-life/life-in-death paradox of the mystic.

Most commentators would undoubtedly be less churlish about such poetry and point with approval at the intertextual layers: the terminology of the mystics and the rational, abstract formulations of the *cancionero* poets. I, however, interpret the poem as a dead-end in the poeticization of Woman; I take the final simile at face value as an indication of the fate of such a metaphysics of love. Even in the hyper-ideal world of Salinas there is nothing more invisible than invisibility, and there is, after all, a final 'beyond'.

Posterity may well come to value a work like *La voz a ti debida*, however, precisely because of the moribund, end-of-the-line quality I see in it rather than because of the opposite view, whereby it allegedly revives (yet one more time!) the centuries-old tradition of male poets writing about female objects. For this poem by Salinas suggests that the courtly Petrarchan tradition is neither inexhaustible nor ahistorical. It clearly had a beginning and so perhaps it has an end. Even if this will appear too apocalyptic for some, it is evident that Spanish poetry since the mid twentieth century has shown signs of the abandonment or the renunciation of the tradition.

Significant in this shift in the ethos of love poetry has been the rise to prominence of women love poets. This is important of course as a reflection of social realities: the change in our perceptions of gender-roles. It is not, however, a matter merely of entering new territory; it is, radically, the clearance of space for that purpose. Women poets have by and large reacted critically and creatively to the formidable male legacy stretching from the Renaissance Petrarchists through Bécquer and the Romantics to Neruda and Salinas. In one way such a process echoes Harold Bloom's dictum about poems being about other poems; in another way the involvement of women poets does not square with his quasi-Oedipal theory of the struggle between a (male) poet and his father

In the following poem by Gioconda Belli the 'male gaze' is inverted: it is the man who is the object of wonder and contemplation. He has taken woman's place on the pedestal:

> Dios te hizo hombre para mí.
>
> Te admiro desde lo más profundo
> de mi subconsciente,
> con una admiración extraña y desbordada
> que tiene un dobladillo de ternura.
>
> Tus problemas, tus cosas
> me intrigan, me interesan
> y te observo
> mientras discurres y discutes

> hablando del mundo
> y dándole una nueva geografía de palabras.[14]

> God made you man for me. I admire you from the the depths of my
> subconscious, with a strange and overflowing admiration which has a hem
> of tenderness. Your problems, your things intrigue and interest me, and I
> observe you when you ponder and discuss, talking of the world and giving
> it a new geography of words.

The poem's title – 'De la mujer al hombre' ('From woman to man') –
implies the reversal of the conventional amatory trajectory. Here woman is
the origin and creator, man the destination and repository. The opening line
enhances the subversive effect by re-writing the Genesis myth of the creation
of woman from man. Gender stereotyping is also inverted in the mockingly
dismissive reference to men's 'problems' and 'things'; man is here portrayed
as the source of a detached interest on the part of the poet. The final line
from the part of the poem that has been quoted provides an equivalent of
the kind of hyperbole indulged in by male poets when they refer to how
the beloved adds a new dimension to reality. In short, the poem comes over
as a riposte to such statements of male control and whim as we find at the
very opening of *La voz a ti debida*:

> Tú vives siempre en tus actos.
> Con la punta de tus dedos
> pulsas el mundo, le arrancas
> auroras, triunfos, colores,
> alegrías; es tu música.
> La vida es lo que tú tocas.[15]

> You always live in your activities. With the tip of your fingers you pluck
> the strings of the world, you draw from it dawns, triumphs, colours, joys;
> it is your music. Life is what you touch.

There is, however, a certain tension in Belli's poetry between a clear-cut
disassociation from the ethos of male poets writing about women and a
willingness seemingly to yield to the detail of its associated rhetoric. I say
'seemingly' because there are ambivalences. In the first line of another of
her poems there is a clear reminiscence of the opening line of the poem we
have just examined:

> Y Dios me hizo mujer,
> de pelo largo,
> ojos,
> nariz y boca de mujer.
> Con curvas
> y pliegues
> y suaves hondonadas.[16]

> And God made me woman, with long hair, eyes, nose and mouth of a
> woman. With curves and folds and smooth hollows.

This reads like a latter-day version of the Petrarchist portrait, but there is one
crucial difference, which is that of the speaking voice. This is a female self-
representation, and the resemblance in detail to the male–centred conception
of woman counts for less than the control of the text. Thus the conclusion
is as resonantly egocentric for the woman's cause as a Renaissance love
poem would be for the man's: 'me levanto orgullosa / todas las mañanas / y
bendigo mi sexo' ('I get up proudly every morning and I bless my sex').

Even more energetic than Belli in her undermining of the rhetoric and
conventions of masculine love poetry is Ana Rossetti. Part of her success
resides in her sheer ability to shock: she evidently relishes ignoring the
etiquette and coyness of the standard male poetic discourse. Consider, for
instance, the opening lines of a poem entitled 'París' which, despite the
suggestion that it may refer to the city because of the reference to an avenue
in the first line, turns out to be an allusion to the god of that name and
his judgement of the beauty of the three goddesses. The focus in Rossetti's
poem, however, is not upon the three female contestants in the legendary
beauty contest but on the judge himself, who, in an unexpected *volte face*, is
subjected to a detailed and highly sexualized portrait. The recondite vocabulary, including architectural terms, and the flexible syntax, however, make
this poetry as mannered as many a Renaissance poem:

> Dime, en dónde, en qué avenida tus pies,
> por dónde el rastro, en qué sendero.
> Tus piernas, esas cintas que el vello deshilacha
> y en la ojiva, el pubis, manojo de tu vientre,
> la dovela.
> Crece en tu torno el gladiolo,
> llave anal, violador perenne,
> y tres diosas
> quieren morder contigo la manzana.[17]

> Tell me where, in which avenue are your feet, where is the trail, in which
> path. Your legs, those ribbons that the hairs fray and in the pointed arch,
> the pubis, your belly's bundle, the voussoir. The gladiolus grows around
> you, anal key, perennial violator, and three goddesses want to bite the
> apple with you.

Despite this utilization of an elevated style, Rossetti's poetry, like that of
Belli, frequently emerges as a counter-text to the amatory verse written by
men about women. Indeed, far more than in the case of the Nicaraguan poet,
Rossetti's texts engage in a trenchant discussion with those of Renaissance
poets. This is most obvious in her choice of language: a diction that is

artificial and pompous – a cross between the Latinism of Góngora and the recondite terminology of Rubén Darío. This is evident in the opening of a poem whose title – 'Cierta secta feminista se da consejos prematrimoniales' ('A certain feminist sect gives itself prematrimonial advice') – smacks, like many of Rossetti's, of the extravagant fussiness of baroque poetry, rather like the titles that Quevedo's first editor, González de Salas, was to supply for his poetry. The opening subjunctives echo the famous injunction of the Latin drinking-song, 'Gaudeamus igitur juvenes dum sumus':

> Y besémonos, bellas vírgenes, besémonos.
> Démonos prisa desvalijándonos
> destruyendo el botín de nuestros cuerpos.
> Al enemigo percibo respirar tras el muro,
> la codicia se yergue entre sus piernas.
>
> Y besémonos, bellas vírgenes, besémonos.
> No deis pródigamente a la espada,
> oh viril fortuna, el inviolado himen.
> Que la grieta, en el blanco ariete
> de nuestras manos, pierda su angostura.
>
> (p. 36)

So let's kiss each other, pretty virgins, let's kiss each other. Let us make haste and ransack ourselves, destroying the booty of our bodies. I sense the enemy is breathing behind the wall, and his greed is rising up between his legs. And let us kiss each other, pretty virgins, let us kiss each other. Do not wastefully give to the sword, o virile fortune, your unviolated hymen. Let the crack lose its tightness through the white battering-ram of our hands.

This is extraordinary not only because of the frankness of its subject, touching on lesbianism and masturbation. Rossetti also usurps the Medieval metaphor of love as war and converts it into a feminist weapon. Perhaps the most remarkable feature, though, is the energy and conviction of the speaking voice – a world away both from the feigned humility of the courtly Petrarchan lover and from the schoolboy smut of Renaissance erotica.

Rossetti's re-writing, however, involves more than the appropriation of the language of men's love poetry. It is again a matter of inversion and parody, as when in another poem she envisages the man's body in terms of flowers. She apes not only the detail but also the lubricious approach and the tendency of Petrarchists to fragmentation of the body when they focus on separate attributes:

> Flores, pedazos de tu cuerpo;
> me reclamo su savia.
> Aprieto entre mis labios

la lacerante verga del gladiolo.
Cosería limones a tu torso,
sus durísimas puntas en mis dedos
como altos pezones de muchacha . . .
En mis muslos contengo los pétalos mojados
de las flores. Son flores pedazos de tu cuerpo.

(p. 22)

Flowers, pieces of your body; I claim their sap for myself. I squeeze
between my lips the cutting rod of the gladiolus. I would sew lemons onto
your torso, their rock-hard tips in my fingers like the raised nipples of a
girl . . . In my thighs I hold the wet petals of flowers. Pieces of your body
are flowers.

Where male love poetry, however, sharply differentiates between the sexes,
Rossetti is content to ascribe to her male object female attributes – 'pezones
de muchacha' ('nipples of a girl'). And whereas the male approach is above
all visually oriented – a kind of restrained voyeurism – Rossetti's depiction
involves the other senses – touch, taste and smell – in a heady celebration
of carnal indulgence that includes not only a graphic description of oral sex
but the use of a vulgar colloquialism for penis ('verga').

Masculine love poetry commonly portrays the woman as pure and innocent; such a perception is as evident in the popular tradition, represented
by the *pastorelas* or *serranillas* (see Chapter 5), as in the Petrarchan ideal. The
dichotomy of the knowing, controlling male and the vulnerable, exposed
female is brilliantly reversed in Rossetti's 'A un joven con abanico' ('To a
youth with a fan'). The title does not so much imply an effeminate youth
or one of ambivalent sexuality as a male object who is supplied with a conventional object of femininity – the fan – as though to underline the role
reversal that the poem will articulate:

Y qué encantadora es tu inexperiencia.
Tu mano torpe, fiel perseguidora
de una quemante gracia que adivinas
en el vaivén penoso del alegre antebrazo.
Alguien cose en tu sangre lentejuelas
para que atravieses
los redondos umbrales del placer
y ensayas a la vez desdén y seducción . . .
Y mientras, adorable
y peligrosamente, te desvías.   (p. 49)

And how charming is your inexperience. Your clumsy hand, faithful
pursuer of a burning gracefulness that you imagine in the embarrassing
toing and froing of the joyous forearm. Someone sews sequins in your
blood so that you can cross the round thresholds of pleasure and you try

out scorn and seduction at the same time . . . And meanwhile, adorably
and dangerously, you shy away.

If such poems were to be merely inversions of the male–female relationship,
and relied in the main on shock effects they would soon pall. Rossetti, however, is wickedly inventive. The mocking tone of the opening is a distinctive
touch, so alien to the predominantly rapt but respectful contemplation of
the male poet. Notable too is the concluding sentence that describes the
youth's awkwardness in terms that would once have been used for the elusive
Petrarchan lady – 'te desvías' ('you shy away') – though, characteristically,
Rossetti adds a patronizing sting in the adverb 'adorable[mente]' ('adorably').

Rossetti's poetry is, above all, extraordinarily vehement. Its explicitness is
readily experienced but what an awareness of the pre-history of male poetry
helps us to savour is its anger. It is as though she feels compelled to avenge
poetic lies and injustices, and to right a poetic imbalance:

> Es tan adorable introducirme
> en su lecho, y que mi mano viajera
> descanse, entre sus piernas, descuidada,
> y al desenvainar la columna tersa . . .
> presenciar la inesperada expresión
> de su anatomía que no sabe usar
> aún . . .
> . . .
> . . . Es adorable pervertir
> a un muchacho, extraerle del vientre
> virginal esa rugiente ternura
> tan parecida al estertor final
> de un agonizante, que es imposible
> no irlo matando mientras eyacula.
>
> (p. 32)

> It is so adorable for me to gain access to his bed, and for my wandering
> hand to rest casually, between his legs, and when it unsheathes the smooth
> column . . . to witness the unexpected reaction of his anatomy which as yet
> he does not know how to use . . . It is adorable to pervert a a boy, to draw
> out of his virginal belly that roaring tenderness so like the rattle of the
> dying that it is impossible not to continue killing him as he ejaculates.

There is a positive relish here in the corruption of a male virgin that constitutes more than a mere inversion of the *carpe diem* approach, while the
concluding metaphor of orgasm as death, that figured in Renaissance love
poetry, is the culmination of what has been nothing less than a female sexual
assault.

Rossetti also strays from the conventions of masculine love poetry by her
references to homosexuality, male as well as female. The subject has been

by no means uncommon or disguised in Spanish poetry since the death of
Franco, and is most conspicuous in the work of Luis Antonio de Villena
(1951–), one of the most flamboyant and colourful figures in Spanish
cultural life of recent years. Villena's poetry is far more than an assertion of
sexuality, which would have been merely to kick at an open door. As Chris
Perriam has shown, it involves issues of life-style and culture, as in a poem set
in Verona with its 'thorough-going, joyful disruption of any merely solemn
faith in old cultural values':[18]

> La noche cayó sobre una estatua del Dante
> entre un aire suave y los trinos de Verdi o Donizetti . . .
> . . .
> la efigie del poeta bajo la inmensa luna,
> los arcos, las *loggie*, las arias y su melodrama.
> Y aquellos muchachos que querían llevarnos a un concierto
> de *rock* . . .
> Yo pensaba que el Amor vendría a asaltarme
> en una esquina
> . . .
> Aquel Amor con la melena larga y camiseta Wrangler.[19]

> Night fell on a statue of Dante, between a gentle breeze and the trills of
> Verdi or Donizetti . . . the effigy of the poet under the immense moon, the
> arches, the loggias, the arias and their melodrama. And those boys who
> wanted to take us to a rock concert . . . I thought that Love would come to
> assault me on a street corner . . . That Cupid with his long hair and
> Wrangler tee-shirt.

Before the twentieth century, however, the portrayal of homosexuality
was as much a rarity poetically as it was a taboo socially. It would, however,
be simplistic to relate the two aspects in terms of cause and effect. As we have
seen in the work of such poets as Neruda and Rossetti the inescapable point
of reference is literary; it is what could be termed the courtly Petrarchist
consensus that sets the agenda, however much questioning and challenge
there may be. A particular danger in approaching a homosexual poet is
over-interpretation: reading in a layer of meaning by the identification of
supposedly distinctive homosexual images or symbols. This is a critical deficiency to which modern poets are particularly subject. Nobody would contemplate such an approach to a seventeenth-century poet like Villamediana,
who was either homosexual or bisexual. If he had been writing in our
times, however, it could be imagined that lines such as the following from
two of his sonnets would be understood as an indication of a forbidden
sexuality:

> ¡Oh cuánto dice en su favor quien calla,
> porque, de amar, sufrir es cierto indicio,

y el silencio el más puro sacrificio
y adonde siempre Amor mérito halla![20]

O, how much he says in his own favour he who is silent, because to suffer
is a sure sign of loving, and silence the purest sacrifice wherein Love
always finds merit.

Sufrir quiero y callar; mas si algún día
los ojos descubrieren lo que siento,
no castiguéis en mí su atrevimiento,
que lo que mueve Amor no es culpa mía.

(p. 100)

I wish to keep silent and to suffer, but if one day my eyes were to reveal
what I feel, do not punish me for my daring, for what Love provokes is
not a fault of mine.

The secrecy of love and the dangers and daring associated with it, however,
are conventions of courtly poetry and readily accepted as such. It has been
very different, however, for a poet such as Lorca, whose work has encouraged
intensive searches for homosexual textual traits, whether in individual images
or in the subject-matter of those poems that have a narrative element. This
is not to say that his poetry would have been the same had he not been
a homosexual. It is to suggest, however, that his points of reference are
above all with other poets, whether heterosexual or homosexual or, for
that matter, male or female. To deny him this priority is to diminish the
poetry to no more than a reflection, however oblique, of the life. In such a
critical pursuit, understanding will be stunted – confined principally to an
appropriately homosexual decoding of phrase and image.

Thus our appreciation of a poem like 'Arbolé, arbolé' considered in the
last chapter (p. 114) is enhanced by our knowledge that it follows in
the tradition of encounter poems. It may be that the negative and melancholy rendering of the subject is consistent with a homosexual viewpoint
but there is an evident danger in making such assertions as 'Lorca set out
to describe the plight of the homosexual' because it assumes what is unknown and irrelevant: the poet's intention when he wrote. In any case it
is not necessary to be either a woman or a homosexual to re-write traditional forms or subjects. Modern poets are not so different from their
predecessors in this regard even though their methods may differ. Just as
Rossetti and Lorca react creatively to well-established poetic conventions,
so too does Gil de Biedma in a poem entitled 'Albada', which is a modern
dawn-song:

Despiértate. La cama está fría
y las sábanas sucias en el suelo.

Por los montantes de la galería
    llega el amanecer,
con su color de abrigo de entretiempo
    y liga de mujer.

Despiértate pensando vagamente
que el portero de noche os ha llamado.
Y escucha en el silencio: sucediéndose
hacia lo lejos, se oyen enronquecer
los tranvías que llevan al trabajo.
    Es el amanecer.

Irán amontonándose las flores
cortadas, en los puestos de las Ramblas,
y silbarán los pájaros – cabrones –
desde los plátanos, mientras que ven volver
la negra humanidad que va a la cama
    después de amanecer.[21]

Awake. The bed is cold and the dirty sheets are on the floor. Through the
fan-lights of the balconies dawn arrives, with its colour of a lightweight
coat and a woman's garter. Awake, vaguely thinking that the night porter
has called you. And listen in the silence: the trams creaking hoarsely as
they follow each other into the distance taking people to work. It is
daybreak. The cut flowers will be piled up in heaps on the stalls in the
Ramblas, and the blasted birds will whistle from the plane trees, while
there can be seen the return of the dark humanity that goes to bed after
dawn.

This is a model of how a traditional form may be updated. Metrically, in
its mix of hendecasyllabic and heptasyllabic lines it is Spanish Renaissance
rather than Medieval poetry that is evoked. There is a flirtation with rhyme
rather than a fixed scheme. The repeated allusions to dawn and waking
echo the sadness of lovers parting at dawn in the traditional *alba*; when the
poet curses the birds he mimics the dejection of his Medieval predecessor.
Unlike the original form, however, which is invariably located in a rural
setting, Gil de Biedma's is set in a modern city with its trams, its night-
workers returning home, and the flower-sellers setting up their stalls for the
new day in one of the busiest streets in Barcelona. It is thus a poem that
suggests a double source of familiarity: identifiable terms of reference and a
recognizable genre.

    For an example of a modern love poem, however, that transcends its
model and genuinely enhances the form there can be few better than an
alba by Claudio Rodríguez (1934–99), a poem entitled 'Sin leyes' ('Without
laws'). It serves to remind us that imitation, as we saw in Chapter 3, can be
emulation, for the concluding lines of this poem, describing the lovers lying

together as dawn breaks, have a concentrated pathos that the early lyric –
the *poesía de tipo tradicional* – can only suggest:

> Como una guerra sin
> héroes, como una paz sin alianzas,
> ha pasado la noche. Y yo te amo.
> Busco despojos, busco una medalla
> rota, un trofeo vivo de este tiempo
> que nos quieren robar. Estás cansada
> y yo te amo. Es la hora. ¿Nuestra carne
> será la recompensa, la metralla
> que justifique tanta lucha pura
> sin vencedores ni vencidos? Calla,
> que yo te amo. Es la hora. Entra ya un trémulo
> albor. Nunca la luz fue tan temprana.[22]

> Night has gone like a war without heroes, like a peace without alliances.
> And I love you. I look for spoils, I look for a broken medal, a live trophy of
> this time that they want to steal from us. You are tired and I love you. It is
> time. Will our flesh be the compensation, the shrapnel that justifies so
> much sheer struggle with neither victors nor vanquished? Be quiet, for I
> love you. It is time. Now a tremulous dawn enters. Never was light so
> early.

It is a serious and tender poem: the development of the military metaphor,
common in the courtly lyric, is not as inappropriate as it seems. Its combination with the brief declarations of love creates an effect that is unsettling
and poignant. Moreover, the repeated invocations of the *alba* – 'es la hora'
('it is time') – and the gentle exasperation of the final phrase convey both the
precariousness of passion and how valuable it is in its very precariousness.
The poem emerges as a confirmation and consolidation of the genre; it is
entirely apt that Rodríguez should have cited an anonymous Medieval *alba*
as an epigraph: 'Ya cantan los gallos, / amor mío. Vete: / cata que amanece'
('Now the cocks crow, my love. Go away: take heed that it is dawn').

Chapter 7

Religious and moral poetry

The poem in which the following lines appear has sometimes been referred to as one of the most erotic in Spanish:

> ¡O noche que guiaste!,
> ¡o noche, amable más que el aluorada!,
> ¡o noche que juntaste
> Amado con amada,
> amada en el Amado transformada!
>
> En mi pecho florido,
> que entero para él solo se guardaua,
> allí quedó dormido,
> y yo le regalaua,
> y el ventalle de cedros ayre daua.
>
> El ayre de la almena,
> quando yo sus cabellos esparcía,
> con su mano serena
> en mi cuello hería,
> y todos mis sentidos suspendía.
>
> Quedéme y olvidéme,
> el rostro recliné sobre el Amado;
> cesó todo y dejéme,
> dejando mi cuidado
> entre las açucenas olvidado.[1]

Oh, night that guided, night more delightful than the dawn; oh night that joined Lover with beloved, the beloved transformed into the Lover! In my flowering breast, that kept itself intact for him alone, there he stayed asleep as I regaled him, and the cedars were a fan that made a breeze. The breeze came from the battlements when I stroked his hair, and he wounded my neck with his calming hand, causing all my senses to be suspended. I stayed still and forgot myself, I laid my face upon my Lover, everything stopped and I abandoned myself, leaving my cares forgotten among the lilies.

Yet it found no place in the previous chapter because it does not fall into that area of experience that we commonly understand as material for a

155

love poem. These last four stanzas of San Juan de la Cruz's 'Noche oscura' ('Dark night') refer to the experience of a mystic. Indeed the title is only a convenient shorthand mode of reference that picks up a phrase from the first line of the poem:

> En una noche oscura,
> con ansias, en amores inflamada,
> ¡o dichosa uentura!,
> salí sin ser notada,
> estando ya mi casa sosegada.

> In a dark night with my desires inflamed by love, oh happy fortune! I went out unnoticed as my house was now at peace.

The full title – long as it is – accurately describes the nature of the experience: 'Canciones del alma que se goza en auer llegado al estado de la perfección, que es la unión con Dios, por el camino de la negación espiritual' ('Verses of the soul that takes delight in having reached the state of perfection, that is the union with God, along the path of spiritual negation'). The union that is represented so unmistakably in the ecstatic stammering of the first of the four stanzas quoted previously – the fifth of the poem – is that of the soul and God. The former is envisaged as a lovesick girl leaving her house in the dead of night to meet her lover, who is God. Even a recognition of the coded significance, however, does not entirely prepare us for the sheer sensuousness and abandon of the poem's conclusion, for the afterglow of the union is conceived in terms of physicality as well as luminosity. As it sought God the soul was enveloped in a necessary darkness – the emptiness (to change metaphor) that precedes and is required by fulfilment. In another poem San Juan refers to dark caverns being suffused by light and heat. What is notable here, however, is the detail and delicacy: the exchange of caresses in the wake of the love-making, the bliss of stasis and oblivion.

Only in the most partial reading, though, could this be taken for a love poem. To do so would be to ignore not only such obvious clues as the title but also a long tradition of biblical and religious interpretation. The principal source of San Juan's poetry is the *Song of Solomon* (or *Song of Songs*), a collection of Jewish love songs attributed to King Solomon, son of King David. The 'Song' was believed to refer either to his marriage to the daughter of the Pharaoh or to his fabled meeting with the Queen of Sheba. For most of its existence, however, the collection has been understood metaphorically. For Jewish commentators the woman was Israel, while subsequent Christian readings have variously identified the Bride as the embattled Christian Church and, as with San Juan, the individual human soul in search of divine love.

It is not only mystical poets such as San Juan, however, who engage in the interchange of the concepts and images of the sacred and the secular. In the courtly love tradition the extremes of both praise and lament led poets into blasphemy. Thus the beloved could be envisaged as God, the source of all that was good and beautiful; and obtaining a favourable response from her could transport the lover from the hell of unrequited love to the heaven of whatever amatory indulgence she might permit him. By a reverse process the religious poet setting out to write in praise of the Virgin would avail himself of the attitudes and terminology of the courtly love poet addressing the superior lady, laying stress on her virtues and ability to inspire and ennoble him. The most celebrated instance of such an application of the courtly to the religious in Peninsular poetry is Alfonso X's prologue to his *Cantigas de Santa Maria*, written in Galician-Portuguese.

Berceo's *Milagros de Nuestra Señora*, written a little earlier than the Alfonsine collection, opens with an Introduction the source of which has not been found. Presumably, it would have been a Latin prose text, as for the miracle-stories themselves. The main purpose of the Introduction is to outline the many qualities of the Virgin. This is partly achieved by straightforward metaphor; thus she is a star, a queen, a temple, a good neighbour, a medicine and so on. The predominant method of description in the Introduction, however, is allegory. An allegory is a narrative or story with a secondary meaning; it is a development of metaphor insofar as it comprises a set of connected images for which there are similarly constructed referents. It is perhaps used mainly for didactic religious purposes, but it would be as much an error to believe that it was consequently easy to follow as it would be to think that symbolism has to be difficult or complex. In the Introduction to the *Milagros*, for instance, we discover eventually that the idyllic meadow into which the weary poet-persona has strayed is an image of the Virgin. Berceo self-consciously points to the solution of the riddle:

> Sennores e amigos,   lo que dicho avemos
> palavra es oscura,   esponerla queremos:
> tolgamos la corteza,   al meollo entremos,
> prendamos lo de dentro,   lo de fuera dessemos.[2]

> Good people and friends, what we have said is obscure and so we wish to clarify it: let us take away the shell and get to the heart of it, let us take what is within and abandon what is on the outside.

It is not exaggerating to think of the process in terms of a puzzle, as the significance of the allegory is by no means obvious – not as clear-cut as, say, the best-known allegory in English literature, Bunyan's *Pilgrim's Progress*. Initially we might have assumed that Berceo's meadow was a representation of heaven, conceived as it was as a *locus amoenus* or 'pleasance' with religious overtones. Stanza 14 is therefore misleading:

Semeja esti prado   egual de paraíso,
en qui Dios tan grand graçia tan grand bendiçión miso;
él que crió tal cosa   maestro fue anviso:
omne que ý morasse   nunque perdríe el viso.

This meadow seems identical to Paradise wherein God placed such grace and blessing; he who created such a thing was a wise master: he who would dwell there would never lose his sight.

Berceo's practice – or perhaps that of the author of the lost source of the Introduction – appears subtle when set alongside other religious allegories. Poets of the late sixteenth and early seventeenth centuries were especially alert to the educational power of allegorical verse. Indeed San Juan himself supplied commentaries on his major poems in order that the Carmelite nuns might derive illumination from his work. His method was reductive and limiting: forcing a single meaning on symbols of considerable potency, and applying a mechanistic logic by isolating words and explaining their significance as though they were part of a minutely detailed allegory. Thus he 'explains' a simple expression of not succumbing to temptation, conveyed clearly in a line of verse as 'ni cogeré las flores' ('I shall not pick the flowers'), in the following terms:

todos los gustos y contentamientos y deleites que se le pueden ofrecer en esta vida que le podrían impedir el camino si cogerlos y admitirlos quisiese, los cuales son en tres maneras: temporales, sensuales y espirituales

all the pleasures and joys and delights which can be offered to him in this life, which could block his way if he were to wish to gather and keep them, and which are of three kinds: temporal, sensual and spiritual.

Such a heavy-handed treatment, with its stress on lists of three in the didactic manner of the theologian, does no favours either to the poetry or to the reader, and it is perhaps significant that in his commentaries San Juan refers to himself in the third person, not the first, as though to underline the distance between the inspiration of the poem and the dry-as-dust exegesis.

The instructive element implicit in such an approach dominates the religious art of the period in which San Juan wrote as it was compatible with the ethos of Counter Reformation Spain. It became even more important with the intervention of the Jesuits in Spanish education and literature. In the work of religious poets such as José de Valdivielso (1560–1638) and, more especially, Alonso de Ledesma (1562–1633), allegory becomes a vital tool for explaining the facts and mysteries of the Gospels and the Sacraments in everyday terms. To this end secular material was appropriated for doctrinal purposes with greater enthusiasm than ever. The outcome was frequently coarse; one commentator refers to Ledesma's 'barbarous imagination' and cites the following passage as an instance of how distasteful his allegorical realizations might seem to a modern sensibility. The conception of Christ is envisaged in terms of a king entering a hermitage called Santa María:

> Viene por cumplir un voto
> que prometido tenía,
> estando Adán a la muerte
> de achaque de una comida.
> No es voto de nueve horas,
> ni aun de solos nueve días,
> que nueve meses estuvo
> sin salir de la capilla.[3]

> He comes to fulfil a vow that he had promised, when Adam had died from the affliction of what had been eaten. This was not a nine-hour vigil, nor one of nine days, because he did not go out of the chapel for nine months.

Just as shocking in its familiarity is the depiction of Christ's transfiguration and death through the allegory of an 'indiano', that is a Spaniard who emigrated to the New World, made his fortune and then returned home. At the opening there is a pun on 'Santa María', which is both the name of the Virgin and that of the Spanish port – Puerto de Santa María – to which the 'indiano' returned:

> Aquel perulero rico,
> que para nuestro remedio
> dessembarco en las Indias
> en santa María del puerto.[4]

> That rich man, returning from Peru, who to redeem us, disembarked from the Indies in the port of Santa María.

What may also appear grotesque about Ledesma's work is the sheer profusion of analogies; the birth of Christ is compared, among other things, to a process of debt, a disguised suitor, imprisonment, a knife-fight, a father threatening his son, and a garment cut to another's measurement.

Ledesma is not, however, representative of the poetry of Counter Reformation Spain. His work is only one thread in a rich tapestry, albeit one that is luridly popularizing. If we fail to look beyond him then indeed we might conclude that the Counter Reformation was no more than a reactionary movement that re-asserted Medieval values in the face of the religious Reformation of the sixteenth century. At worse it would conform to Protestant stereotyping and bear out what Johan Huizinga, in a celebrated study, saw as a characteristic of spiritual life at the end of the Middle Ages: the reduction of all that was meant to stimulate spiritual consciousness to an 'appalling commonplace profanity, to a startling worldliness in other-worldly guise'.[5]

Crucial in the revivification in Spain of the traditional culture of Christendom were the Jesuits. The Society of Jesus, founded by St Ignatius Loyola, set great store by education, and many of the finest writers of the Golden Age – Cervantes, Lope de Vega, Quevedo – were educated by them. The most identifiable contribution of the Jesuits to Spanish poetry comes from the *Spiritual Exercises* of St Ignatius. In the exercises the meditator begins by visualizing clearly the subject of his meditation, what is sometimes referred to as the 'composition of place'. Next he applies the 'three powers of the soul' – memory, understanding and will – to the features chosen for meditation. The process ends with a colloquy addressed to God or Christ or the Virgin, often of a familiar or informal nature.

Rather than adhering fully to such a scheme many poems of Counter Reformation Spain betray symptoms of it. The most important aspects are the visualization of a sacred scene and the colloquy. In the following anonymous sonnet both features are prominent:

> No me mueve, mi Dios, para quererte,
> el cielo que me tienes prometido,
> ni me mueve el infierno tan temido
> para dejar por eso de ofenderte.
>
> Tú me mueves, Señor; muévenme el verte
> clavado en esa cruz, y escarnecido;
> muévenme el ver tu cuerpo tan herido,
> muévenme tus afrentas, y tu muerte.
>
> Muéveme, al fin, tu amor, y en tal manera,
> que aunque no hubiera cielo, yo te amara,
> y aunque no hubiera infierno te temiera.
>
> No me tienes que dar porque te quiera;
> pues aunque lo que espero no esperara,
> lo mismo que te quiero te quisiera.[6]

> It is not the heaven that You have promised me that moves me, my God, to love You, nor is it fearsome hell that moves me to cease offending You. It is You who move me, Lord; to see You nailed to that Cross and despised moves me; seeing Your body so wounded moves me, as too the insults You suffered and Your death. Your love, finally, moves me, and in such a way that even if there were no heaven I would love You and even if there were no hell I would fear You. You need not give me anything to make me love You; for even if I did not hope for what I do, I would love You just as I do.

The colloquy is there from the start, preceding the brief but intense visualization: the description of Christ on the Cross in the second quatrain. The poem has a directness enhanced by the arresting opening with its negative that immediately wrong-foots the reader: we wonder what kind of claim it will make about the nature of faith. Not the least of its achievements is to have adapted the stylistic features of *cancionero* verse – anaphora and polyptoton – to a speaking voice that blends a simple logic with a fervent conviction. A similarly blunt but more tender realization of aspects of the Ignatian scheme is evident in one of Lope de Vega's *Rimas sacras*. In the opening quatrain the visualization of the scene of the Crucifixion is combined with a trait that relates to the practice of typology, a mode of biblical scholarship that searches for the prefiguration of events in the life of Christ in the Old Testament, whereby, for example, the wood in the tree in the Garden of Eden presages (or even *is*) the wood that went into the making of the Cross. In Lope's sonnet, the poet addressing Christ in the colloquy observes how the wood of the Cross is used to make the staff of the Good Shepherd:

> Pastor que con tus silbos amorosos
> me despertaste del profundo sueño:
> tú, que hiciste cayado de ese leño
> en que tiendes los brazos poderosos.[7]

> Shepherd, who with your lover's whistles awoke me from my deep sleep: you who made a crook out of this wood on which you stretch your powerful arms.

The tendency to familiarity that leads to the bizarre extravagance of some of Ledesma's analogies emerges in the conclusion of the Lope sonnet as a graphic reminder of the suffering of Christ. It will be for individual tastes to determine whether this is shockingly trivial or touchingly devout:

> Espera, pues, y escucha mis cuidados...
> Pero ¿cómo te digo que me esperes
> si estás para esperar los pies clavados?

> Wait, then and listen to my worries... But, why do I need to tell you to wait for me if your nailed feet make you wait?

This kind of direct approach is certainly disconcerting in its uncompromising candour, akin to the portraits of saints by El Greco. As I have already indicated, however, the religious poetry of the Golden Age is richly varied, and lines like the following by Luis de León relate to another strand, philosophic in origin:

> Ve cómo el gran maestro,
> aquesta inmensa cítara aplicado,
> con movimiento diestro
> produce el son sagrado,

con que este eterno templo es sustentado.
   Y, como está compuesta
de números concordes, luego envía
consonante respuesta;
y entrambas a porfía
mezclan una dulcísima armonía.[8]

It sees how the great master, playing that immense zither, with skilled movement, produces the sacred sound by which this eternal temple is supported. And as it is composed of a concord of numbers, it sends forth a matching response; and the two vying with each other yield the sweetest harmony.

This extract from 'A Francisco Salinas' is a succinct version of the Aristotelian or pre-Copernican world-picture: a cosmogonic theory that postulates that the earth, not the sun, is at the centre of the universe. According to this long-established theory, unanimously accepted up to the sixteenth century, the planets and stars that move around the earth each emit a different musical note; these notes harmonize with each other to produce the music of the spheres. Luis de León's poem is largely a metaphor of this notion: a description of how hearing his friend, the blind musician Francisco Salinas, playing the organ reminds him of the heavenly music. Thus 'el... maestro' is an image of God controlling the universe.

   The opening of the poem alludes to another philosophical idea:

   El aire se serena
y viste de hermosura y luz no usada,
Salinas, cuando suena
la música extremada,
por vuestra sabia mano gobernada.
   A cuyo son divino
mi alma, que en olvido está sumida,
torna a cobrar el tino
y memoria perdida
de su origen primera esclarecida.
   Y como se conoce,
en suerte y pensamientos se mejora;
el oro desconoce,
que el vulgo ciego adora,
la belleza caduca, engañadora.

The air becomes calm and is clothed in beauty and unused light, Salinas, at the sound of the consummate music produced by your skilled hand. At this divine sound, my soul, which is sunk in oblivion, recovers its senses and the memory of its illustrious prime origin that it had lost. And as it gets to know itself, it improves in fate and thoughts; it ceases to recognize the gold that the blind mob adores, a perishable and deceptive beauty.

The idea that the soul is oblivious of its heavenly origin is one that dates back to pre-Socratic philosophy. These lines reveal how in Platonism and Neoplatonism – a later refinement of Platonism – Renaissance humanists encountered a non-Christian spiritual tradition that in its ethical and spiritual dimension was akin to Christianity itself. The emphasis on higher spiritual values at the expense of base material ones – in effect the dichotomy of body and soul – is a central tenet of Christianity.

That Luis de León should have represented inferior values in terms of gold had an added significance at the time he wrote. Classical moralists such as Horace, a favourite poet of Luis de León, had written of the folly of men who in pursuit of wealth would risk their lives by crossing dangerous seas. Such a topos had a striking relevance for the sixteenth-century Spaniard with the discovery and colonization of the Americas, which held the potential of untold wealth for the adventurer. The theme of the danger of surrendering to material instincts is present in another of Luis de León's poems, 'Vida retirada', previously mentioned in Chapter 1 (see p. 33):

> Ténganse su tesoro
> los que de un flaco leño se confían;
> no es mío ver el lloro
> de los que desconfían,
> cuando el cierzo y el ábrego porfían.
>   La combatida antena
> cruje, y en ciega noche el claro día
> se torna; al cielo suena
> confusa vocería,
> y la mar enriquecen a porfía.[9]

Let those who entrust themselves to a fragile bark have their treasure; it is not for me to witness the weeping of those who lose their certainty when the north wind blows against the south. The stricken mast creaks, and bright day becomes blind night; the confused cries resound to heaven, and they vie with each other to make the sea rich.

The topic of the foolish gold-seeker, however, is in fact only a subsidiary subject. The principal concern, as the poem's title implies, is the contrast of court and country. Classical poets, notably Horace again, had written of the simple pleasures of country life, though it was given a distinctive development in the literature of sixteenth-century Spain. A seminal work was Antonio de Guevara's *Menosprecio de corte y alabanza de aldea* ('Scorn of the court and praise of the village') (1539). Luis de León's poem fits squarely into the antithetical pattern defined in Guevara's title:

> ¡Qué descansada vida
> la del que huye el mundanal rüido,

y sigue la escondida
senda, por donde han ido
los pocos sabios que en el mundo han sido!

  Que no le enturbia el pecho
de los soberbios grandes el estado,
ni del dorado techo
se admira, fabricado
del sabio moro, en jaspes sustentado.

What a restful life is that of he who flees the noise of the world, and
follows the hidden path along which have gone the few wise men who
have been in the world! For his breast is not disturbed by the condition of
the proud grandees, nor does he admire the golden roof, built by the
clever Moor, and sustained by jasper columns.

The sharpness of the contrast is underscored by the use of the same word
('sabios – sabio') with an opposing significance at structurally parallel points.
'Pocos sabios' in the last line of the first stanza refers to those possessed of
genuine wisdom who shun the bustle of the city, while 'sabio moro' represents an ill-directed and merely apparent wisdom associated with worldly
splendour. The visual contrast between the hidden path and the golden roof
adds to the vigour of the antithesis.

Indeed the whole poem betrays considerable skill and sensitivity in the
marshalling of words and images; Luis de León's formidable training as a
biblical scholar obviously supplies a cutting edge to a poetic talent.[10] Among
the many telling details there is the juxtaposition in a passage near the end
where the scene of the shipwreck abruptly yields to the idyllic picture of
the poet in his country retreat:

    al cielo suena
confusa vocería,
y la mar enriquecen a porfía.
      A mí una pobrecilla
mesa, de amable paz bien abastada,
me baste   (p. 74)

the confused cries resound to heaven, and they vie with each other to
make the sea rich. Let a poor little table laden with the joys of peace be
enough for me

It is not so much the opposition of the concepts of wealth and poverty in
successive lines that catches the eye but, rather, the irony. Those who had
sought to enrich themselves perish wretchedly, bestowing their bodies as a
booty to the sea as well as the gold and treasure that they jettison, while the
humble table – of wood, we might presume, unlike the gold from which
the roof designed by the 'wise Moor' was made – represents the true riches
of the soul.

We have moved in the course of this chapter from a brand of religious poetry that is inspirational to one that is doctrinal – from the mystical to the moral. Until recent times distinguishing between the religious and the moral would have been fatuous; indeed, as the poetry of Luis de León reveals, for a Golden Age poet the term 'religion' encompassed theology, philosophy and morality. There was nothing new in this, even if the terms in which the issues were explored betrayed the hallmarks of Italian Humanism. Indeed there are few poems more concerned with the practicalities of how to lead a good life than Jorge Manrique's *Coplas por la muerte de su padre* ('Verses on the death of his father') written in the fifteenth century. In the later part of the poem he outlines an exemplary individual life – that of his father, Rodrigo Manrique – but the opening stanzas in particular are concerned with life in the most general sense, and especially with an acute awareness of what the world is and should be. What is most important about the world is that it is the scene of the Incarnation:

> Este mundo bueno fue
> si bien usásemos dél
> como debemos . . .
> Aun aquel fijo de Dios
> para sobirnos al cielo
> descendió
> a nescer acá entre nos,
> y a vivir en este suelo
> do murió.[11]

> This world would be good if we used it as well as we ought . . . And to raise us to heaven indeed that son of God came down to be born here among us and to live on this earth where He died.

This stanza is preceded by the plain articulation of the symbol of life as a journey, with a beginning and an end:

> Este mundo es el camino
> para el otro, qu'es morada
> sin pesar . . .
> Partimos cuando nascemos,
> andamos mientras vivimos,
> e llegamos
> al tiempo que feneçemos.

> This world is the path to the other, which is a dwelling without sorrow . . . We leave when we are born, we walk while we are alive, and we arrive at the moment of our death.

Manrique's vision is serene, especially when compared to the anguished expressions of late Medieval writing about death. The same cannot be said of a number of compositions on death by Quevedo, written in the early part of the seventeenth century. To speculate on causes, whether by reference to biography or history, is, as we have seen, fruitless, but there is no mistaking the disquiet in the effect. Lines like the opening of a sonnet that the poet's principal editor rather arbitrarily designates a metaphysical poem indicate one way in which the journey of life seems particularly fraught:

> Vivir es caminar breve jornada,
> y muerte viva es, Lico, nuestra vida,
> ayer al frágil cuerpo amanecida,
> cada instante en el cuerpo sepultada.[12]

> To live is to walk a short day's journey, and our life, Lico, is a living death, yesterday dawning in the fragile body, and buried at each moment in the body.

Here life is a living death; what Quevedo perhaps invites us to acknowledge is that it is its very brevity that makes it so. In two other sonnets this concept of the fleeting nature of life is given an extraordinary realization. Phrases such as the following come across as a *reductio ad absurdum* of the commonplace that life is short. In one we read:

> ¡Fue sueño ayer; mañana será tierra!
> ¡Poco antes, nada; y poco después, humo![...]
> ya no es ayer; mañana no ha llegado;
> hoy pasa, y es, y fue, con movimiento
> que a la muerte me lleva despeñado.
>   (p. 5)

> Yesterday it was a dream; tomorrow it will be earth! A little before it was nothing; and a little after, smoke! it is no longer yesterday; tomorrow has not arrived; today passes away, and is, and was, with movement that carries me precipitously to death.

In the other sonnet, obviously a companion piece, this extreme vision of accelerated time is translated into a morphological disruption as finite verbs are converted into nouns:

> Ayer se fue; mañana no ha llegado;
> hoy se está yendo sin parar un punto:
> soy un fue, y un será, y un es cansado.
>   (p. 4)

> Yesterday went away; tomorrow has not arrived; today is going away without stopping for a moment: I am a was, a will be, and an is that is weary.

Allied to the intuition of fugitive time is that of its imperceptible character, though 'stealthy' would be a more appropriately emotive way of describing it:

> Huye sin percibirse, lento, el día,
> y la hora secreta y recatada
> con silencio se acerca, y, despreciada,
> lleva tras sí la edad lozana mía.
>
> La vida nueva, que en niñez ardía,
> la juventud robusta y engañada,
> en el postrer invierno sepultada,
> yace entre negra sombra y nieve fría.
>
> No sentí resbalar, mudos, los años;
> hoy los lloro pasados, y los veo
> rïendo de mis lágrimas y daños.
>
> Mi penitencia deba a mi deseo,
> pues me deben la vida mis engaños,
> y espero el mal que paso, y no le creo.
>   (p. 7)

The day flees slowly and imperceptibly, and the secret and demure hour approaches in silence, and bears away in its wake my youthful age that it scorns. New life, which glowed in childhood, energetic youthfulness that was deceived, now lies buried in its final Winter, between black shadow and cold snow. I did not sense the slipping away of the silent years; today I weep at their passing, and I see them laughing at my tears and pains. Let my penitence be indebted to my desire, since my deceits owe me life, and I wait for the ills that I undergo, and I do not believe it.

The sonnet contains many words to do with periods of time and the stages of life (day, hour, age, childhood, youth, Winter). There is an ethical and psychological consideration. The poet bemoans his past life and recognizes the need for repentance, but the last line is complex and surprising. He believes (and we must understand these as simultaneous thoughts and experiences) that as he awaits death ('espero') he is already in a sense undergoing it ('paso') since such life is by its nature already death, as with the amatory metaphor of the death in life. But so deceived is he – so attracted to and diverted by life – that even now he cannot fully appreciate the significance of what is happening to him ('no le creo'). The whole thrust of the sonnet seemed to be leading by argument and illustration to self-knowledge and a realization of error that would provoke an appropriate response. In the end, however, we don't get that response. It is as if the poet were to be saying: 'yes, I am aware of all this, but I *feel* differently'.

As with Luis de León, Quevedo's moral poetry draws on both Christian and classical sources; his view of life and death relates to Catholicism and Stoicism. Ethically these have points in common insofar as they suggest a mode of conduct and a reaction towards suffering that incorporates patience and fortitude. Stoicism parts company with Christianity, though, in its advocacy of suicide as an acceptable solution. Christianity does not envisage death merely in negative terms as the end of suffering but positively as the start of a new and better life. Life is valuable in that, properly lived, it prepares the way for the after-life. Even if Quevedo's moral poems are rooted in these partly complementary, partly conflicting, traditions, however, they are far from being classic expositions of these doctrines. They emerge as shocking and apparently deviant, such is their ability to manipulate language and through it the reader's emotions. The way in which he speaks with horror of the onset of death owes little either to the Stoic's detachment or to the Christian's faith, as in the quatrains of a sonnet that supplies one of the most terrifying personifications of death in all poetry:

> ¡Cómo de entre mis manos te resbalas!
> ¡Oh, cómo te deslizas, edad mía!
> ¡Qué mudos pasos traes, oh muerte fría,
> pues con callado pie todo lo igualas!
>
> Feroz, de tierra el débil muro escalas,
> en quien lozana juventud se fía;
> mas ya mi corazón del postrer día
> atiende el vuelo, sin mirar las alas.
>
> (p. 33)

Oh, how you slip away between my hands! Oh, how you slide off, my life! What silent steps you bring, oh cold death, as with silent foot you render everything the same! Fiercely, you scale the fragile wall of earth that vigorous youth relies upon; but now my last-day heart observes the flight, without looking at the wings.

Such a conception does not allow us to retain our bearings. No sooner has one image registered than it is elbowed aside to make way for another, yet more fearsome. The ebbing sands of life yield to the muffled footsteps of death's arrival, which in turn give way to an enemy that easily storms the human castle, and finally, most frighteningly, the beating of wings that bear away the soul on its flight to death.

It is tempting to see in such febrile evocations what some cultural commentators have described as a baroque sensibility. The use of a term like this requires an understanding of artistic evolution as a continuous process involving reaction and counter-reaction. Thus the darkness and disorder of baroque art arises as a response to the balance and poise of the Renaissance; in turn the baroque will yield to the measured restraint of the neo-classical art of the eighteenth century, and so on.

The danger with this way of designating and relating successive movements is not that it exaggerates but that it simplifies. Lurid or extreme portrayals of death were not a baroque novelty even if the mode of expression obviously was. The bleakness of Quevedo's complaints at death has a parallel in Medieval poetry, notably in the long elegy that the Archpriest of Hita wrote on the death of the go-between in *Libro de buen amor*, the aptly named Trotaconventos (literally 'trots round the convents'). Just as the paintings of Hieronymus Bosch had inspired some of Quevedo's more graphic visions, so the representation of the all-powerful nature of death that is celebrated and cursed in Juan Ruiz also has a visual source: the *Danse macabre* or Dance of Death, which envisages death as the great leveller, carrying away Popes, kings and emperors as well as paupers and beggars:

> ¡Ay Muerte, muerta seas, muerta e mal andante!
> Mataste a mi vieja, ¡matasses a mí ante!
> Enemiga del mundo, que non as semejante,
> de tu memoria amarga non es que non se espante.
>
> Muerte, al que tú fieres, lievas te lo de belmez:
> al bueno e al malo, al rrico e al rrefez,
> a todos los eguales e los lievas por un prez;
> por papas e por rreyes non das una vil nuez.
>
> Non catas señorío, debdo nin amistad;
> con todo el mundo tienes continua enamistat;
> non ay en ti mesura, amor nin piedad,
> si non dolor, tristeza, pena e grand crueldad.[13]

> Oh, Death! Would that you die and be cursed! You killed the old woman! You should have killed me first! Enemy of the world, without equal; there is nobody who does not fear your bitter memory. When you wound someone there is no defence. You carry away the good and the evil, the nobleman and the slave; you make them all equal and you take them all for one price; you don't give two hoots for popes or kings. You have no regard for lordship, for family or friendship; you are the world's constant enemy; you have no courtesy, no love, no pity; nothing save pain, sadness, grief and great cruelty.

Indeed the repeated fixation on bodily decay, unsurprising in the century of the great plagues, is a feature that is less marked in Quevedo, preoccupied as he was with the peculiarly psychological terror of death.

Moreover, in the same years in which Quevedo was writing his bleakest sonnets on time and death Góngora was creating the imposing artifices of the *Polifemo* and the *Soledades* that, notwithstanding their shadows, strike us as exuberant and life-enhancing. Nor was the response to mortality in seventeenth-century poetry invariably as anguished as Quevedo's. Spanish literature of this period is notable too for the control and asceticism of the playwright Calderón and the scepticism of the essayist and prose-writer Gracián. This aloof manner, far removed from the hyper-ventilation of some baroque art, is well conveyed in a sonnet by the leading poet of the second half of the seventeenth century, the Mexican nun, Sor Juana Inés de la Cruz (1651–95):

> Verde embeleso de la vida humana,
> loca esperanza, frenesí dorado,
> sueño de los despiertos intrincado,
> como de sueños, de tesoros vana;
> alma del mundo, senectud lozana,
> decrépito verdor imaginado;
> el hoy de los dichosos esperado
> y de los desdichados el mañana:
> sigan tu nombre en busca de tu día
> los que, con verdes vidrios por anteojos,
> todo lo ven pintado a su deseo;
> que yo, más cuerda en la fortuna mía,
> tengo en entrambas manos ambos ojos
> y solamente lo que toco veo.[14]

> Green spell-binder of human life, mad hope, golden frenzy, the dream of those awake, confused, as in dreams, futile in her treasure; soul of the world, blossoming senility, imagined decrepit greenness; the today longed for by the lucky and the tomorrow by the unlucky: let them follow your name in search of your day, those who wear green glass in their spectacles, and see it all painted as they desire it; for I, wise in my fortune, hold in both hands both eyes and see only what I touch.

The sonnet is constructed in the classical fashion, characteristic of Sor Juana's use of the form; despite her indebtedness to Góngora in other compositions she shows no inclination to experiment in the manner of her major predecessors. Nonetheless the poem contains deft touches. The quatrains, addressed to Hope, comprise a lengthy denunciation by enumeration. The syntactic components that constitute this attack, however, are considerably varied. The opening phrase occupying a whole line is followed by two terse noun and adjective combinations, while the repetition of the preposition 'de' in the third and fourth lines evokes unease and potential disorder. The second quatrain opens with arrestingly contradictory ideas: the oxymoron 'senectud lozana' speaks for itself but the conjunction of soul and world also links two terms normally in opposition to each other – the world is traditionally the enemy of the soul. The chiasmus in lines 7 and 8 highlights both the clear contrast of 'dichosos' and 'desdichados' and the use of the adverbs 'hoy' and 'mañana' as nouns, rather in the manner of Quevedo. At the end, clear-sighted rationalism emerges in the appropriately crisper phrase-structuring, and the notion of having eyes on one's hands is remarkable. It affirms the control over the senses that was lacking in those who cherished hope, to which the final line adds an icy caution.

Notwithstanding the scepticism of this sonnet and the apparent nihilism of Quevedo's sonnets on time there is no sense of a spiritual crisis, even less a wavering of belief. It is in the poetry of the last century and a half that we discover in Spanish literature, as elsewhere, expressions of doubt and questioning. We saw in Chapter 2 how the poetry of Rosalía de Castro is imbued with spiritual misgivings and religious anguish. For these qualities alone she deserves to be regarded as the most innovative and forward-looking poet in Spain in the second half of the nineteenth century. Not for nothing was Miguel de Unamuno an admirer. Unamuno is unusual among the many poets cited in this study in that he is nowadays hardly rated as a poet. This is due to his eminence as a novelist and an essayist rather than to the quality, or indeed the quantity, of his verse. In his vast output, religious poetry holds a special place. As with other parts of his work Unamuno's sense of the Spanish inheritance is uniquely acute and passionate; in his vast poem *El Cristo de Velázquez* ('The Christ of Velazquez') he seemingly distils, via a meditation on a painting by the seventeenth-century artist and a pattern of glosses on scriptural quotations, a whole national religious sensibility. The most distinctive and moving passages of the work are perhaps those that focus on Christ's humanity and suffering:

> Abandonado de tu Dios y padre,
> que con sus manos recojió su espíritu,
> Te alzas en ese trono congojoso
> de soledad, sobre la escueta cumbre
> del teso de la calavera, encima
> del bosque de almas muertas que esperaban
> tu muerte, que es su vida. ¡Duro trono
> de soledad...!¹⁵

> Abandoned by Your God and father, who with His hands gathered His spirit, You rise up on that anguished throne of loneliness, on the succinct summit of the skull's crest, above the forest of dead souls who waited for Your death, which is their life. Harsh throne of loneliness

Unamuno's own spiritual uncertainty and crisis of faith is achingly conveyed in the late novel *San Manuel bueno, mártir*. Years previously, however, the same insistent questions and haunting doubts appeared in such poems as 'Salmo I':

> Señor, Señor, ¿por qué consientes
> que te nieguen ateos?
> ¿Por qué, Señor, no te nos muestras
> sin velos, sin engaños?
> ¿Por qué, Señor, nos dejas en la duda,
> duda de muerte?
> ¿Por qué te escondes?
> ¿Por qué encendiste en nuestro pecho el ansia
> de conocerte,
> el ansia de que existas,
> para velarte así a nuestras miradas?
> ¿Dónde estás, mi Señor; acaso existes?
> ¿Eres Tú creación de mi congoja,
> o lo soy tuya?   (p. 217)

Lord, Lord, why do You permit atheists to deny you? Why, Lord, do You not show Yourself to us without veils, without deceits? Why, Lord, do You leave us in doubt, the doubt of death? Why do You hide Yourself? Why did You kindle in our breast the anxiety to know You, the anxiety that You might exist, only to hide Yourself to our glances? Where are You, my Lord; do You by chance exist? Are You a creation of my anguish, or am I of Yours?

(Readers familiar with the novel *Niebla* will recognize a premonition of the dialogue between Augusto Pérez and Unamuno in the final question.) These lines have something of the manner of the Ignatian scheme in the earnestness of the questioning. Their content, of course, strays into areas that would have been uncharted though, for a Counter Reformation poet. The issue of doubt – put more radically, the non-existence of God – is central to the flow of interrogation and occasional rebuke that extends to over 250 lines. Indeed the terror in this tormented poem does not reside in any lack of will to believe but in the failure to encounter the divine presence. There are repeated references to a hidden God:

> ¡Quiero verte, Señor, y morir luego,
> morir del todo;
> pero verte, Señor, verte la cara,
> saber que eres!
> ¡saber que vives!
> ¡Mírame con tus ojos,
> ojos que abrasan;
> mírame y que te vea!
> ¡que te vea, Señor, y morir luego!
>   (p. 218)

I want to see You, Lord, and then die, die completely; but to see You, Lord, to see Your face, to know that You are, to know that You live! Look at me with Your eyes, eyes that burn; look at me and may it be that I see You, that I may see You, Lord, and then die!

There are unavailing echoes here of the mystic's experience, of a *copla* divinized by both San Juan de la Cruz and Santa Teresa:

Vivo sin vivir en mí,
Y de tal manera espero,
Que muero porque no muero.

I live without living in me, and I hope in such a way that I die because I do not die.

As often happens with intertextual references the reminiscence is highly emotive, underlining through the poignancy of the contrast the later poet's failure to achieve the desired vision. Appropriately Unamuno's poem is open-ended. Nothing has been glimpsed or guaranteed and the problem of God's existence is unresolved:

Tú me abrirás la puerta cuando muera,
la puerta de la muerte,
y entonces la verdad veré de lleno,
sabré si Tú eres
o dormiré en tu tumba. (p. 220)

You will open the door for me when I die, the door to death, and then I shall see the truth in its fullness, I shall know if You are, or I shall sleep in Your tomb.

This does not have the terror of the void that is evoked at times in Rosalía de Castro, but it communicates a sense of precariousness that prevents us labelling it by something as weak as mere 'curiosity'. Unamuno's attitude in poems such as this is akin to the condition described in one of Antonio Machado's early poems: 'pobre hombre en sueños, / siempre buscando a Dios entre la niebla' ('a poor man who dreams, always looking for God in the mist').[16] Machado, too, occasionally expresses a desperate desire for belief, especially after the untimely death of his wife. In 'Poema de un día', a ruminative meditation, this longing is impulsive:

razón y locura
y amargura
de querer y no poder
creer, creer, creer!
(p. 554)

reason and madness and bitterness of wanting and not being able to believe, believe, believe!

In later poetry Machado cultivated a whimsical philosophical tone and adopted a heteronymic mode of expression, inventing poets to whom he ascribed poems and essays. In a review of the work of one such heteronym, Abel Martín, Machado explains how Martín entertained a nihilist concept of God: 'Dios regala al hombre el gran cero, la nada o cero integral, es decir, el cero integrado por todas las negaciones de cuanto es' ('God presents man with the gift of the great zero, the nothingness or integral zero, that is, the zero composed of all the negations of all that is') (p. 693). This review also cites poetic illustrations of this negative theology, but these are less impressive than the poems about as well as attributed to Abel Martín, the finest of which perhaps is the one that describes his death. The fifth and final section moves from a kind of spiritual anguish characteristic of Unamuno to a resigned acceptance of the void, the 'great zero':

> Y sucedió a la angustia la fatiga,
> que siente su esperar desesperado . . .
> la sed que el agua clara no mitiga,
> la amargura del tiempo envenenado . . .
> ¿El que todo lo ve no le miraba?
> ¡Y esta pereza, sangre del olvido!
> ¡Óh, sálvame, Señor! . . .
> Abel tendió su mano
> hacia la luz bermeja
> de una caliente aurora de verano,
> ya en el balcón de su morada vieja.
> Ciego, pidió la luz que no veía.
> Luego llevó, sereno,
> el limpio vaso, hasta su boca fría,
> de pura sombra – ¡oh, pura sombra! – lleno.
>
> (p. 735)

And weariness followed his anguish, sensing his wait without hope, the thirst that clear water does not assuage, the bitterness of poisoned time. . . . And he who sees all was not looking at him? And this listlessness, the blood of oblivion! Oh, save me, Lord! . . . Abel stretched out his hand towards the vermilion light of a warm Summer dawn, now on the balcony of his old house. In his blindness he asked for the light he could not see. Then he lifted, serenely, the clean glass towards his cold mouth, full of pure shadow, pure shadow!

In its subtle detailing of place and time this passage is emotionally vibrant if understated, with the result that the contradiction in the final line, following the irony of the warm Summer dawn as the time of death, does not seem contrived even if it is not direct in the way that Unamuno is. The later poetry of Machado, however, has provoked little critical or imitative interest. It was viewed almost as a dead-end, not because atheism or nihilism are of their nature unsuitable as poetic material but because later poets found the kind of religious crisis articulated by Unamuno a more attractive model.

The poetry of Blas de Otero (1916–79) often comes across as a development of the uncertainty and vulnerability that are keynotes of Unamuno's. Politically to the left, he found in religious questioning an outlet for political dissent in the period of the Franco regime. We encounter the same interrogative method as with Unamuno:

> Sé que el mundo, la Tierra que yo piso,
> tiene vida, la misma que me hace.
> Pero sé que se muere si se nace,
> y se nace, ¿por qué?, ¿por quién quiso?
>
> Nadie quiso nacer. Ni nadie quiere
> morir. ¿Por qué matar lo que prefiere
> vivir? ¿Por qué nacer lo que se ignora?[17]

> I know that the world, the Earth that I tread, has life, the same that makes me. But I know that one dies if one is born, and one is born, why? for who wanted it? Nobody wanted to be born. Nor does anyone wish to die. Why kill what prefers to live? Why bring to life what is not known?

At the heart of this existential probing is an awareness of man's isolation: the hidden God of Unamuno's 'Salmo I' becomes the silent God of Otero's sonnet 'Hombre' ('Man'):

> Luchando, cuerpo a cuerpo, con la muerte,
> al borde del abismo, estoy clamando
> a Dios. Y su silencio, retumbando,
> ahoga mi voz en el vacío inerte.
>
> Oh Dios. Si he de morir, quiero tenerte
> despierto. Y, noche a noche, no sé cuándo
> oirás mi voz. Oh Dios. Estoy hablando
> solo. Arañando sombras para verte.
>
> Alzo la mano, y tú me la cercenas.
> Abro los ojos: me los sajas vivos.
> Sed tengo, y sal se vuelven tus arenas.
>
> Esto es ser hombre horror a manos llenas.
> Ser – y no ser – eternos, fugitivos.
> ¡Ángel con grandes alas de cadenas!

(p. 41)

Struggling, hand-to-hand with death at the edge of the abyss, I am shouting to God. And his silence, echoing, drowns my voice in the lifeless void. Oh God. If I must die, I want to have you awake. And, night after night, I do not know when you will hear my voice. Oh God. I am talking alone. Scratching shadows in order to see you. I raise my hand, and you chop it off. I open my eyes: you cut them open as I gaze. I am thirsty, and your sands turn into salt. This is what it is to be a man – horror with my hands full. To be – and not to be – eternal, elusive. Angel with huge wings of chains.

More than Unamuno Otero envisages the pain of life and the threat of death in images: 'abismo' ('abyss') and 'vacío' ('void') in the opening quatrain suggest man at the brink. We further appreciate the urgency of the poet's plight in the disrupted articulation of the second quatrain. We have already seen how good sonneteers can create tension by disregarding the structural norms we expect of the form, and accordingly we discover here the combination of a sentence that is no more than a sigh, enjambements with the consequent pause in the middle of the line, and a syntactically incomplete sentence. Likewise, the grammatical looseness of the final tercet with its wavering between the singular ('hombre', 'ángel') and the plural ('eternos', 'fugitivos') suggests disorientation, to which the slightly varied citation of Hamlet's famous phrase adds a grimly dramatic note.

The most arresting feature, however, is perhaps the sense of violence evoked in the first tercet. The silent God is also a vindictive one who mutilates with a cruel precision: he attacks the very hands and eyes that are the instruments of a desperate supplication. In this tercet, too, the restoration of a syntax that operates within rather than against the expected metrical pattern emphasizes the feeling of spurned aspiration: each of the three lines opens with a terse phrase that invites a positive response, only for this to be ruthlessly unfulfilled in what follows.

Despite its negative theology this poem still follows in the familiar line of Spanish religious poetry in its single-minded concern with the relationship of man and God, highly fraught though that is here. Such a concentrated focus is, however, unusual in modern poetry. Existential questions are frequently ill-defined; the notion of the absurdity of life, cultivated especially by French writers of the mid twentieth century, is a product in part of a failure of analysis or an inability to define. These traits are evident in a poem by César Vallejo entitled 'Los heraldos negros' ('The dark heralds'), written some time before the emergence of French existential philosophy:

Hay golpes en la vida, tan fuertes . . . Yo no sé!
Golpes como del odio de Dios; como si ante ellos,
la resaca de todo lo sufrido
se empozara en el alma . . . Yo no sé!

Son pocos; pero son . . . Abren zanjas oscuras
en el rostro más fiero y en el lomo más fuerte.
Serán tal vez los potros de bárbaros atilas;
o los heraldos negros que nos manda la Muerte.

Son las caídas hondas de los Cristos del alma,
de alguna fe adorable que el destino blasfema.
Esos golpes sangrientos son las crepitaciones
de algún pan que en la puerta del horno se nos quema.

Y el hombre . . . Pobre . . . pobre! Vuelve los ojos, como
cuando por sobre el hombro nos llama una palmada;
vuelve los ojos locos, y todo lo vivido
se empoza, como charco de culpa, en la mirada.
Hay golpes en la vida, tan fuertes . . . Yo no sé![18]

There are blows in life, so strong . . . I don't know! Blows as of the hatred
of God; as if before them, the surge of all that has been suffered were to
well up in the soul . . . I don't know! They are few; but they exist . . . They
open dark ditches in the most fierce face and on the strongest back. They
are perhaps the steeds of barbarous Attilas; or the dark messengers sent to
us by Death. They are the deep falls of the Christs of the soul, of some
precious faith that Destiny blasphemes. Those bloody blows are the
crackling of a loaf of bread that burns at our oven door. And what about
man? Wretched . . . wretched! He turns his eyes, as when we are
summoned by a hand on our shoulders; he turns his mad eyes, and the
whole of what he has lived wells up, like a puddle of guilt, in his glance.
There are blows in life, so strong . . . I don't know!

Here the vindictive God is apparently no more than a figure of speech,
whether in the simile in line 2 or the metaphor in lines 9 and 10. Unlike
Otero, Vallejo does not specify the causes of man's suffering. The poem's
closing line does no more than repeat the fact of suffering and its inexplic-
able nature. Like Otero, however, Vallejo has recourse to vivid imagery, but
the effect is more alienating because the images do not relate to each other.
For example, the obvious menace in the metaphors of the second stanza –
the 'bárbaros atilas' and the eponymous dark heralds – yields to the homely
and thus incongruous idea of bread baking in the oven. This odd conjunction bears out the poet's bewilderment at the harshness of life. Ultimately,
however, his depiction of hapless humanity – cowed and frightened – is in
the long line of Hispanic expressions of what Unamuno termed 'the tragic
sense of life'. Vallejo's concept of man as victim falls squarely in a tradition
that stretches from the disturbing sonnets on time and death by Quevedo.

Chapter 8

Satire, burlesque and poetry as celebration

The previous two chapters had a clear thematic basis and were concerned with subjects that relate to identifiable and universal human experiences. As a result the poems that figured in them could be said to have a *pretext*, if not necessarily in the sense that the poem depends upon a prior happening (which is, more precisely, a pretext) that is 'translated' into the text, then insofar as the poem is prompted by considerations that are outside it. Merely to make this point may strike some as surprising: does not all poetry have a pretext in either or both senses of the word? The aim of this chapter is to address this question – to consider the possibility that poetry, rather than than having to be 'about something', whether love, time or death, can be about itself: that it can be its own subject and thus its own justification.

The genre that supplies a suitable way-in to this issue is satire. Satire may at first sight lead in the opposite direction, since it is most clearly about something other than itself. As it involves criticism and mockery, however, satire connects both with the moral vision that was the concern of the previous chapter and the ludic impulse that will be an important factor for an assessment of the viability of the poem as a thing in its own right. What distinguishes the satirist from the moralist is the importance of ridicule and irony. It is not that moralists do not avail themselves of these tools for their attack but, rather, that they are not as integral to the criticism. A satirist's works, therefore, will often be perceived as burlesques. Moreover, a moralist may focus on a defect or vice that is common to humankind or may be provoked into writing by a failing in a particular individual or by a deficiency peculiar to the age in which he lives. The satirist is like the moralist in that his attack may be general or specific. In this case, however, the specificity or otherwise of the attack will more crucially affect how we read and categorize the poem, concretely for present purposes whether it has an exterior motive (a pretext) or whether it is self-contained or auto-referential.

Let us consider first a poem by the Nicaraguan poet–priest Ernesto Cardenal (1925–). The focus is political: the absolute tyranny of the Somoza family in the middle decades of the twentieth century. The surprise that is registered in the opening lines is the seed from which Cardenal's attack will grow:

> 2 A.M. Es la hora del oficio Nocturno, y la iglesia
> en penumbra parece que está llena de demonios.[1]

> 2 a.m. It is the time for the Evening Service, and the church in the
> half-light appears to be full of demons.

We do not expect churches to be inhabited by demons, and it is on this topsy-turvy premiss that the poem unfolds. Cardenal describes the unavailing or unconcerned response of official religion to everyday outrage and atrocity. The poet's sense of personal responsibility and helplessness appears in the repeated quasi-confessional line: 'Y mi pecado está siempre delante de mí' ('And my sin is always before me'). In the course of the poem he re-introduces the opening phrase ('es la hora') as though to remind us of religion's failure and its abdication of responsibility:

> Es la hora en que brillan las luces de los burdeles
> y las cantinas. La casa de Caifás está llena de gente.
> Las luces del palacio de Somoza están prendidas.
> Es la hora en que se reúnen los Consejos de Guerra
> y los técnicos en torturas bajan a las prisiones.
> La hora de los policías secretos y de los espías,
> cuando los ladrones y los adúlteros rondan las casas
> y se ocultan los cadáveres. – Un cuerpo cae al agua.

> It is the time when the lights shine in the brothels and the bars. The house
> of Caiaphas is full of people. The lights of Somoza's palace are switched
> on. It is the time when the Councils of War have their meetings and the
> torture specialists go down to the cells. The time of secret police and
> spies, when thieves and adulterers prowl around the houses and when
> corpses are hidden. A body falls into the water.

The reference to Caiaphas, the High Priest to whom Jesus was led before being crucified, serves to point out the distance between the life of Christ and the role of the Church in Somoza's Nicaragua. The conclusion confirms the Church's malevolence:

> Y la iglesia está helada, como llena de demonios,
> mientras seguimos en la noche recitando los salmos.

> And the church is freezing, as if full of demons, while we continue to
> recite the psalms in the night.

Cardenal's poem is an attack on the alliance of Church and state, an appropriate priority for a priest sympathetic to Liberation Theology and later a minister in the Sandinista government, who earned a rebuke from

Pope John Paul II for his political stance. A more covert mode of satire is provided by Cardenal's Spanish contemporary, Gil de Biedma, in a mocking poem entitled 'El arquitrabe' ('The Architrave'):

> Uno vive entre gentes pomposas. Hay quien habla
> del arquitrabe y sus problemas
> lo mismo que si fuera primo suyo
> –muy cercano, además.
>
> Pues bien, parece ser que el arquitrabe
> está en peligro grave. Nadie sabe
> muy bien por qué es así, pero lo dicen.
> Hay quien viene diciéndolo desde hace veinte años.
>
> Hay quien hable, también, del enemigo:
> inaprensibles seres
> están en todas partes, se insinúan
> igual que el polvo en las habitaciones.
>
> Y hay quien levanta andamios
> para que no se caiga: gente atenta.
> (Curioso, que en inglés *scaffold* signifique
> a la vez andamio y cadalso.)
>
> Uno sale a calle
> y besa a una muchacha o compra un libro,
> se pasea, feliz. Y le fulminan:
> *Pero cómo se atreve?*
>   ¡El arquitrabe . . .![2]

One lives among pompous people. There is one who speaks of the architrave and its problems just as though it were a cousin of his, a close one besides. Well then, it seems that the architrave is in serious danger. Nobody knows very well why it is like that, but they say so. There is someone who has been saying it now for twenty years. There is someone who also speaks of the enemy: individuals who are hard to pin down are everywhere, they insinuate themselves like dust in rooms. And there is someone who erects scaffolds so that it doesn't fall: prudent people. (Strange that in English *scaffold* means both scaffolding and a gallows.) One goes out into the street and kisses a girl or buys a book, one goes for a walk, quite happy. And they berate you: *But how dare you?* The architrave!

The opening sentence raises the expectation of a social satire, perhaps of a deflation of the self-important members of society. The following illustration, however, deflects such an anticipation for it appears to be an attack on a narrowly specialist area: the architectural expert. The introduction, however, of the time reference in line 8, which, though apparently casual, would have corresponded closely enough to the period that Franco had been in power, alerts us to a new development. Accordingly the second illustration is politically pointed. The allusion is evidently to the enemies within: those hostile, albeit in a silenced and necessarily stealthy manner, to the regime. Gil de Biedma next cleverly links the architectural and the political – the subjects of the first two illustrations – by the incorporation of a word in English ('scaffold') that, as he tells us directly, has a double meaning – relating both to buildings (hence architectural) and to executions (hence political). The colloquial and parenthetical mode of explanation enhances rather than downplays the satirical edge. Finally, in the face of the censure provoked by everyday activities indicative of individual freedom (buying a book, going for a walk), there is nothing left except the retreat into the triviality and irrelevance of our architectural enthusiast.

Political satire is not an exclusively modern sub-genre. One of the most remarkable poems of the fifteenth century is an anonymous satirical poem, the *Coplas de ¡ay panadera!* It provides an account of the battle of Olmedo in 1445 where the armies of Juan II of Castile and the supporters of his favourite Alvaro de Luna defeated the mixed forces of Juan I of Navarre and dissident Castilian nobles. The narrator is a camp-follower (the 'panadera') whose view of the struggle is highly jaundiced. The emphasis is on the cowardice displayed by both sides, and the poem ridicules the aristocrats on display. For the most part it comprises a dismissive cataloguing of the deficiencies of the combatants, devoting one stanza to each of the principal figures. The poet is politically impartial and no less even-handed when it comes to ladling out insults embellished by graphic and scatalogical detail:

> La persona tabernera
> del vil conde de Medina
> el cual será muy aína
> echado en una buitrera,
> lleno de figos de sera
> e de torreznos e vino,
> fizo más suçio camino
> que xamás hombre fiziera.[3]

> The tavern-loving personage of the ghastly Count of Medina, who would be very quick off the mark in a hunt for vultures, full of figs, bacon and wine, took the dirtiest road that was ever taken.

Among the targets, too, is Rodrigo Manrique, the subject of his son Jorge's *Coplas*:

> Con lengua brava e parlera
> y el coraçón de alfeñique,
> el comendador Manrique
> escogió bestia ligera,
> y dio tan gran correndera

fuyendo muy a deshora
que seis leguas en un hora
dexó tras sí la barrera.

(p. 134)

With his quarrelsome, busy tongue and his weedy heart, Comendador
Manrique chose a fast mount, and, riding away at just the wrong time, set
off at such a rapid pace that within an hour he was six leagues from the
battlefront.

This depiction of the loud-mouthed coward is at a far remove from the
exemplary Christian knight in his son's poem. Manrique Junior, however,
was also capable of using poetry as a vehicle for personal insult. Such attacks
were, even by the time he was writing, a common poetic mode, with its
roots in Provençal satirical poetry and, more immediately, the Galician-
Portuguese *cantigas d'escarnho e de maldizer* ('Songs of scorn and mockery').
Manrique may have left his father a shining monument but he was moved
to spite when he wrote about his step-mother, who was also his sister-in-
law. He imagines inviting her to a feast in her honour but everything that
he envisages about the event is a grotesque inversion of the etiquette of
hospitality and entertainment. The unfortunate lady will be forced to enter
the castle through the stable, while her ladies-in-waiting have to suffer the
indignity of going in through the sewer; their beds will be full of fleas; they
will be served by naked servants; undergarments will be used as their table
napkins. The meal that is to be served, as can be readily imagined, will be
appropriately disgusting:

Verná luego un ensalada
de cebollas albarranas
con mucha estopa picada
y cabeçuelas de ranas;
vinagre vuelto con hiel
y su azeyte rosado...
Y el arroz hecho con grassa
d'un collar viejo, sudado,
puesto por orden y tassa,
para cada uno un bocado:
por açucar y canela,
alcrevite por ensomo.[4]

Next will come a salad with bitter onions, with an abundance of minced
burlap and frogs' heads; vinegar mixed with gall and half-frozen oil...
And rice prepared with the grease from an old and sweaty collar, carefully
and scrupulously served, so every one had a portion: in place of sugar and
cinnamon, sulphur was spread on top.

Evidently Manrique needed a poem like this to get his feelings about his
step-mother off his chest. One should be wary, however, about making any

deductions about either the step-mother or the father on the basis of what we read in these poems. It would be futile to try and determine whether the image of the father in his own poem was truer than the one in the *Coplas de ¡ay panadera!* They are both, to a considerable extent, the product of their genre, with the result that individual traits are recycled according to the dictates of the moral or satirical mode.

More than with other genres perhaps, when satire becomes conventional it can become gratuitous. As we have seen, it thrives on grievance and injustice, however profound or trivial they may be. This does not of course mean that a poet writing on a long-established topic such as anti-clericalism is necessarily less than serious. The adoption, however, of what are considered the stock subjects of satire allows poets the opportunity to engage self-consciously with their predecessors, in other words with *precursor texts* rather than *pretexts*.

Such is the case with much poetry, or indeed literature, that is conveniently designated anti-feminist. With its roots in classical literature, and with the ideological backing of Medieval theologians, by the Renaissance the attack on women had become as conventional as its opposite manifestation: the courtly Petrarchan idealization. It should therefore no more surprise us that Quevedo, the author of the poems to Lisi, should pen vitriolic verses against women than that Rodrigo Manrique should have been considered both a good Christian knight and a cowardly knave. To consider Quevedo a misogynist merely because he wrote anti-feminist diatribes is clearly an error. Even to make the claim on the grounds of the peculiar vehemence of the attack is no less mistaken. What is demonstrated is poetic accomplishment, a virtuosity that is not dependent on truth or strength of feeling, as when Quevedo describes a prostitute:

> Antoñuela, la Pelada,
> el vivo colchón del sexto,
> cosmógrafa que consigo
> medía a estados el suelo[5]

> Antoñuela, with her shaved head, the live mattress of the Sixth Commandment, a cosmographer who with herself marked the earth with her spread body

Other than the obviously sexual metaphor of cartography here, two details need explaining in order to savour the density of Quevedo's attack: the bald head is a sign of someone suffering from syphilis, while the Sixth Commandment is the one that forbids adultery. Such poetry may strike us as unappealing because the choice of such easy targets – predominantly old women and prostitutes – suggests an abuse of satire. It is possible to enjoy this poetry by separating manner from matter and admire it for its linguistic brilliance while deploring its subject. Such an attitude, common among Quevedo scholars, will strike some as an evasion of critical responsibility. It is, however, an unfortunate fact that, in order to have the freedom to attack the powerful and the corrupt, poets require the licence to be unconcerned about matters of good taste and common decency. Both political correctness and its opposite come at a price.

What is not at issue, however, is the nature of such a poem. It is essentially a burlesque – a mode of satire that belongs to aesthetics (though some may flinch at the use of the term in this context) rather than ethics. Burlesque is a derisive imitation or send-up of a literary work. It thus betrays a ludic impulse, even if it is a game that is outmoded or not to the taste of a particular epoch. The spirit of play, however, is a powerful motive in poetic composition. We saw in Chapter 1 the importance of academies and *tertulias* as a source of poetic stimulus through competition, but the very form of some poems betrays a ludic intent. The riddle – a verbal puzzle that dates back over thousands of years – is a clear instance of a playing *in* words. It is also an excellent vehicle for illustrating the importance of the listener's or reader's intervention in the making of the poem, an issue that was also discussed in Chapter 1. Erotic poetry, frequently dependent on double meanings, is very suitable for the riddle as is evident in a Golden Age compilation of 72 'enigmas' entitled *Libro de diferentes cosicosas* ('The book of various bits and pieces'). The anonymous poet dedicates his collection to 'la sola hermosa' ('the sole beauty') rather as with the Petrarchan sequence, but amatory aspiration in this case is, to put it mildly, more direct. Yet as this example illustrates it is not simply a matter of indecent suggestion:

> Tengo un miembro largo, liso y duro,
> por el un cabo peludo,
> por el otro agujereado.
> Métolo en una concavidad honda y escura,
> y estáse un rato mojando;
> y, un cierto licor echando,
> me estoy con él un rato holgando.[6]

> I have a member that is long, smooth and hard, with hairs at one end and a hole at the other. I put it in a deep, dark hollow, and it stays a moment getting wet; and as it releases its liquid I spend some time enjoying myself with it.

Each of the riddles is prefaced by a title, which is the solution with the letters reversed so as not to spoil the game. In the case of the above poem the title is *Al amulp*, the inverted form of 'la pluma', meaning a quill pen, one that operated by having to be constantly dipped in the inkwell. The cryptic title thus allows a turning of the tables. Could not the poet claim that the indecency was in the eye of the beholder – specifically the woman to whom he addresses these riddles? This reversal lends an extra edge to this adolescent joke; it is the poet who can play the role of the innocent party while the duped reader will have been forming obscene – supposedly false – conclusions.

Both this riddle and Quevedo's cruel burlesques depend on playful ingenuity. Such a quality also typifies some of the poetry written in Spain in the 1920s, partly, as we have seen, as a reaction to the overblown rhetoric of *modernismo* and the over-earnest ideology of the Generation of 1898. Jocularity is not always a light-hearted matter though; the members of the *avant-garde* movements following the First World War also had an agenda and were as passionate and dogmatic as the *modernistas*. Indeed they are as important for what they signalled to the new generation of poets who would come to prominence in the 1920s as for any individual work of their own; for the most part their poetry appeared in literary journals rather than as books. The Generation of 1927 thus had a double and conflicting inheritance, which contributed to the richness and complexity of their work. They respected the poetry of past centuries – whether Gil Vicente or Góngora – but also revealed an irreverent streak, acquired from their *avant-garde* predecessors. Even if the specific kind of poetics advocated by a movement like *creacionismo* was no longer being heeded, the iconoclastic impulse remained. The adoption of, or at least the flirtation with, Surrealism, discernible in Alberti, Lorca and Cernuda, is symptomatic of the rebellious spirit and experimental manner, but so too are less momentous manifestations. When Lorca was a student at the Residencia de Estudiantes in Madrid in the early 1920s he and his fellow-students, including Salvador Dalí and Luis Buñuel, would meet in Lorca's room to compose *anaglifos*, nonsense poems made up of three nouns, the second of which had to be 'la gallina' ('chicken') and the third of which was to have no connection with the first, and could even be a nonsense word as here:

> El té,
> el té,
> la gallina
> y el Teotocópuli.[7]

The tea, the tea, the hen and the Teotocopuli.

The cultivation of nonsense poetry was one way in which the old orthodoxy could be mocked. Widening poetry's frame of reference by looking beyond prescribed subjects and settings was another. Here the example of the Futurists and the Italian theorist, Marinetti, was important. If poetry could pay homage to the machine age and its inventions then it could also celebrate cultural novelties, as when Alberti dedicates a whole book of poems to the stars of the silent cinema, or when the title of a jazz song is the trigger for a poem by Cernuda. The spirit of innovation also led a number of Spanish poets of the 1920s to experiment with the very appearance of their poetry on the page, what is termed *poésie concrète*. Some of the compositions that fall into this category push orthography and lay-out to the very limits. Thus in the poem entitled 'Fuegos artificiales' ('Fireworks') by Francisco Vighi (1890–1962) the text is separated into two columns, enabling both vertical as well as horizontal reading. We are supplied with the sound effects of the spectacle and a humour achieved by irreverent invocations of saints on whose feast-days there would have been firework displays. I cite the opening and closing chunks (for want of a better word) of the poem:

Fchsss . . . . ¡¡Pon!!   Serpentina de magnesio y latín
Empezó la función   a cargo de San Agustín.

                        . . .

¡Cataplún! ¡Cataplón!
dio dos estornudos   Un trueno profundo
San Cristobalón.   Terrible explosión.
                                             Se acabó el mundo.
                                             ¡¡¡Poon!!![8]

This is not all by way of the (appropriately) verbal pyrotechnics, for the poet scatters the letters that make up the words 'fuegos artificiales' ('firework') within the two columns of text, in large upper-case and in a varied presentation: back to front, upside down and on their side. The poem thus registers essentially, as would indeed a firework display, as a visual 'happening'.

   Other minor poets of the 1920s were even more extreme in their experiments with *poésie concrète* while the major figures shunned such radical innovations as if aware of the dangers, and perhaps because at heart they were wedded to the traditions of Spanish poetry. Lorca's forays in 'Teorías', the first section of *Canciones*, are timid when compared with those of lesser contemporaries such as his friend Adriano del Valle (1895–1957), Guillermo de Torre (1900–71) and Juan Larrea (1895–1980). Significantly, even Gerardo Diego (1896–1987), the most distinguished of the *creacionistas*, is less concerned with shape than verbal detailing. In his poem 'Columpio' ('Swing') the back and forth motion is conveyed in a pattern that is oral/aural rather than visual:

                        Bandadas de flores
Flores de sí   Flores de no
                        Cuchillos en el aire
                        que las rasgan las carnes
                        forman un puente
Sí   No

> Cabalga el soñador
> Pájaros arlequines
> cantan el sí   cantan el no[9]

> Flocks of flowers   Flowers of yes   Flowers of no   Knives in the air that
> tear the flesh form a bridge   Yes   No   The dreamer rides harlequin
> birds   they sing yes   they sing no

Even though the separation of words and phrases across the page is prompted by the distinctive movement of the swing, the effect is less a visual equivalent than an aid to intonation. Moreover the description is metaphorical rather than merely pictorial, as when the energetic regularity of the motion is compared to knives and a bridge.

Although Diego and Lorca were interested in innovation, they clearly did not want to undermine what they understood to be the indispensable assumptions of the poetic act. Indeed even when Guillermo de Torre wrote of the need to break with the continuity of logical discourse and to promote a fragmentary perception – a feature we observed in Alberti's *Sobre los ángeles* in Chapter 5 – he is still advocating the primacy of the word, and re-asserting the conceptual as well as verbal priority of poetry.

For all their rebelliousness, however, the *creacionistas* and the members of the *avant garde* were not *against* poetry. That, however, is what a Chilean poet of a slightly later generation, Nicanor Parra (1914–), the brother of the folksinger Violeta, would appear to be when he wrote *antipoemas* ('antipoems'). The term is not of his coining: it had previously been employed by Huidobro. Parra shared many of the aims of the earlier *avant-garde* writers but he differed by eschewing the air of self-promotion – the bardic aura – that the *ultraístas* and *creacionistas*, no less than their Romantic-minded predecessors, were disposed to adopt. His 'Manifiesto' is a rebuke to his spiritual antecedents:

> Señoras y señores
> Esta es nuestra última palabra.
> –Nuestra primera y última palabra–
> Los poetas bajaron del Olimpo.[10]

> Ladies and gentlemen, this is our last word. – Our first and last word –
> The poets have come down from Mount Olympus.

The use of set phrases from formal speech, such as in the first line of the above quotation, colloquialisms, acronyms, proper names and foreign words are all ways in which Parra sought to make poetry not 'un objeto de lujo' ('a luxury object') but 'un artículo de primera necesidad' ('an article of prime necessity'). Yet his poetry clearly belongs in a satirico-burlesque tradition: in some poems he cocks a snook at bourgeois taste and etiquette, and in others engages in humour for its own sake. He has a particular penchant for jokes based on religion – a distinctively Hispanic trait – as when he supplies an unexpected gloss on the words of the thief crucified alongside Christ in Luke xxxiii, 42: 'Acuérdate de mí cuando estés en tu reino' ('Remember me when you are in your kingdom'). The phrase 'remember me' is appropriated to its use when one is seeking a favour or a job, as is immediately evident:

> Acuérdate de mí cuando estés en tu reino
> Nómbrame presidente del Senado
> Nómbrame Director del Presupuesto
> Nómbrame Contralor General de la República.
>
> (p. 79)

> Remember me when you are in your kingdom / Appoint me President of the Senate / Appoint me Chief of the Budget / Appoint me General Comptroller of the Republic.

The final request is wickedly humorous, given the source of the quotation:

> En el peor de los casos
> Nómbrame Director del Cementerio

> In the last resort / make me the head of the Cemetery

Twentieth-century Spanish and Spanish American poetry, then, like literature and the arts generally in this period, reveals a readiness to push forms to the limit and to question, if not to abolish, conventional modes of expression. For such an aim, satire and burlesque are, clearly, suitable tools. Moreover, as the previous pages have implied, modern poets have been preoccupied with their own activity as poets, not merely as a subject for ancillary theoretical writing but as an issue that is inscribed in the poem itself. In other words, the making of the poem and the awareness of what it means to write a poem are themselves subjects for poetry. This metapoetics is an interesting but perhaps logical progression from the Petrarchan ethos of the lyric as an individualization of the poet as man to the modern (auto-) justification of the poet as poet. There has been a shift in emphasis from the experience being written about to the writing about the experience. In his essay on one of Marianne Moore's poems, Wallace Stevens wonders if 'the question as to Miss Moore's poem is not in respect to its meaning but in respect to its potency as a work of art'.[11] And, more generally, Jonathan Culler argues that there is a convention 'especially useful in the case of obscure or minimalist poems, where the fact that they are presented as poems is the one thing we can be certain of, [which] is the rule that poems are significant if they can be read as reflections on or explorations of the problems of poetry itself'.[12]

It seems appropriate to conclude a broad-based survey on poetry by addressing such a fundamental issue. The first point to make is that while this 'worrying' about poetry is a modern obsession, the poet's awareness of his / her poetic craft also emerges with varying degrees of sophistication in earlier Spanish poetry. The word 'craft' is especially appropriate for a poet like Berceo who defined his role – essentially a mix of translator, versifier, refiner – literally in terms of work: 'leal obrero de Dios' ('God's loyal worker'). For the Golden Age poets there was no lack of theoretical justification or assistance, and, occasionally, literary precepts and principles are integrated in the text. In his Third Eclogue, Garcilaso describes how a group of four nymphs utilize the materials of the natural world – leaves, sand, dyes – to create pictures of mythological tales that reflect the poem's principal concern: the death of a loved one. The poem comprises a development of the second part of the First Eclogue which, as we saw in Chapter 1, was concerned with Nemoroso's lament for the death of Elisa. This event is incorporated into the world of myth in the other poem as it constitutes the last of the four depictions created by the nymphs. What is especially striking is the way Garcilaso envisages their activity. He compares their representational skills to those of the Greek painters Apeles and Timantes, renowned for their ability to create pictures which give the illusion of real life. There is, however, another analogy:

> Las telas eran hechas y tejidas
> del oro que'l felice Tajo envía,
> apurado después de bien cernidas
> las menudas arenas do se cría,
> y de las verdes ovas, reducidas
> en estambre sotil cual convenía
> para seguir el delicado estilo
> del oro, ya tirado en rico hilo.[13]

> The tapestries were made and woven from the gold that the joyous Tagus provides, refined after the fine sands where it was produced had been sieved, and from the green spawn crushed into a delicate material, as was fitting to follow the delicate style of the gold, now drawn into a rich thread.

Words such as 'convenía' ('was fitting') and 'estilo' ('style') bring to mind the terminology of Renaissance theories of poetic decorum: the principle whereby poets choose the forms and diction appropriate for the subject. The poet's task is to dress up his ideas in a garment that suits the occasion – that is, the immediate poetic purpose.

A similar encounter between the poet's craft and the poem's material is evident in Góngora's *Soledades*. Although the first *Soledad* contains the court–country debate common in sixteenth-century literature, as we have seen in the poetry of Luis de León (see Chapters 1 and 7), both Michael Woods and Arthur Terry have cautioned against extending the dichotomy to nature and art.[14] For country people, nature is there to be exploited:

> Vence la noche al fin, y triunfa mudo
> el silencio, aunque breve, del rüido:
>   sólo gime ofendido
> el sagrado laurel del hierro agudo;
> deja de su esplendor, deja desnudo
> de su frondosa pompa al verde aliso
>   el golpe no remiso
> del villano membrudo.[15]

> Night is victorious at last, and dumb silence triumphs, albeit briefly, over the noise: only the sacred laurel moans, offended by the sharp axe; the unremitting blows of the well-built peasant strip the green elder of its splendour, of its leafy pride.

Nature is an artifice that mirrors what Terry has described as the 'ultimate artifice': 'the poem itself, the complex structure of words in whose shaping the reader is made to collaborate'.[16] Moreover, Terry suggests, there is a connection between the natural world and the act of poetic creation through 'the process of verbalization'. He illustrates this by citing a passage, that Góngora later discarded, where a river is compared to the act of speaking, as a 'torcido discurso' ('twisted discourse') whose sentences are interrupted by the parentheses of islands:

> en brazos divididos caudalosos
> de islas, que paréntesis frondosos
> al período son de su corriente.

> divided into abundant branches of islands, which are leafy parentheses in the period of its course.

The passages we have just encountered in Garcilaso and Góngora raise a further issue. It is that nature in Spanish poetry is seldom perceived as a thing in its own right. The significance of landscape is not often merely pictorial, and unlike in English poetry there is not that particular fondness for minutiae or humble details. A comparison of the role of nature in Bécquer with its treatment by the English Romantics would be illuminating. Again, the harsh landscape of Castile is seldom described for its own sake, and is for the most part a prompt for historical or personal meditation in Antonio Machado's *Campos de Castilla*. More often, Spanish poets writing about nature are celebrating the ability of the poet to describe or merely perceive it. What is lacking is a poet like Clare, Lawrence or Hughes, for whom the landscape itself becomes all-consuming. For Spanish poets nature is the starting-point for an aesthetic musing. As a consequence the understanding of the natural world is, more than with English poets, dictated by fashion. We are invited – sometimes implicitly, sometimes directly – to look beyond, and what we invariably see is the poem itself. The preoccupation is ultimately the form or the making of the poem.

So when we are confronted by a passage like the following by Meléndez Valdés (1754–1817), we may cast only the most cursory of glances with the inner eye to the scene being described:

> ¡Cuál vaga en la floresta
> el céfiro süave!
> ¡Cuál con lascivo vuelo
> sus frescas alas bate,
> sus alas delicadas,
> que forman al mirarse
> del sol en los reflejos
> mil visos y cambiantes!
> ¡Cuál licencioso corre
> de flor en flor y afable
> con soplo delicioso
> las mece y se complace!
> Ahora a un lirio llega,
> ahora el jazmín lame,
> la madreselva agita
> y a los tomillos parte.[17]

> How the gentle breeze wanders in the grove! How with lecherous flight it beats its fresh wings, its delicate wings, which, as they look at themselves in the sun, form a thousand varied rays of light! How licentiously it runs from flower to flower and pleasantly with its exquisite breath it takes delight in making them sway! Now it reaches a lily, now it licks the jasmine, it stirs the honeysuckle, and divides the thyme.

It is not only the developed personification of the breeze that may prevent us from imagining the scene in purely visual terms. We are likely to be particularly exercised by what the poem generates by way of technical effects, which are largely independent of the context. There is, for example, the bright assonance on *a* in lines 4–5, assisted by the inversion of the object in 'sus frescas alas bate' ('it beats its fresh wings'). The repeated use of hyperbaton in the second stanza appropriately provides a more complex, elaborate phrasing for the myriad reflections of sunlight. There are sensuous alliterations in successive lines in the third and fourth stanzas: 'mece' / 'complace'; 'lirio' / 'llega'. The positioning of the verbs at the end of each of the lines of the fourth stanza creates an impression of balance and harmony, while underpinning a *crescendo* in the semantic significance: 'llega' ('it reaches'), 'lame' ('it licks'), 'agita' ('it stirs'), 'parte' ('it divides'). When we read a passage like this we think in terms of *style* rather than *scene*, even allowing for the propensity of neo-classical art to stylization. It also serves us to remind us that the distinction Paul Auster made between Shakespeare and Racine, and implicitly between English and French literature, could also be applied to Spanish poetry, especially to someone like Meléndez Valdés writing in a century dominated by French models: 'Whereas Shakespeare, for example, names more than five hundred flowers in his plays, Racine adheres to the single word "flower".'[18]

The same conclusion could be drawn from a poem dating from the first decade of the twentieth century. With the following piece by Juan Ramón Jiménez we exchange the Rococo delicacy of Meléndez Valdés for the *fin-de-siècle* aestheticism that owes much to the French Symbolists, and which is a more private poetry than that of Darío and the *modernistas*. Anyone familiar with the poetry of Housman or Edward Thomas, contemporaries of Jiménez, however, will note again the distinction between landscape as focus and landscape as pretext:

> Todo el ocaso es amarillo limón;
> en el cenit cerrado, bajo las nubes mudas,
> bandadas negras de pájaros melancólicos
> rayan, constantes, el falso cielo de lluvia.
>
> Por el jardín, sombrío de los plúmbeos nimbos,
> las rosas tienen una morada veladura,
> y el crepúsculo vago, que cambia las verdades,
> pone en todo, al rozarlo, pálidas gasas húmedas . . .
>
> Lívido, deslumbrado del amarillo, torvo,
> del plomo, en mis oídos, como una mosca, zumba
> una ronda monótona que yo no sé de dónde
> viene . . . que tiene lágrimas . . . que dice: nunca . . . nunca.[19]

All of the western sky is a lemon yellow; at the closed zenith, beneath the mute clouds, black flocks of melancholy birds unceasingly mark the false sky like rain. In the garden, dark with its leaden haloes, the roses are veiled in a violet light, and the uncertain dusk, which undermines truth, imbues everything that it touches with unknown vapours. Livid, dazzled by the yellow, and leaden-grim, in my ears like a horsefly, there comes from I know not where the hum of a monotonous serenade . . . which has tears . . . which says: never . . . never.

Even before we reach the last stanza with its incorporation of a mysterious emotional element we are directed by the poem's very preciosity to the way of saying rather than the thing said. Detail is a matter less of visual perception and more of linguistic fastidiousness, as with the precise allocation of an adjective to almost every noun, in order to suggest a controlling presence through the symmetrical understanding. The fact that I should be defining the effect in abstract terms is an indication of how I have been drawn away from the notion of landscape as material world.

According to Andrés Sánchez Robayna, the poetic language of Jiménez 'converges' with that of Jorge Guillén, a member of the Generation of 1927, in an essential point: 'la visión de la materia verbal como un "diseño" (abstracto en ocasiones), una voluntad de construcción y estructuración' ('the vision of verbal substance as a "design" (sometimes abstract), a desire for the construct and for structuring').[20] In Guillén, however, the poetic act is associated with a larger concept than landscape: life itself. To say that Guillén's poetry is a celebration of existence, however, invites two qualifications. Firstly, much of his later work has dark overtones that make the celebration, at best, a muted one. More importantly, though, as with Meléndez Valdés and Jiménez, the ultimate focus of celebration is the poem itself. This is overwhelmingly evident in the very structure of his first and principal work, *Cántico*. Guillén worked on this book for thirty years, publishing interim editions until he terminated the project in 1950; thus the first edition of 1928 contained only 75 poems, while the definitive one had 334. These statistics alone, however, do not reveal the extraordinary attention to symmetry; more than any other work perhaps, *Cántico* reminds us that the etymology of 'poem' involves a Greek word meaning 'thing made'. Preoccupied as it is with numerology, it is a kind of structure that the Renaissance creators of sonnet sequences would have appreciated more than modern sensibilities in search of emotional authenticity and spontaneity. It is in five parts, all with titles, some of which are further sub-divided: the first and fifth both have three sections, while the third – like a microcosm of the whole work – has five. It is a design with a powerful sense of centre: the central section of the central third part is the seventh of the entire work, and distinguished by being the only place in the work where sonnets appear.

Although 3 and 7 are both significant numbers because of their religious and magical associations, the dominant numerological concept in *Cántico* is 5. Many of the individual poems are divided into 5 sections and many poems and parts of poems have 5 stanzas; the opening poem, 'Más allá' ('Beyond'), has sections of 15 (that is, 3 times 5) and 5 stanzas. Moreover, Guillén is partial to the *décima*, a poem of 10 (2 times 5) lines with a fixed rhyme. In the following example of the form there is an important symbolic and structural detail:

> Queda curvo el firmamento,
> Compacto azul, sobre el día.
> Es el redondeamiento
> Del esplendor: mediodía.

Todo es cúpula. Reposa,
Central sin querer, la rosa,
A un sol en cenit sujeta.
Y tanto se da el presente
Que el pie caminante siente
la integridad del planeta.[21]

The firmament is rounded, compactly blue, above the day. It is the
circling of splendour: midday. Everything is a cupola. The rose, at the
centre without wishing it, reposes, subject to a sun at its highest point.
And the present surrenders so much that the walking foot experiences the
wholeness of the planet.

The notion of perfection is conceived in spatial and temporal terms: the
geometry of circularity and centrality and the matching astronomical ap-
propriateness of midday. It is moreover at the very centre of the poem –
the start of line 6 – that we find the word 'central', associated not only
with the mood of serene tranquillity but with a number of mandala objects:
the rose, the sun, the cupola. 'Mandala' is a Sanskrit word meaning 'magic
circle', but its symbolism includes all concentrically arranged figures, all
radial or spherical patterns, and all circles or squares with a central point.
Mandalas are employed in many religions, including Christianity, but also
have a wider spiritual application, figuring for example in Jungian psychology and in meditative practices. With Guillén the presence of the mandala
suggests fulfilment and wholeness; indeed the last part of *Cántico* is entitled
'Pleno ser' ('Full being').

Poetry cannot be made out of numbers, though, any more than it can
be made out of shapes, and the ultimate test of the credibility of Guillén's
celebration – the sub-title of the work is 'Fe de vida' ('Faith in life') –
will be how numerology and symbolism are integrated into a verbal pattern
that encourages the reader to make a matching or complementary response.
Guillén sometimes betrays a tendency – present, as we have seen, in *La voz
a ti debida* by his friend Pedro Salinas – to rely too much on the reiteration
of abstract phraseology. In fact, the sense of 'beyondness' that was a preoccupation in Salinas is much in evidence in *Cántico* as the title of the opening
poem indicates. Enthusiasm for life in the form of a poetry of statement and
exclamation will tend to pall or, worse, lead to readerly resistance because
through its earnestness it may strike the reader as a pose.

What exempts *Cántico* (but perhaps not *La voz a ti debida*) from this
criticism is Guillén's capacity to make us accept the validity of the poem
as *poem* – that he can make us believe or accept, for the duration of the
poem at least, that his envisaging of 'faith in life' warrants our involvement.
This prompts the general reflection that whether we engage actively with a
poem is more important than whether we subscribe to the ideas that could

be extracted from it or which apparently went into it. In the last resort this implies that we ought to feel that the poem is *doing* something to us, such as pleasing us, disturbing us or intriguing us. As a consequence, in another *décima* entitled 'Equilibrio' ('Equilibrium'), rather than a line like 'Todo me obliga a ser centro del equilibrio' ('Everything obliges me to be the centre of the equilibrium') with its peremptory manner, *telling* us that the poet feels himself an integral part of the ineffable harmony of existence, it is through an earlier line that we intuitively comprehend this condition:

> Y si la luz se posa como una paz sin peso...
>
> (p. 309)

> And if the light alights like a weightless peace...

This wonderfully stately yet elegant line – the fourteen-syllable form of the Medieval *mester de clerecía* – epitomizes this equilibrium. The division of the line into two equal halves is already a metrical balance, but there is a complementary alliteration: '*se posa*' is beautifully echoed by the morphologically dissimilar '*sin peso*' at the exactly corresponding point in the second half of the line. It is not necessary to read this aloud to appreciate its impact, and because we discover and *feel* the 'equilibrium' in our reading we cannot resist acknowledging the well-being that is at the heart of the poem.

The word 'maravilla' ('wonder') at the opening of 'Equilibrio' is of a kind that abounds in the work:

> Es una maravilla respirar lo más claro.

> It is a wonder to breathe that which is brightest.

Cántico frequently suggests a quasi-mystical experience appropriate for the heightened perception of reality, as is evident too in the first line of 'Viento saltado' ('Leaping wind'):

> ¡Oh violencia de revelación en el viento...!

> Oh violence of revelation in the wind

A similarly mystical or magical understanding of the phenomenal world is acutely registered in 'Milagro de la luz' ('Miracle of Light') by Angel González (1925–):

> Milagro de la luz: la sombra nace,
> choca en silencio contra las montañas,
> se desploma sin peso sobre el suelo
> desvelando a las hierbas delicadas.
> Los eucaliptos dejan en la tierra

la temblorosa piel de su alargada
silueta, en la que vuelan fríos
pájaros que no cantan.
Una sombra más leve y más sencilla,
que nace de tus piernas, se adelanta
para anunciar el último, el más puro
milagro de la luz: tú contra el alba.[22]

Miracle of light: the shadow is born, crashes in silence against the
mountains, collapses weightlessly onto the floor, uncovering the delicate
herbs. The eucalyptus trees leave on the ground the trembling skin of
their lengthened silhouette, where cold birds that do not sing fly. A lighter
and simpler shadow, that is born from your legs, advances to announce
the ultimate and purest miracle of the light: you against the dawn.

The opening phrase has an obvious affinity with Guillén's poetry. As with
the first poem of *Cántico*, González communicates the idea of a world in the
making, rather than just in being. Notwithstanding the delicate precision
of detail, however, there is a sense in which the landscape, if not inert,
is inadequate. It is completed in one way by the evocation of a miracle
that is greater than that of the effects of light: the presence of the other,
presumably the beloved. Such a feature is consistent with what I suggested
was the distinctively anthropocentric priority of Spanish poets as compared
with their English counterparts. And the scene is completed in another way
by the poem itself. This is not just in the obvious sense of a poet transferring
an impression to the page, but, as with the examples from Garcilaso and
Góngora cited above, in the way in which the poem both reflects and
reflects *upon* the poetic act. In the case of González's poem it is through
contrast. For all its visual energy the scene is explicitly silent. This muted
quality is not only indicated by the birds who do not sing but underscored
by the oxymora of 'choca en silencio' ('silently collides') and 'se desploma
sin peso' ('collapses weightlessly'), referring to the shadow. If it is the human
presence that 'announces' the ultimate miracle, it is the poem that uniquely
has the capacity to proclaim both.

Although the poems of Guillén and González often appear to have an
Olympian quality, their focus is most often the world about us and everyday
objects. In 'Equilibrio', Guillén observes succinctly that 'lo diario es lo bello'
('the everyday is what is beautiful'), while in his *ars poetica*, 'A la poesía' ('To
Poetry'), Gónzalez states that he would like to take poetry out into the
street, with her unkempt hair blowing in the wind:

Y sacarte a las calles,
despeinada,
ondulando en el viento
–libre, suelto, a su aire–

tu cabello sombrío
como una larga y negra carcajada.

(p. 172)

And to take you into the streets, with your sombre hair uncombed,
waving in the wind – free and loose in its breeze – like a long and black
burst of laughter.

It is perhaps to a work like Neruda's *Odas elementales* that we need to turn,
however, to discover the full force of González's 'larga y negra carcajada'
('long and black burst of laughter'). The three books of odes comprise dozens
of poems that are in praise of virtually every conceivable aspect of reality
and experience: the natural world, animals, birds, plants, places, buildings,
people, emotions, articles of clothing and, especially, food. As Neruda's
translator, Margaret Sayers Peden, points out, while the poet's concept of
the ode is a traditional one, derived from classical literature, and while he
adheres to the celebratory intent, as is evident in his repeated recourse to
the verb 'cantar' ('to sing'), his poems do not betray an elevated tone even
though they exalt their subject-matter.[23] It seems apt to end this survey by
juxtaposing a poem like Neruda's 'Oda a los calcetines' ('Ode to my socks')
alongside the very different celebrations of Guillén and González:

Me trajo Maru Mori
un par
de calcetines
que tejió con sus manos
de pastora,
dos calcetines suaves
como liebres.   (p. 174)

Maru Mori brought me a pair of socks knitted with her own hands of a
shepherdess, two socks as soft as rabbits.

This juxtaposition epitomizes the constant and unfailingly productive tensions in poetry written in Spanish over many centuries: between the artistic
and the popular, between speech and song, between the private and the
public, between the esoteric and the accessible. What Neruda's ode com-
memorates above all, however, is the versatility of poetry, a salutary reminder
to those who would regulate its emotional and thematic scope through taste
and criticism. In lines like these, with their blend of extravagant metaphor
and plain speaking, there is an artistic celebration of the happiest kind –
the poetry is an enhancement of life, and life is the justification for the
poem:

Violentos calcetines,
mis pies fueron

dos pescados
de lana,
dos largos tiburones
de azul ultramarino
atravesados
por una trenza de oro,
dos gigantescos mirlos,
dos cañones:
mis pies
fueron honrados
de este modo
por
estos
celestiales
calcetines.

(p. 174)

Violent socks, my feet were two woollen fish, two long sharks of lapis blue colour, shot through with a golden thread, two gigantic blackbirds, two cannons: my feet were honoured in this way by these celestial socks.

Appendix. Chronological list of poets cited

Only poets whose works are quoted in the text are listed. Other poets figure in the Index of Names. Names of Spanish American poets are printed in italics.

The Middle Ages

Anon. (attributed to Per Abat), *Poema de mío Cid* 1207?
Gonzalo de Berceo *c.* 1196–1260?
Juan Ruiz, Archpriest of Hita 1283?–1350/1?
Marqués de Santillana 1398–1458
Hugo de Urries early fifteenth century – post 1492
Jorge Manrique 1440–79
Gil Vicente 1456?–1537

The Golden Age (sixteenth and seventeenth centuries)

Garcilaso de la Vega 1501/3–36
Fray Luis de León 1527–91
Alonso de Ercilla 1533–94
Fernando de Herrera 1534–97
Francisco de Aldana 1537–78
San Juan de la Cruz 1542–91
Luis de Góngora 1561–1627
Lope de Vega 1561–1635
Alonso de Ledesma 1562–1633
Francisco de Quevedo 1580–1645
Conde de Villamediana 1582–1622
Sor Juana Inés de la Cruz 1651–95

Eighteenth and nineteenth centuries

Gaspar Melchor de Jovellanos 1744–1811
José Iglesias de la Casa 1748–91

Juan Meléndez Valdés 1754–1817
Alberto Lista y Aragón 1775–1848
Duque de Rivas 1791–1865
José de Espronceda 1808–42
José Zorrilla 1817–93
José Hernández 1834–86
Gaspar Núñez de Arce 1834–1903
Gustavo Adolfo Bécquer 1836–70
Rosalía de Castro 1837–85

Twentieth century

Miguel de Unamuno 1864–1936
Rubén Darío 1867–1916
Manuel Machado 1874–1947
Antonio Machado 1875–1939
Juan Ramón Jiménez 1881–1958
Francisco Vighi 1890–1962
Pedro Salinas 1891–1951
Jorge Guillén 1893–1986
Vicente Huidobro 1893–1948
César Vallejo 1895–1937
Gerardo Diego 1896–1987
Federico García Lorca 1898–1936
Jorge Luis Borges 1899–1986
Rafael Alberti 1902–99
Luis Cernuda 1902–63
Pablo Neruda 1904–73
Miguel Hernández 1910–42
Nicanor Parra 1914–
Octavio Paz 1914–98
Blas de Otero 1916–79
Gloria Fuertes 1918–98
Ernesto Cardenal 1925–
Ángel González 1925–
Luis Jiménez Martos 1926–
Jaime Gil de Biedma 1929–90
José Ángel Valente 1929–2000
Claudio Rodríguez 1934–99
Víctor Jara 1938–73

Notes

Introduction

1. *Lírica española de tipo popular*, ed. Mergit Frenk, 11th edn (Madrid: Cátedra, 1997), p. 37. Unless otherwise indicated, all translations are by D. Gareth Walters.
2. *Poema de Mío Cid*, ed. Colin Smith, 20th edn (Madrid: Cátedra, 1996), p. 145.
3. Gonzalo de Berceo, *Milagros de Nuestra Señora*, ed. Michael Gerli, 3rd edn (Madrid: Cátedra, 1988), p. 69.
4. Garcilaso de la Vega, *Poesías castellanas completas*, ed. Elias L. Rivers, 2nd edn (Madrid: Castalia, 1972), p. 205. Compare the analogous passage in Virgil: 'My Galatea, Lady of the Sea, sweeter to me than Hyblaean thyme, more lovely than pale ivy, brighter than any swan' (Virgil, *The Pastoral Poems*, translated by E. V. Rieu (Harmondsworth: Penguin Books, 1967), p. 83).
5. Francisco de Quevedo, *Poesía original completa*, ed. J. M. Blecua (Barcelona: Planeta, 1981), p. 531.
6. Luis de Góngora, *Polyphemus and Galatea. A Study in the Interpretation of a Baroque Poem*, ed. Alexander A. Parker with a verse translation by Gilbert Cunningham (Edinburgh University Press, 1977), p. 110.
7. *Antología de los poetas prerrománticos españoles*, ed. Guillermo Carnero (Barcelona: Barral, 1970), p. 53.
8. *Ibid.*, p. 199.
9. José de Espronceda, *El estudiante de Salamanca and Other Poems*, ed. Richard A. Cardwell (London: Tamesis Texts, 1980), p. 126.
10. *Ibid.*, p. 80.
11. Gaspar Núñez de Arce, *Poesías completas*, ed. Ramón Villasuso, 2nd edn (Buenos Aires: Sopena, 1944), p. 165.
12. Rubén Darío, *Prosas profanas y otros poemas*, ed. Ignacio M. Zulueta (Madrid: Clásicos Castalia, 1983), p. 139.
13. Antonio Machado, *Campos de Castilla*, ed. Geoffrey Ribbans, 7th edn (Madrid: Cátedra, 1989), p. 102.
14. Vicente Huidobro, *Antología poética*, ed. Hugo Montes (Madrid: Clásicos Castalia, 1990), p. 41.
15. Rafael Alberti, *Marinero en tierra*, ed. Robert Marrast (Madrid: Clásicos Castalia, 1972), p. 101.

16. Luis Cernuda, *La realidad y el deseo [1924–1962]*, 7th edn (Mexico City: Fondo de Cultura Económica, 1982), p. 29.
17. Gloria Fuertes, *Obras incompletas* (Madrid: Cátedra, 1981), p. 192.
18. Ana Rossetti, *Indicios vehementes: Poemas 1979–1984* (Madrid: Hiperión, 1985), p. 99.
19. Garcilaso de la Vega, *Poesías castellanas completas*, p. 119.

1. Poets and readers

1. Raman Selden, *A Reader's Guide to Contemporary Literary Theory*, 2nd edn (New York: Harvester Wheatsheaf, 1989), pp. 3–4.
2. Terry Eagleton, *Literary Theory: An Introduction* (Oxford: Basil Blackwell, 1983), p. 74.
3. Garcilaso de la Vega, *Poesías castellanas completas*, p. 121.
4. See G. W. Connell, 'The autobiographical element in *Sobre los ángeles*', *Bulletin of Hispanic Studies*, 40 (1963), 160–73 (at p. 170).
5. Rafael Alberti, *Sobre los ángeles. Yo era un tonto y lo que he visto me ha hecho dos tontos*, ed. C. Brian Morris (Madrid: Cátedra, 1981), p. 131.
6. Quevedo, *Poesía original completa*, p. 11.
7. Antonio Machado, *Campos de Castilla*, p. 106.
8. Michael Predmore, *Una España joven en la poesía de Antonio Machado* (Madrid: Ínsula, 1981), p. 138.
9. Federico García Lorca, *Poeta en Nueva York*, ed. María Clementina Millán, 7th edn (Madrid: Cátedra, 1996), p. 125.
10. Derek Harris, *García Lorca: Poeta en Nueva York*, Critical Guides to Spanish Texts no. 24 (London: Grant and Cutler, 1978), p. 32.
11. Stanley Fish, *Is There a Text in This Class? The Authority of Interpretive Communities* (Cambridge, Mass., and London: Harvard University Press, 1980), p. 163.
12. Federico García Lorca, *Libro de poemas*, ed. Mario Hernández (Madrid: Alianza, 1984), p. 218.
13. Fray Luis de León, *Poesía*, ed. Juan Alcina (Madrid: Cátedra, 1997), p. 72.
14. Rosalía de Castro, *En las orillas del Sar*, ed. Xesús Alonso Montero (Madrid: Cátedra, 1985), p. 93.
15. Luis Cernuda, *Prosa I*, ed. Derek Harris and Luis Maristany (Madrid: Siruela, 1994), p. 645.

2. The interrelationship of texts

1. Maurice Blanchot, *Le livre à venir* (Paris: Gallimard, 1959), p. 330.
2. Roland Barthes, 'The death of the author', in David Lodge (ed.), *Modern Criticism and Theory. A Reader* (London and New York: Longman, 1988), pp. 167–72.

3. 'The history of literature . . . is a sum of very few ideas, and of very few original tales, – all the rest being variation of these'; 'I am very much struck in literature by the appearance, that one person wrote all the books' (*The Collected Works of Ralph Waldo Emerson. Volume III. Essays: Second Series* (Cambridge, Mass., and London: The Belknap Press of Harvard University Press, 1983), pp. 28, 137).

4. Harold Bloom, *The Anxiety of Influence: A Theory of Poetry*, 2nd edn (Oxford University Press, 1997), p. 94.

5. J. Hillis Miller, *Theory Now and Then* (New York: Harvester Wheatsheaf, 1991), p. 120.

6. Julia Kristeva, *The Revolution in Poetic Language*, trans. Margaret Waller (New York: Columbia University Press, 1984), p. 60.

7. Mikhail Bakhtin, 'From the prehistory of novelistic discourse', in *The Dialogic Imagination: Four Essays*, ed. Michael Holquist, trans. Caryl Emerson and Michael Holquist (Austin: University of Texas Press, 1981), pp. 41–83, cited in Lodge (ed.), *Modern Criticism and Theory. A Reader*, p. 145.

8. Fernando de Herrera, *Poesía castellana original completa*, ed. Cristóbal Cuevas (Madrid: Cátedra, 1985), p. 356. The phonetic orthography is Herrera's own. The quotation from Iglesias comes from *Poetas líricos del siglo XVIII*. Biblioteca de autores españoles, vol. 61 (Madrid: Rivadeneyra, 1869), p. 410.

9. Quevedo, *Poesía original completa*, p. 516.

10. Francesco Petrarca, *Il Canzoniere*, ed. Dino Provenzal (Milan: Rizzoli, 1954), p. 333.

11. Garcilaso de la Vega, *Poesías castellanas completas*, p. 37.

12. Lope de Vega, *Poesías líricas I*, ed. José F. Montesinos (Madrid: Espasa-Calpe, 1960), p. 155.

13. Quevedo, *Poesía original completa*, p. 24.

14. Garcilaso de la Vega, *Poesías castellanas completas*, p. 193.

15. The theme of the immortality of art combined with a praise of the beloved is the subject of Shakespeare's sonnet 'Shall I compare thee to a summer's day' which concludes: 'So long lives this, and this gives life to thee'.

16. Quevedo, *Poesía original completa*, p. 513.

17. Arthur Terry, *Seventeenth-Century Spanish Poetry: The Power of Artifice* (Cambridge University Press, 1993), p. 172.

18. José Ángel Valente, *Noventa y nueve poemas*, ed. José-Miguel Ullán (Madrid: Alianza, 1981), p. 25.

19. Andrew P. Debicki, however, states unequivocally that it is the beloved's hand (*Poetry of Discovery: The Spanish Generation of 1956–1971*) (Lexington: The University Press of Kentucky, 1982), p. 109).

20. Douglas C. Sheppard, 'Resonancias de Quevedo en la poesía española del siglo veinte', *Kentucky Foreign Language Quarterly*, 9 (1962), 105–13.

21. Octavio Paz, *La centena (Poemas: 1935–1968)* (Barcelona: Barral Editores, 1972), p. 134.

22. Antonio Machado, *Poesía y prosa. Tomo II: Poesías completas*, ed. Oreste Macrí (Madrid: Espasa-Calpe, 1988), p. 470.
23. Bloom, *The Anxiety of Influence*, pp. 93–5.
24. Harold Bloom, *A Map of Misreading* (Oxford University Press, 1980), pp. 19–20.
25. *Ibid.*, p. 12.
26. Manuel Machado, *Alma. Ars moriendi*, ed. Pablo del Barco (Madrid: Cátedra, 1988), p. 101.
27. Federico García Lorca, *Poesía inédita de juventud*, ed. Christian de Paepe (Madrid: Cátedra, 1994), p. 189.
28. Federico García Lorca, *Poema del cante jondo. Romancero gitano*, ed. Allen Josephs and Juan Caballero, 8th edn (Madrid: Cátedra, 1985), p. 146.
29. Rubén Darío, *Cantos de vida y esperanza*, 12th edn, Colección Austral no. 118 (Madrid: Espasa-Calpe, 1971), p. 47.
30. Bloom, *The Anxiety of Influence*, p. 14.
31. García Lorca, *Libro de poemas*, p. 204.
32. Bloom, *The Anxiety of Influence*, p. 94.
33. Castro, *En las orillas del Sar*, p. 136.
34. Luis de León, *Poesía*, p. 109.
35. San Juan de la Cruz, *Poesías*, ed. Paola Elia (Madrid: Clásicos Castalia, 1990), p. 117.
36. Bécquer, *Rimas*, ed. José Carlos de Torres (Madrid: Castalia, 1982), p. 112.
37. Castro, *En las orillas del Sar*, p. 75.
38. For an account of how a contemporary Spanish poet is influenced by Bécquer see Robin W. Fiddian, 'Rewriting Bécquer: "Julia" by Luis Alberto de Cuenca', *Siglo XX / 20th Century* (1993), 31–47.
39. Gioconda Belli, *Poesía reunida* (Mexico City: Editorial Diana, 1989), p. 147.
40. Bécquer, *Rimas*, p. 112.
41. Belli, *Poesía reunida*, p. 54.

3. The epic and the poetry of place

1. C. M. Bowra, *Heroic Poetry* (London: Macmillan, 1952), p. 5.
2. *Poema de mío Cid*, pp. 203–4.
3. Mircea Eliade, *Myth and Reality* (New York: Harper and Row, 1963), p. 6.
4. P. N. Dunn, 'Levels of meaning in the *Poema de mío Cid*', *Modern Language Notes*, 85 (1970), 109–19 (at p. 118).
5. Terry, *Seventeenth-Century Spanish Poetry*, p. 187.
6. Alonso de Ercilla, *La Araucana*, ed. Marcos A. Moringo and Isías Lerner, 2 vols. (Madrid: Clásicos Castalia, 1979), vol. I, p. 127.
7. Pablo Neruda, *Canto general*, ed. Enrico Mario Santí (Madrid: Cátedra, 1997), p. 175.

8. Quoted in Harold Bloom, *The Western Canon: The Books and School of the Ages* (London: Macmillan, 1995), p. 479.
9. Luis de Góngora, *Soledades*, ed., trans., intro., notes and biblio. Philip Polack (Bristol Classical Press, 1997), p. 16.
10. John Felstiner, *Translating Neruda: The Way to Macchu Picchu* (Stanford University Press, 1980), p. 12.
11. Paz, *La centena*, p. 97.
12. Antonio Machado, *Campos de Castilla*, p. 103.
13. Jaime Gil de Biedma, *Las personas del verbo* (Barcelona: Seix Barral, 1981), p. 82.
14. Natalia Calamai, *El compromiso en la poesía de la guerra civil española* (Barcelona: Laia, 1979), p. 145.
15. Cernuda, *La realidad y el deseo*, p. 182.
16. Trevor J. Dadson, 'The reappropriation of poetic language from Francoism: the case of Guillermo Carnero's *Dibujos de la muerte*', *Donaire*, 2 (1994), 12–23 (at p. 14).
17. Guillermo Carnero, *Ensayo de una teoría de la visión (Poesía 1966–1977)*, 2nd edn (Madrid: Hiperión, 1983), p. 80.
18. Jorge Luis Borges, *Selected Poems 1923–1967* (London: Penguin Books, 1985), p. 224.

4. The ballad and the poetry of tales

1. *Spanish Ballads*, ed. C. Colin Smith (Oxford: Pergamon, 1964), p. 5.
2. *Ibid.*, p. 111.
3. García Lorca, *Poema del cante jondo. Romancero gitano*, p. 265.
4. Juan de Valdés, *Diálogo de la lengua*, ed. José F. Montesinos (Madrid: Clásicos castellanos, 1964), p. 168.
5. *Romances de ciegos*, ed. Julio Caro Baroja (Madrid: Taurus, 1966), p. 186.
6. *Ibid.*, p. 176.
7. José de Espronceda, *Poesías líricas y fragmentos épicos*, ed. Robert Marrast (Madrid: Clásicos Castalia, 1970), p. 226.
8. Miguel Hernández, *El hombre y su poesía*, ed. Juan Cano Ballesta (Madrid: Cátedra, 1974), p. 115.
9. *Spanish Ballads*, p. 117.
10. El Marqués de Santillana, *Poesías completas*, 2 vols, ed. Manuel Durán (Madrid: Clásicos Castalia, 1975 and 1980), vol. II, p. 214.
11. Duque de Rivas, *Romances históricos*, 8th edn (Madrid: Espasa-Calpe, 1976), p. 80.
12. José Zorrilla, *Leyendas*, ed. Salvador García Castañeda (Madrid: Cátedra, 2000), p. 151.
13. *Spanish Ballads*, p. 136.
14. *Ibid.*, p. 191.

15. Lope de Vega, *Poesías líricas I*, p. 41.
16. José Hernández, *Martín Fierro*, ed. Ángel J. Battistessa (Madrid: Clásicos Castalia, 1994), p. 53.
17. I am grateful to Dr Ann MacLaren for graciously allowing me to quote from her unpublished verse translation of parts of this poem.
18. *Spanish Ballads*, pp. 30–1.
19. *Ibid.*, p. 207.
20. *Ibid.*, p. 208.
21. Luis de Góngora, *Romances*, ed. Antonio Carreño (Madrid: Cátedra, 1982), p. 147.
22. See, for example, the opening of the fourth *romance*: 'Al pie de un roble escarchado / donde Belardo el amante / desbarató un tosco nido / que habían tejido las aves' ('At the foot of a frost-covered oak where Belardo, the lover, ruined a clumsily made nest that the birds had assembled') (*Poesías líricas I*, p. 8).
23. Both Lope's *romances* to Filis and the Garcilaso poem have as an autobiographical base the theme of the poet's exile. Garcilaso was banished to an island in the Danube after incurring the disfavour of Charles V, while Lope was exiled in Valencia as a result of a libel against the family of his mistress, Elena Osorio, the Filis of the series of ballads.
24. Antonio Machado, *Campos de Castilla*, p. 156.
25. García Lorca, *Poema del cante jondo. Romancero gitano*, p. 238.
26. In a comment made in 1926 Lorca claimed not to know what the poem was about. Although the ballad possessed 'una gran sensación de anécdota... nadie sabe lo que pasa ni aun yo' ('a considerable sense of anecdote ... nobody, not even myself, knows what happens') ('Imaginación, inspiración, evasión', in Federico García Lorca, *Obras completas*, ed. Arturo del Hoyo, 13th edn (Madrid: Aguilar, 1967), pp. 85–91 (at p. 86)).
27. Federico García Lorca, *Gypsy Ballads. Romancero gitano*, trans. with intro. and commentary by Robert G. Havard (Warminster: Aris and Phillips, 1990), p. 158.

5. Songs and sonnets – popular and learned poetry

1. *Lírica española*, p. 186.
2. *Ibid.*, p. 36.
3. *Ibid.*, p. 93.
4. Dámaso Alonso and José Manuel Blecua (eds.), *Antología de la poesía española. Lírica de tipo tradicional*, 2nd edn (Madrid: Gredos, 1964), p. 41.
5. *Lírica española*, p. 87.
6. Santillana, *Poesías completas*, vol. I, p. 45.
7. Arcipreste de Hita, *Libro de buen amor*, ed. G. B. Gybbon-Monypenny (Madrid: Castalia, 1988), p. 325.

8. Federico García Lorca, *Canciones y Primeras canciones*, ed. Piero Menarini (Madrid: Espasa-Calpe, 1986), p. 121.
9. *Lírica española*, p. 90.
10. Lope de Vega, *Poesías líricas I*, p. 75.
11. Bécquer, *Rimas*, p. 188.
12. *Ibid.*, p. 123.
13. Robert Pring-Mill, *'Gracias a la vida': The Power and Poetry of Song*, The Kate Elder Lecture 1 (London: Queen Mary and Westfield Department of Spanish, 1989).
14. Quoted *ibid.*, p. 50.
15. Javier Heraud, 'Palabra de guerrillero', in *Our Word: Guerrilla Poems from Latin America*, trans. Edward Dorn and Gordon Brotherston (London: Cape Goliard Press, 1968), n.p.
16. Pring-Mill, *'Gracias a la vida'*, p. 14.
17. Octavio Paz, *Los hijos del limo. Del romanticismo a la vanguardia* (Barcelona: Seix Barral, 1974), p. 140.
18. Hernando del Castillo, *Cancionero general*, ed. J. M. Aguirre (Salamanca: Anaya, 1971), p. 59.
19. Garcilaso de la Vega, *Poesías castellanas completas*, p. 77.
20. *Ibid.*, p. 59.
21. Luis de Góngora, *Sonetos completos*, ed. Biruté Ciplijauskaité, 3rd edn (Madrid: Castalia, 1978), p. 230.
22. See, for example, his sonnet beginning 'Menos solicitó veloz saeta' (*Sonetos completos*, p. 247).
23. Jorge Luis Borges, *El hacedor* (Madrid: Alizanza, 1995), p. 88.
24. Simile and analogy are used extensively by those Spanish poets who immediately follow Garcilaso (sometimes called the First Generation of Spanish Petrarchists) largely as a result of imitating the fifteenth-century Catalan poet Ausiàs March.
25. Fernando de Villena, *Poesía (1980–1990)*, with a preliminary study by José Lupiáñez (Granada: A. Ubago, 1993), p. 334.
26. César Vallejo, *Obra poética completa*, intro. Américo Ferrari (Madrid: Alianza Tres, 1982), p. 205.
27. Cited in Luis de Góngora, *Poems of Góngora*, ed. R. O. Jones (Cambridge University Press, 1966), p. 6.
28. Góngora, *Polyphemus and Galatea*, p. 108. The passage is brilliantly analysed by A. A. Parker on pp. 60–2 of this edition.
29. Alberti, *Sobre los ángeles*, p. 73.

6. Love poetry

1. A. J. Krailsheimer (ed.), *The Continental Renaissance* (Harmondsworth: Penguin Books, 1971), p. 15.

2. Quevedo, *Poesía original completa*, p. 510.
3. R. O. Jones, *A Literary History of Spain. The Golden Age: Prose and Poetry* (London: Ernest Benn, 1971), p. 29.
4. Herrera, *Poesía castellana original completa*, p. 396.
5. The clearest exposition of this hypothesis is provided by Keith Whinnom, *La poesía amatoria de la época de los Reyes Católicos* (University of Durham, 1981).
6. *Poesía erótica del Siglo de Oro*, ed. Pierre Alzieu, Robert Jammes and Yvan Lissorgues (Barcelona: Editorial Crítica, 1984), p. 50.
7. *Ibid.*, p. 86.
8. Francisco de Aldana, *Poesías castellanas completas*, ed. José Lara Garrido (Madrid: Cátedra, 1985), p. 131.
9. In his study on Petrarchism, Leonard Forster has what he terms a 'Tailpiece on the survival of Petrarchan commonplaces', including their use in advertising (*The Icy Fire* (Cambridge University Press, 1969), p. 191).
10. Quevedo, *Poesía original completa*, p. 615.
11. Bécquer, *Rimas*, p. 114.
12. Pablo Neruda, *Veinte poemas de amor y una canción desesperada*, ed. Hugo Montes (Madrid: Clásicos Castalia, 1987), p. 47.
13. Pedro Salinas, *La voz a ti debida. Razón de Amor. Largo Lamento*, ed. Montserrat Escartín (Madrid: Cátedra, 1995), p. 111.
14. Belli, *Poesía reunida*, p. 18.
15. Salinas, *La voz a ti debida*, p. 105.
16. Belli, *Poesía reunida*, p. 11.
17. Rossetti, *Indicios vehementes*, p. 19.
18. Chris Perriam, *Desire and Dissent: An Introduction to Luis Antonio de Villena* (Oxford/Washington, DC: Berg, 1995), p. 43.
19. Luis Antonio de Villena, *Poesía 1970–1984* (Madrid: Visor, 1988), p. 311.
20. Conde de Villamediana, *Obras*, ed. José Manuel Rozas (Madrid: Castalia, 1969), p. 83.
21. Gil de Biedma, *Las personas del verbo*, p. 86.
22. Claudio Rodríguez, *Antología poética*, ed. Philip W. Silver (Madrid: Alianza, 1981), p. 95.

7. Religious and moral poetry

1. Juan de la Cruz, *Poesías*, p. 116.
2. Berceo, *Milagros de Nuestra Señora*, p. 72.
3. See Jones, *A Literary History of Spain. The Golden Age*, p. 147.
4. Alonso de Ledesma, *Conceptos espirituales y morales*, ed. Francisco Almagro (Madrid: Editora Nacional, 1978), p. 60.
5. Johan Huizinga, *The Waning of the Middle Ages* (Harmondsworth: Penguin Books, 1965), p. 147.

6. *The Penguin Book of Spanish Verse*, p. 163.
7. Lope de Vega, *Poesías líricas I*, p. 156.
8. Luis de León, *Poesía*, p. 82.
9. *Ibid.*, p. 73.
10. See D. Gareth Walters, 'On the structure, imagery and significance of *Vida retirada*', *Modern Language Review*, 81 (1986), 71–81.
11. Jorge Manrique, *Poesía*, ed. J. M. Alda Tesán, 18th edn (Madrid: Cátedra, 1997), p. 151.
12. Quevedo, *Poesía original completa*, p. 11.
13. Arcipreste de Hita, *Libro de buen amor*, p. 424.
14. Sor Juana Inés de la Cruz, *Obras completas I: Lírica personal*, ed. Alfonso Méndez Plancarte (Mexico City: Fondo de Cultura Económica, 1951), p. 280, repr. in *The Penguin Book of Spanish Verse*, p. 316.
15. Miguel de Unamuno, *Obras completas VI: Poesía* (Madrid: Escelicer, 1969), p. 450.
16. Antonio Machado, *Poesía y prosa*, p. 481.
17. Blas de Otero, *Angel fieramente humano. Redoble de conciencia*, 2nd edn (Buenos Aires: Losada, 1973), p. 43.
18. Vallejo, *Obra poética completa*, p. 59.

8. Satire, burlesque and poetry as celebration

1. Ernesto Cardenal, *Gethsemaní, KY* (Mexico DF: Ediciones Ecuador, 1964), p. 46, repr. in *The Penguin Book of Latin American Verse*, ed. E. Caracciolo-Trejo (Harmondsworth: Penguin Books, 1971), p. 311.
2. Gil de Biedma, *Las personas del verbo*, p. 51.
3. *Poesía crítica y satírica del siglo XV*, ed. Julio Rodríguez-Puértolas (Madrid: Castalia, 1981), p. 135.
4. Manrique, *Poesía*, p. 146.
5. Quevedo, *Poesía original completa*, p. 1117.
6. *Poesía erótica*, p. 300.
7. Cited in C. B. Morris, *A Generation of Spanish Poets* (Cambridge University Press, 1969), p. 83.
8. *Poesía española de la vanguardia (1918–1936)*, ed. Francisco Javier Díez de Re-venga (Madrid: Clásicos Castalia, 1995), p. 184.
9. *Ibid.*, p. 204.
10. Nicanor Parra, *Poesía y antipoesía*, ed. Hugo Montes Brunet (Madrid: Clásicos Castalia, 1994), p. 82.
11. Wallace Stevens, *The Necessary Angel* (London: Faber and Faber, 1984), p. 94.
12. Jonathan Culler, *Structuralist Poetics: Structuralism, Linguistics and the Study of Literature* (London: Routledge and Kegan Paul, 1975), p. 177.
13. Garcilaso de la Vega, *Poesías castellanas completas*, p. 197.

14. M. J. Woods, *The Poet and the Natural World in the Age of Góngora* (Oxford University Press, 1978), p. 156; Terry, *Seventeenth-Century Spanish Poetry*, p. 85.
15. Góngora, *Soledades*, p. 40.
16. Terry, *Seventeenth-Century Spanish Poetry*, p. 86.
17. Juan Meléndez Valdés, *Poesías selectas. La lira de marfil*, ed. J. H. R. Polt and Georges Demerson (Madrid: Clásicos Castalia, 1981), p. 113.
18. Paul Auster, 'Twentieth-century French poetry', in *The Red Notebook* (London: Faber and Faber, 1995), p. 48.
19. Juan Ramón Jiménez, *Melancolía*, prologue by Francisco Javier Blasco (Madrid: Taurus, 1981), p. 201.
20. Andrés Sánchez Robayna, *La luz negra* (Madrid: Ediciones Júcar, 1985), p. 57.
21. Jorge Guillén, *Cántico* (Barcelona: Seix Barral, 1984), p. 241.
22. Ángel González, *Poemas*, edited by the author, 7th edn (Madrid: Cátedra, 1998), p. 54.
23. Pablo Neruda, *Elemental Odes*, selected, trans. and intro. by Margaret Sayers Peden (London: Libris, 1991), p. 1.

Bibliography

Primary sources

Alberti, Rafael, *Marinero en tierra*, ed. Robert Marrast, Madrid: Clásicos Castalia, 1972.
    Sobre los ángeles. Yo era un tonto y lo que he visto me ha hecho dos tontos, ed. C. Brian Morris, Madrid: Cátedra, 1981.
Aldana, Francisco de, *Poesías castellanas completas*, ed. José Lara Garrido, Madrid: Cátedra, 1985.
Alonso, D. and Blecua, J. M. (eds.), *Antología de la poesía española. Lírica de tipo tradicional*, 2nd edn, Madrid: Gredos, 1964.
Antología de los poetas prerrománticos españoles, ed. Guillermo Carnero, Barcelona: Barral, 1970.
Bécquer, Gustavo Adolfo, *Rimas*, ed. José Carlos de Torres, Madrid: Castalia, 1982.
Belli, Gioconda, *Poesía reunida*, Mexico City: Editorial Diana, 1989.
Berceo, Gonzalo de, *Milagros de Nuestra Señora*, ed. Michael Gerli, 3rd edn, Madrid: Cátedra, 1988.
Borges, Jorge Luis, *El hacedor*, Madrid: Alianza, 1995.
    Selected Poems 1923–1967, London: Penguin Books, 1985.
Cardenal, Ernesto, *Gethsemaní, KY*, Mexico DF: Ediciones Ecuador, 1964.
Carnero, Guillermo, *Ensayo de una teoría de la visión (Poesía 1966–1977)*, 2nd edn, Madrid: Hiperión, 1983.
Castillo, Hernando del, *Cancionero general*, ed. J. M. Aguirre, Salamanca: Anaya, 1971.
Castro, Rosalía de, *En las orillas del Sar*, ed. Xesús Alonso Montero, Madrid: Cátedra, 1985.
Cernuda, Luis, *La realidad y el deseo (1924–1962)*, 7th edn, Mexico City: Fondo de Cultura Económica, 1982.
Darío, Rubén, *Cantos de vida y esperanza*, 12th edn, Colección Austral no. 118, Madrid: Espasa-Calpe, 1971.
    Prosas profanas y otros poemas, ed. Ignacio M. Zulueta, Madrid: Clásicos Castalia, 1983.
Ercilla, Alonso de, *La Araucana*, ed. Marcos A. Moringo and Isías Lerner, 2 vols., Madrid: Clásicos Castalia, 1979.
Espronceda, José de, *El estudiante de Salamanca and Other Poems*, ed. Richard A. Cardwell, London: Tamesis Texts, 1980.

Poesías líricas y fragmentos épicos, ed. Robert Marrast, Madrid: Clásicos Castalia, 1970.

Fuertes, Gloria, *Obras incompletas*, Madrid: Cátedra, 1981.

García Lorca, Federico, *Canciones y Primeras canciones*, ed. Piero Menarini, Madrid: Espasa-Calpe, 1986.

Gypsy Ballads. Romancero gitano, trans. with intro. and commentary by Robert G. Havard, Warminster: Aris and Phillips, 1990.

Libro de poemas, ed. Mario Hernández, Madrid: Alianza, 1984.

Obras completas, ed. Arturo del Hoyo, 13th edn, Madrid: Aguilar, 1967.

Poema del cante jondo. Romancero gitano, ed. Allen Josephs and Juan Caballero, 8th edn, Madrid: Cátedra, 1985.

Poesía inédita de juventud, ed. Christian de Paepe, Madrid: Cátedra, 1994.

Poeta en Nueva York, ed. María Clementa Millán, 7th edn, Madrid: Cátedra, 1996.

Garcilaso de la Vega, *Poesías castellanas completas*, ed. Elias L. Rivers, 2nd edn, Madrid: Castalia, 1972.

Gil de Biedma, Jaime, *Las personas del verbo*, Barcelona: Seix Barral, 1981.

Góngora, Luis de, *Poems of Góngora*, ed. R. O. Jones, Cambridge University Press, 1966.

Polyphemus and Galatea. A Study in the Interpretation of a Baroque Poem, ed. Alexander A. Parker with a verse trans. by Gilbert Cunningham, Edinburgh University Press, 1977.

Romances, ed. Antonio Carreño, Madrid: Cátedra, 1982.

Soledades, ed. with trans., intro., notes and biblio. by Philip Polack, Bristol Classical Press, 1997.

Sonetos completos, ed. Biruté Ciplijauskaité, 3rd edn, Madrid: Castalia, 1978.

González, Ángel, *Poemas*, ed. González, 7th edn, Madrid: Cátedra, 1998.

Guillén, Jorge, *Cántico*, Barcelona: Seix Barral, 1984.

Hernández, José, *Martin Fierro*, ed. Ángel J. Battistessa, Madrid: Clásicos Castalia, 1994.

Hernández, Miguel, *El hombre y su poesía*, ed. Juan Caro Ballesta, Madrid: Cátedra, 1974.

Herrera, Fernando de, *Poesía castellana original completa*, ed. Cristóbal Cuevas, Madrid: Cátedra, 1985.

Hita, Arcipreste de, *Libro de buen amor*, ed. G. B. Gybbon-Monypenny, Madrid: Castalia, 1988.

Huidobro, Vicente, *Antología poética*, ed. Hugo Montes, Madrid: Clásicos Castalia, 1990.

Jiménez, Juan Ramón, *Melancolía*, prologue Francisco Javier Blasco, Madrid: Taurus, 1981.

Juan de la Cruz, San, *Poesías*, ed. Paola Elia, Madrid: Clásicos Castalia, 1990.

Juana Inés de la Cruz, Sor, *Obras completas I: Lírica personal*, ed. Alfonso Méndez Plancarte, Mexico City: Fondo de Cultura Económica, 1951.

Ledesma, Alonso de, *Conceptos espirituales y morales*, ed. Francisco Almagro, Madrid: Editora Nacional, 1978.

León, Fray Luis de, *Poesía*, ed. Juan Alcina, Madrid: Cátedra, 1997.

Lírica española de tipo popular, ed. Mergit Frenk, 11th edn, Madrid: Cátedra, 1997.

Machado, Antonio, *Campos de Castilla*, ed. Geoffrey Ribbans, 7th edn, Madrid: Cátedra, 1989.

  Poesía y prosa. Tomo II: Poesías completas, ed. Oreste Macrí, Madrid: Espasa-Calpe, 1988.

Machado, Manuel, *Alma. Ars moriendi*, ed. Pablo del Barco, Madrid: Cátedra, 1988.

Manrique, Jorge, *Poesía*, ed. J. M. Alda Tesán, 18th edn, Madrid: Cátedra, 1997.

Meléndez Valdés, Juan, *Poesías selectas. La lira de marfil*, ed. J. H. R. Polt and Georges Demerson, Madrid: Clásicos Castalia, 1981.

Neruda, Pablo, *Canto general*, ed. Enrico Mario Santí, Madrid: Cátedra, 1997.

  Elemental Odes, selected, trans. and intro. Margaret Sayers Peden, London: Libris, 1991.

  Veinte poemas de amor y una canción desesperada, ed. Hugo Montes, Madrid: Clásicos Castalia, 1987.

Núñez de Arce, Gaspar, *Poesías completas*, ed. Ramón Villasuso, 2nd edn, Buenos Aires: Sopena, 1944.

Otero, Blas de, *Angel fieramente humano. Redoble de conciencia*, 2nd edn, Buenos Aires: Losada, 1973.

Our Word: Guerrilla Poems from Latin America, trans. Edward Dorn and Gordon Brotherston, London: Cape Goliard Press, 1968.

Parra, Nicanor, *Poesía y antipoesía*, ed. Hugo Montes Brunet, Madrid: Clásicos Castalia, 1994.

Paz, Octavio, *La centena (Poemas: 1935–1968)*, Barcelona: Barral Editores, 1972.

The Penguin Book of Latin American Verse, ed. E. Caracciolo-Trejo, Harmondsworth: Penguin Books, 1971.

The Penguin Book of Spanish Verse, intro. and ed. J. M. Cohen, Harmondsworth: Penguin Books, 1960.

Poema de mío Cid, ed. Colin Smith, 20th edn, Madrid: Cátedra, 1996.

Poesía crítica y satírica del siglo XV, ed. Julio Rodríguez-Puértolas, Madrid: Castalia, 1981.

Poesía erótica del Siglo de Oro, ed. Pierre Alzieu, Robert Jammes, Yvan Lissorgues, Barcelona: Editorial Crítica, 1984.

Poesía española de la vanguardia (1918–1936), ed. Francisco Javier Díez de Revenga, Madrid: Clásicos Castalia, 1995.

Poetas líricos del siglo XVIII, Biblioteca de autores españoles, vol. 61, Madrid: Rivadeneyra, 1869.

Quevedo, Francisco de, *Poesía original completa*, ed. J. M. Blecua, Barcelona: Planeta, 1981.

Rivas, Duque de, *Romances históricos*, 8th edn, Madrid: Espasa-Calpe, 1976.

Rodríguez, Claudio, *Antología poética*, ed. Philip W. Silver, Madrid: Alianza, 1981.

Romances de ciego, ed. Julio Caro Baroja, Madrid: Taurus, 1966.

Rossetti, Ana, *Indicios vehementes: Poemas 1979–1984*, Madrid: Hiperión, 1985.

Salinas, Pedro, *La voz a ti debida. Razón de Amor. Largo Lamento*, ed. Montserrat Escartín, Madrid: Cátedra, 1995.

Santillana, Marqués de, *Poesías completas*, 2 vols., ed. Manuel Durán, Madrid: Clásicos Castalia, 1975 and 1980.

Spanish Ballads, ed. C. Colin Smith, Oxford: Pergamon, 1964.

Unamuno, Miguel de, *Obras completas VI: Poesía*, Madrid: Escelicer, 1969.

Valente, José Ángel, *Noventa y nueve poemas*, ed. José-Miguel Ullán, Madrid: Alianza, 1981.

Vallejo, César, *Obra poética completa*, intro. Américo Ferrari, Madrid: Alianza Tres, 1982.

Vega, Lope de, *Poesías líricas I*, ed. José F. Montesinos, Madrid: Espasa-Calpe, 1960.

Villamediana, Conde de, *Obras*, ed. José Manuel Rozas, Madrid: Castalia, 1969.

Villena, Fernando de, *Poesía (1980–1990)*, with a preliminary study by José Lupiáñez, Granada: A. Ubago, 1993.

Villena, Luis Antonio de, *Poesía 1970–1984*, Madrid: Visor, 1988.

Zorrilla, José, *Leyendas*, ed. Salvador García Castañeda, Madrid: Cátedra, 2000.

Secondary sources

Auster, Paul, 'Twentieth-century French poetry', in *The Red Notebook*, London: Faber and Faber, 1995, pp. 41–76.

Bakhtin, Mikhail, 'From the prehistory of novelistic discourse', in Lodge (ed.), *Modern Criticism and Theory. A Reader*, pp. 125–56.

Barthes, Roland, 'The death of the author', in Lodge (ed.), *Modern Criticism and Theory. A Reader*, pp. 167–72.

Blanchot, Maurice, *Le livre à venir*, Paris: Gallimard, 1959.

Bloom, Harold, *The Anxiety of Influence: A Theory of Poetry*, 2nd edn, Oxford University Press, 1997.

    A Map of Misreading, Oxford University Press, 1980.

    The Western Canon: The Books and School of the Ages, London: Macmillan, 1995.

Bowra, C. M., *Heroic Poetry*, London: Macmillan, 1952.

Calamai, Natalia, *El compromiso en la poesía de la guerra civil española*, Barcelona: Laia, 1979.

Cernuda, Luis, *Prosa I*, ed. Derek Harris and Luis Maristany, Madrid: Siruela, 1994.

Connell, G. W., 'The autobiographical element in *Sobre los ángeles*', *Bulletin of Hispanic Studies*, 40 (1963), 160–73.

Culler, Jonathan, *Structuralist Poetics: Structuralism, Linguistics and the Study of Literature*, London: Routledge and Kegan Paul, 1975.

Dadson, Trevor J., 'The reappropriation of poetic language from Francoism: the case of Guillermo Carnero's *Dibujos de la muerte*', *Donaire*, 2 (1994), 12–23.

Debicki, Andrew P., *Poetry of Discovery: The Spanish Generation of 1956–1971*, Lexington: The University Press of Kentucky, 1982.

Dunn, P. N., 'Levels of meaning in the *Poema de mío Cid*', *Modern Language Notes*, 85 (1970), 109–19.

Eagleton, Terry, *Literary Theory: An Introduction*, Oxford: Basil Blackwell, 1983.

Eliade, Mircea, *Myth and Reality*, New York: Harper and Row, 1963.

Emerson, Ralph Waldo, *The Collected Works of Ralph Waldo Emerson: Volume III. Essays: Second Series*, Cambridge, Mass., and London: The Belknap Press of Harvard University Press, 1983.

Felstiner, John, *Translating Neruda: The Way to Macchu Picchu*, Stanford University Press, 1980.

Fiddian, Robin W., 'Rewriting Bécquer: "Julia" by Luis Alberto de Cuenca', *Siglo XX / 20th Century* (1993), 31–47.

Fish, Stanley, *Is There a Text in This Class? The Authority of Interpretive Communities*, Cambridge, Mass., and London: Harvard University Press, 1980.

Forster, Leonard, *The Icy Fire*, Cambridge University Press, 1969.

Harris, Derek, *García Lorca: Poeta en Nueva York*, Critical Guides to Spanish Texts no. 24, London: Grant and Cutler, 1978.

Huizinga, Johan, *The Waning of the Middle Ages*, Harmondsworth; Penguin Books, 1965.

Jones, R. O., *A Literary History of Spain. The Golden Age: Prose and Poetry*, London: Ernest Benn, 1971.

Krailsheimer, A. J. (ed.), *The Continental Renaissance*, Harmondsworth: Penguin Books, 1971.

Kristeva, Julia, *The Revolution in Poetic Language*, trans. Margaret Waller, New York: Columbia University Press, 1984.

Lodge, David (ed.), *Modern Criticism and Theory. A Reader*, London and New York: Longman, 1988.

Miller, J. Hillis, *Theory Now and Then*, New York: Harvester Wheatsheaf, 1991.

Morris, C. B., *A Generation of Spanish Poets*, Cambridge University Press, 1969.

Paz, Octavio, *Los hijos del limo. Del romanticismo a la vanguardia*, Barcelona: Seix Barral, 1974.

Perriam, Chris, *Desire and Dissent: An Introduction to Luis Antonio de Villena*, Oxford / Washington DC: Berg, 1995.

Petrarca, Francesco, *Il Canzoniere*, ed. Dino Provenzal, Milan: Rizzoli, 1954.

Predmore, Michael, *Una España joven en la poesía de Antonio Machado*, Madrid: Ínsula, 1981.

Pring-Mill, Robert, *'Gracias a la vida': The Power and Poetry of Song*, The Kate Elder Lecture 1, London: Queen Mary and Westfield Department of Spanish, 1989.

Robayna, Andrés Sánchez, *La luz negra*, Madrid: Ediciones Jucar, 1985.

Selden, Raman, *A Reader's Guide to Contemporary Literary Theory*, 2nd edn, New York: Harvester Wheatsheaf, 1989.

Sheppard, Douglas C., 'Resonancias de Quevedo en la poesía española del siglo veinte', *Kentucky Foreign Language Quarterly*, 9 (1962), 105–13.

Stevens, Wallace, *The Necessary Angel*, London: Faber and Faber, 1984.

Terry, Arthur, *Seventeenth-Century Spanish Poetry: The Power of Artifice*, Cambridge University Press, 1993.

Valdés, Juan de, *Diálogo de la lengua*, ed. José F. Montesinos, Madrid: Clásicos castellanos, 1964.

Virgil, *The Pastoral Poems*, trans. E. V. Rieu, Harmondsworth: Penguin Books, 1967.

Walters, D. Gareth, 'On the structure, imagery and significance of *Vida retirada*', *Modern Language Review*, 81 (1986), 71–81.

Whinnom, Keith, *La poesía amatoria de la época de los Reyes Católicos*, University of Durham, 1981.

Woods, M. J., *The Poet and the Natural World in the Age of Góngora*, Oxford University Press, 1978.

Index of names

Subject index